Musical Instruments in Art and History

MUSICAL INSTRUMENTS
IN ART AND HISTORY

PROFESSOR ROGER BRAGARD
Curator of the Musée Instrumental de Bruxelles

DR. FERDINAND J. DE HEN

Translated by
BILL HOPKINS

A Studio Book
THE VIKING PRESS — NEW YORK

Original French edition, *LES INSTRUMENTS DE MUSIQUE DANS L'ART ET L'HISTOIRE*

Published in 1968 by The Viking Press, Inc.
625 Madison Avenue, New York, N.Y. 10022

Distributed in Canada by
The Macmillan Company of Canada Limited,
Library of Congress catalog card number : 68-15484

The photographs in this book are by Messrs. Boucher, Giraudon, Minsart, Roland (Sado), and Scala; also by the photographic services of various museums, libraries and collections. The marginal illustrations were drawn by Marina Ponjaert. The cover and direction of photography are by K. Grunewald. Wespin Photogravure of Brussels assisted with the photographs.

Printed in Belgium by L'Imprimerie Dereume of Brussels under the direction of Messrs. Naumann.

Bound by L'Imprimerie H. Dessain of Malines, Belgium.

ACKNOWLEDGEMENTS

The authors wish to thank, for their generous help, Mme. Thibault-Chambure, Paris; the engineer, R. Liebens, Brussels; Messrs. Baschet, Paris; Dr. Neupert, Bamberg; Hammond Ltd., U.S.A.; the College van Burgemeester en Schepenen of the City of Antwerp, and also the curators of the museums and the authorities given below.

MUSEUMS AND ABBREVIATIONS

B.N.: Bibliothèque Nationale, Paris, France.
B.R.: Bibliothèque Royale, Brussels, Belgium.
G.M.: Gemeentemuseum, The Hague, Netherlands.
K.M.S.K.: Koninklijk Museum voor Schone Kunsten, Antwerp, Belgium.
M.A.C.: Museo de Arte Cataluña, Barcelona, Spain.
M.C.: Musée de Cluny, Paris, France.
M.I.: Musée Instrumental, Brussels, Belgium.
M.L.: Musée du Louvre, Paris, France.
M.R.A.H.: Musées Royaux d'Art et d'Histoire, Brussels, Belgium.
M.R.B.A.: Musées Royaux des Beaux-Arts, Brussels, Belgium.
N.G.: Nationalgalerie, Berlin, Germany.
N.M.: Nationalmuseet, Copenhagen, Denmark.
R.M.O.: Rijksmuseum voor Oudheden, Leiden, Netherlands.
S.B.: Staatsbibliothek, Munich, Germany.
S.K.: Staatliche Kunstsammlung, Cassel, Germany.
U.B.: Universiteitsbibliotheek, Utrecht, Netherlands.
Abbazia, Montecassino, Italy.
Baschet, Paris, France.
Cathedral of Antwerp, Belgium.
Hammond, U.S.A.
Neupert, Bamberg, Germany.
Studio for Electronic Music, Brussels, Belgium.

CONTENTS

LIST OF COLOUR PLATES

PREFACE

Fifty years or so ago, it would have seemed a foolhardy enterprise to devote a lengthy book to the subject of musical instruments and to illustrate it with more than a hundred colour plates. At that time meticulous catalogues were published with a view to giving the specialists accurate information, but no one dreamed of making available to the general public pictures of these fine instruments into whose making so much care had gone, instruments designed as much to "charm the ear as to move the spirit and delight the eye".

It must be admitted that "violin and guitar collectors", as they were slightingly called by Pierre Larousse were, in the last century, looked upon somewhat unfavourably. Indeed, they were regarded as being in the same class as those who hoard "dinner menus, embellished visiting cards, bric-à-brac and old coins".

And yet the instruments of the great makers have been appreciated for centuries and were sought after by professionals and amateurs, by sovereigns, lords and the bourgeoisie in Italy, France, England, Germany and Austria; one has only to recall the collection of Isabella d'Este, marchioness of Mantua, or that of her nephew Alfonso II, Duke of Ferrara; the impressive collection left by Henry VIII — more than two hundred and seventy wind instruments and about a hundred and ten stringed instruments; the famous *Musikkammer* of the bankers Fugger of Augsburg which held about four hundred instruments, almost all of them in ivory or precious exotic woods, among which were a hundred and forty lutes, masterpieces by Laux Maler, Magnus Tieffenbrücker and Laux Bosch; and finally, the two hundred and fifty exquisitely beautiful instruments collected by the Archduke Ferdinand of Tyrol in his château at Ambras, near Innsbruck, which formed the basis of the music collection at the Vienna *Kunsthistorisches Museum*. However, it might be thought that these were not true collections, but rather assemblages of instruments intended to be played; in fact, in the case of an amateur such as Alfonso II, one can distinguish the *usati* from the *non usati* instruments, and the latter would be " displayed in groups, ranged in an ideal order " in a large hall. Sabba da Castiglione tells us that the fashion in about 1545 was to decorate the interiors of palaces with instruments; at that time, they were prized for the beauty of their shape, for their decoration, and even for their rarity. Patrons shared the experiences of the the avant-garde and often financed them, so it is hardly surprising to find in the collection of the Duke of Ferrara the famous enharmonic six-manual harpsichord based on the designs of Nicolà Vicentino, side by side with a case holding instruments of everyday use, a complete set of six crumhorns, preserved today in the Brussels Instrumental Museum (Plate III. - 17).

It was not only kings and great lords who acquired instruments; besides them there existed an extensive clientele: members of professional corporations — it has been calculated that each member, on average, used about ten instruments — organists, "masters of musical instruments and of lutes" and enlightened amateurs. It was easy to find makers who were willing to satisfy their wishes; in sixteenth-century Paris, one had only to enter a shop whose display could be seen from the street, the instruments being exhibited on "small woollen mats", in order to acquire an instrument such as even a modest budget could afford. Before the financial crisis which shook Europe in about 1559, it was possible to buy two citterns of different size — a tenor and a bass — for the price of an oak cabinet; and for half this sum one could buy a lute in a case or a clavichord (*manicordion*).

There were still a large number of firms of makers in the seventeenth century; certain business concerns possessed hundreds of lutes, mandoras, "guyternes", citterns, viols and lyres, three hundred finished instruments and more than twice as many in unvarnished wood.

The lutes of Flanders, Germany, Venice, Padua and even Lyons were as famous as the guitars of Spain, the viols of England and the violins of Brescia, Cremona, Venice and Cambrai; the reputation of the flute-makers of Lyons and Germany extended beyond their home town or country, but who today — but for a number of the more initiated — could give the names of some of these makers who were so renowned in their time? True, the Amatis, Guarneris and Stradivari are widely remembered; but the Parisian "luthiers" of the eighteenth century — Docquay, Lejeune, Guersan, Salomon — are still unknown names.

The revival of the harpsichord at the beginning of this century has brought into due repute once again the names of Rückers of Antwerp, Blanchet and Taskin of Paris and Hasse of Hamburg, but the revival of the recorder has not brought to the notice of the general public the names of Hotteterre, Schlegel and Stanesby; the lute has not yet brought contemporary fame upon Hans Frei, Des Moulins, Sebastian Schelle or Joachim Tielke; the family of Sellas of Venice, to whom we owe so many magnificent theorbos and chitarroni, that of Voboam of Paris who left us admirable guitars, both are still relegated to obscurity.

A book such as the present one will enable us to know and to admire their work; simply to thumb through this book we are confronted with pictures of the past; the trumpets, shawms and trombones (*sackbuts*) bring to mind the gay tableaux in which, perched on a dais (or a scaffold), minstrels livened up the parade and the subsequent dances; the lutes evoke the intimate music of the Renaissance, the melody with accompaniment and also those broken consorts in which the voice was joined by plucked strings and a small organ; as for the "upright flute", we may recall having seen it on a German ivory sculpture from the end of the sixteenth century in the company of a panpipe, a trombone, a transverse flute, a recorder, an oboe, a racket and a cornett.

But such memories and dreams should not divert us from the task in hand. Let us merely point out that the beautiful plates in this book represent only a small part of the collection of instruments to be found in the Brussels Instrumental Museum. This Museum was originally founded by the acquisition of two famous collections: that of Fétis (1872) and that of the Rajah Tagore (1876), and has grown year by year. In 1878 the Tolbecque collection of Niort added nearly a hundred instruments: an Italian positive, a regal, harpsichords by Marius and Tibaut, a guitar by Matteo Sellas; that of Count Pietro Correr of Venice added in 1886 some extremely rare examples of Italian craftsmanship of the sixteenth and seventeenth centuries. Finally, in 1908, the Snoeck collection of Ghent added to this already imposing assemblage instruments from the Low Countries which demonstrate the evolution of instrument making characteristic of that region. To all these elements were joined the private collections of Victor-Charles and Joseph Mahillon besides the individual instruments which these men donated to the Museum and those it acquired in exchanges.

We have not mentioned the collection of instruments from Asia, Africa, North America, South America and Australia: this could be the subject of as sizable a book as the present volume. Today, one cannot help admiring the liveliness of the Brussels Conservatoire Museum: the collections never remain static; a judicious purchasing policy, made possible by the concession of a considerable subsidy, makes it possible to enrich them whenever a valuable piece comes onto the market. In this way, each visit to the Museum is a discovery, and I am sure that those who read this book will want to see the instruments whose existence it will have revealed to them; and they would also doubtless like to hear them. The Museum curator is more and more occupied by the task of restoring the instruments, of giving them back — as far as possible — their original condition, and of providing them with their voice. It now seems a normal enough objective to play a work of the past on those instruments for which it was written; many an artist is successfully devoting himself to this, with the support of some of the recording companies, and once again the instruments are able to fulfil the task ascribed to them by Sabba da Castiglione: "to charm the ear and delight the eye".

G. THIBAULT (Mme H. de CHAMBURE)
Curator of the Musée Instrumental
du Conservatoire National Supérieur de
Musique; Paris.

I - The Prehistoric Ages
The Orient
Greece and Rome

I — 1. Greek vase of the 5th century B.C.

"Magus", *Les Trois Frères.*

THE PREHISTORIC AGES

Our knowledge of the musical instruments used in Europe in prehistoric times is largely based on two types of source: on the one hand there are the results of archaeological excavations (in other words the instruments or fragments thereof which have actually been unearthed), and on the other hand the fair number of pictorial representations which can sometimes throw light on the role these instruments played in the religious and secular life of far-off times.

Such evidence, slender and fragmentary as it is, often requires extremely careful interpretation, for the frescoes and drawings are not always very explicit. An example of this problem is the famous "Magus" in the cave *Les Trois Frères* (Arriège, France) where an object thought by some to be a vertical flute is seen by others as a sort of musical bow.

In order to obtain some idea of what were the first instruments used by man, we need only turn to the primitive peoples of today, and it will be seen that those instruments are none other than the voice, along with the hands and feet which are used as percussion; besides clapping, the hands slap the thighs, the armpits or the shoulders, producing rhythmic sounds which differ according to which part of the body is being struck.

Even though this practice remains largely the preserve of cultures still in the primitive state, it is met with occasionally in civilized countries, as in nursery songs accompanied by hand-clapping or in certain regional European customs such as the Tyrolean *Schuhplattlertanz* (a dance in which even the shoes are struck with the hand).

Before very long, primitive man discovered that, depending on how they were struck, plucked or rubbed, some of his tools and weapons were capable of producing sounds which differed both in pitch and in timbre. It is hardly surprising that he then set about transforming these tools so as to create proper musical instruments.

As early as the Magdalenian era (15,000-10,000 B.C.) we find in France a *scraper,* made of reindeer bone. Archaeologists have found them at Laugerie-Haute (the Dordogne), La Madeleine (the Dordogne), Lorthet (Hautes-Pyrénées) and at L'Abri du Château-lez-Bruniquel (Tarn-et-Garonne).

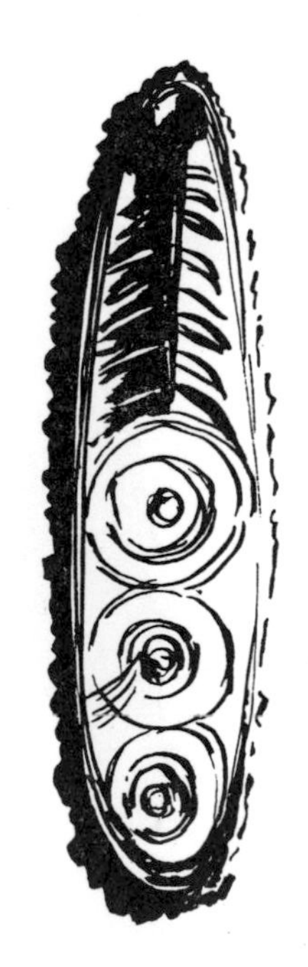
Bull-roarer.

Dating from the same period, *bull-roarers* have been found in the same region, but this time at La Roche-lez-Lalinde (the Dordogne) and at L'Abri du Bois de la Garenne de Saint-Marcel (Indre).

It is interesting to note that the bull-roarer is popular with those Australian tribes who today lead a Stone-Age existence. These tribes make the instrument in the same way as did paleolithic man. It consists of a long piece of bone, flat and oval-shaped, pierced at one end and attached to a long thread. By this means, the instrument may be whirled in the air at varying speeds. Its double movement — through the air and around its own axis — produces an uncanny whirring sound which, in the right circumstances, and in the shadows of the evening, must certainly have startled and even terrified anyone unaware of the reason for the phenomenon. This is why the Papous and the Australian aborigines see it as a sacred instrument by means of which they are able to contact spirits. Men of the Magdalenian civilization must also have felt similarly about the bull-roarer and used it for the same purposes.

Quite clearly, the small number of instruments that have been discovered in excavations do not constitute sufficient evidence for us to be certain of the exact extent of the areas in which they were used. For various reasons these might extend much further than one would imagine from the evidence. The areas in which an instrument was used could vary according to the era. For instance, the *curingas* — present-day Australian bull-roarers — are made of wood. Naturally wood is much more perishable than either bone or stone, so it is logical to suppose that Magdalenian man, and even Solutrian man before him (17,000-15,000 B.C.), made bull-roarers of wood as well as of bone.

What we have said about geographical areas and the dating of the bull-roarer is equally applicable in the case of flutes and whistles.

Whistles.

As a result of the excavations of Dr. Körber, we know that already in the paleolithic age, when bone was used as a basic material, the *vertical flute* was in existence, as shown by the bone flute discovered in the cave at Salzofen (Toten Gebirge). This is constructed in accordance with a very elementary acoustical principle: the player's breath breaks over the edge of the tube, thus setting in vibration the column of air inside the instrument. The same constructioñ is still used by many non-European peoples.

Before very long, man must have found that if a tube was provided with holes at some distance apart down its length it could be made to produce sounds of different pitch by means of the partial or entire blocking of these holes. A fragment of an instrument constructed in this way, dating from the second Aurignacian era (about 25,000 B.C.), has been found at Isturitz (Basses-Pyrénées).

Whistles, too, were known at this period, for some have been found, made of reindeer bone, at Aurignac itself (Haute-Garonne), and at other places: Laugerie-Basse, Les Eyzies, La Madeleine (all in the Dordogne), Solutré (Saône-et-Loire), and even in Belgium, where archaeological findings are proving to be of great interest. Indeed, although the whistle (or one-holed flute) found at Goyat is as recent as the first Magdalenian era (15,000-14,000 B.C.), the one discovered at Trou-de-Sureau (Montaigle) belongs to the second Aurignacian era.

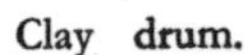

Clay drum.

Paleolithic whistles have also been found in Switzerland, at Schaffouse, as well as in Moravia, at Pekarna, and in Germany, at Petersfels-lez-Engen and at Schüssenried; on the other hand, in the nordic lands such whistles only begin to appear in the Maglemosian civilization (7500-5000 B.C.). Like the much earlier Isturitz flute, some of these were made from a fingerbone.

In mesolithic times (10,000-3000 B.C.), all these instruments continued to exist, but only a few from this period have been found. It was in the neolithic age (3000-1800 B.C.) that clay drums made their appearance. Archaeological museums have complete specimens and fragments, most dating from the Lausitz civilization and more particularly from the Walternienburg (2800-2500 B.C.) and from the Bernburg (2500-1900 B.C.) eras.

From these periods, two forms of drum have come down to us, one cup-shaped and the other in the form of an hour-glass.

The *goblet* (or cup-shaped) *drum* originated in the Near East where a similar drum, the *darabuka*, is in use to this day. Like the darabuka, the goblet drum is distinguished by a head which is a little wider than the body itself; some examples have been found in the Ukraine (Tripoljian civilization), thus forming part of the great Danubian cultures.

The decoration of these drums and drum fragments, being in the form of spiral bands or of dotted lines, or in yet other forms, enables us to define the date of manufacture as being within the span of the neolithic age.

The *hour-glass drums* which have come down to us are too few in number for us to be able to discuss them more fully. The drum does not appear to have been used in the nordic civilizations.

Lur.

The neolithic age also gave us other percussion instruments such as *clay bells* which were played at Tordos (Rumania) and at Knossos (Crete), and the *strung rattle*, a kind of jingle, also of clay, some of which have been found at Kopancs-Kökénydomb (Hungary).

One of the wind instruments of those times was the *conch trumpet*, whose use was not confined to coastal regions, but spread far inland as well; a conch trumpet of this period has been discovered at Budapest.

As before, of course, the fact that clay instruments have survived from the neolithic age does not rule out the possibility that similar instruments, made of wood or even of reed, were in existence both then and in earlier times.

The discovery and exploitation of bronze opened up many new possibilities for man to enrich his material life. Obviously, it was also bound to leave its mark on the making of instruments.

However, the Bronze Age, whose dates may be given roughly as 1800-1000 B.C., was of longer duration in the nordic countries than in the south-west of Europe, where, in fact, the Iron Age supervened much sooner. Thus, as is to be expected, it is in the northern regions, where the Bronze Age lasted longest, that bronze instruments are found to be most highly developed and most fully diversified.

The *horn*, made from the horn of an animal, was at first decorated with the newly discovered metal, but very soon animal horn was abandoned in favour of a similar instrument made entirely of bronze. The new substance being more malleable, it became possible to bring about refinements in the shape of the instrument.

However, neither the animal horn nor the bronze horn found at Lund possesses a mouthpiece. This means that the player would still have to adapt his lips suitably to perform the function of a mouthpiece. Nonetheless, it is at around this time that we see the beginnings of this accessory, still considered essential today. The earliest version was made as a fixed part of the instrument, and it was not until much later that it became a separate part. To return to the new material, bronze enabled man to make longer horns, and thus the short and very wide bore of the animal horn disappeared to be replaced by a longer, finer bore which ended in a less pronounced widening. As a result of these two modifications — in the mouthpiece and in the bore — new sounds came into existence alongside those already available, and the timbre of the instruments became more brilliant. Finally, the shape of the curved horn was replaced by that of the (more or less) straight horn.

However, certain instruments found in the Scandinavian marshlands and called *lurs* do not yet conform with this tendency, and their extremely elegant shape resembles the tusk of a mammoth, an animal we know to have lived in this region well before the manufacture of the lurs which have been unearthed. Thus we may assume that these bronze lurs were an imitation of instruments belonging to an earlier period and made from mammoth tusks.

Most of these bronze lurs have been found intact and, curiously, in identically tuned pairs. It would seem that this was so that two players could play in unison, the one reinforcing the other. We have so little knowledge about the musical practices of such distant times that it would be somewhat bold to claim that these lurs were already being used to create even a rudimentary form of instrumental polyphony, though when used in pairs it would have been possible for them to do so. Rock paintings found in the south of Sweden show that lurs were used in worship.

The Iron Age which followed was the last age preceding our own. It must be admitted that, though they are more recent, the first centuries of the Iron Age tell us nothing new about ancient instruments, some of which have come to light both in excavations and in pictorial representations.

Apparently, besides other materials like wood and reed, bronze continued to be used in the making of instruments as in the previous era, rather than the newly-discovered iron. The rattles found at Blödesheim (Hessen-Rhine) and Wallerfangen (Saar), dating from the beginning of the Iron Age, are all in bronze. Moreover, it would be difficult to maintain that the *lyre* of which we have an illustration from the (strictly Austrian) Hallstatt civilization (1500-1000 B.C.) was made of anything but wood; in bronze or iron its weight would have made it cumbersome to manipulate.

THE ORIENT

Since many of the Greco-Roman and Etruscan instruments have their origins in the East, we must, before examining them, take a look at the evolution of the oriental instruments which influenced their form. In order to follow broadly the phases through which these instruments passed prior to the stage at which they served as points of departure for Western instruments of the same family, we shall investigate their evolution by categories of family and type.

Stringed Instruments

The *arched harp* is found already in Mesopotamia at the time of the Sumerian civilization, depicted on reliefs which often show it and other instruments being played by animals; thus,

I. — 2.

Mural bas-relief of the Assyrian palace at Kujundschik (ruins of Nineveh) from the period of Assurbanipal (668-627 B.C.), showing musicians playing the frame-drum *(me-ze)*, lyres and a pair of cymbals. The name of these lyres, *sabitu,* indicates the number of their strings. The me-ze is still played in these regions today under the name of *dajre.*

Musée du Louvre, Paris.

I. — 3.

Egyptian sistrum of the Middle Empire. It consists of a metal plate bent into the form of a horseshoe on which are mounted five rods, bent back at their ends. When the instrument is shaken, these ends knock against the sides of the plate. The top of this sistrum is decorated with an unidentified animal. Height: *c.* 3¾ ins.

Musées Royaux d'Art et d'Histoire, Brussels. No. R. 101.

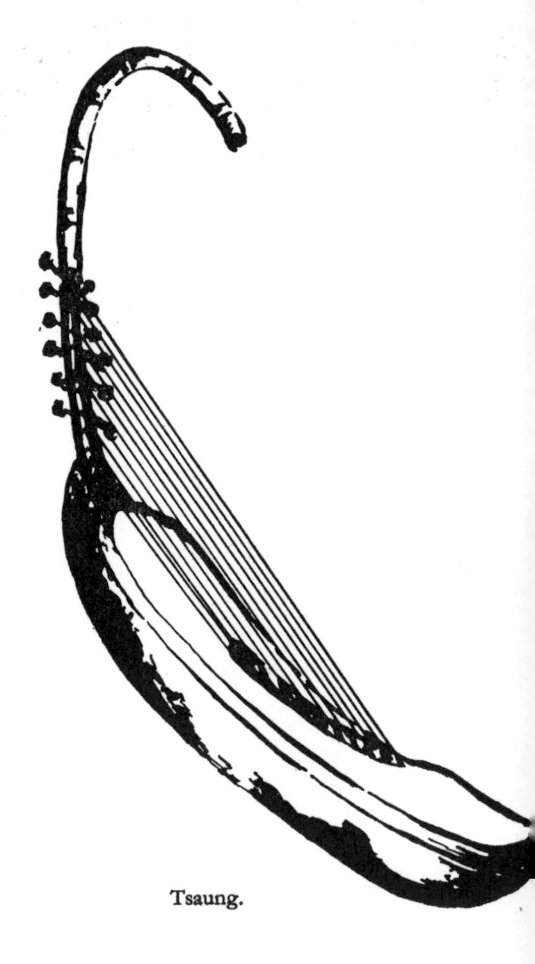

Tsaung.

I. — 2. **Assyrian bas-relief** (668-627 B.C.)

◀ I. — 3. **Egyptian sistrum** (Middle Empire)

I. — 4. **Egyptian harp** (2000-1785 B.C.)

I. — 5. **Egyptian castanets**
(New Empire)

I. — 6. **Hebrew shofarim** ▶

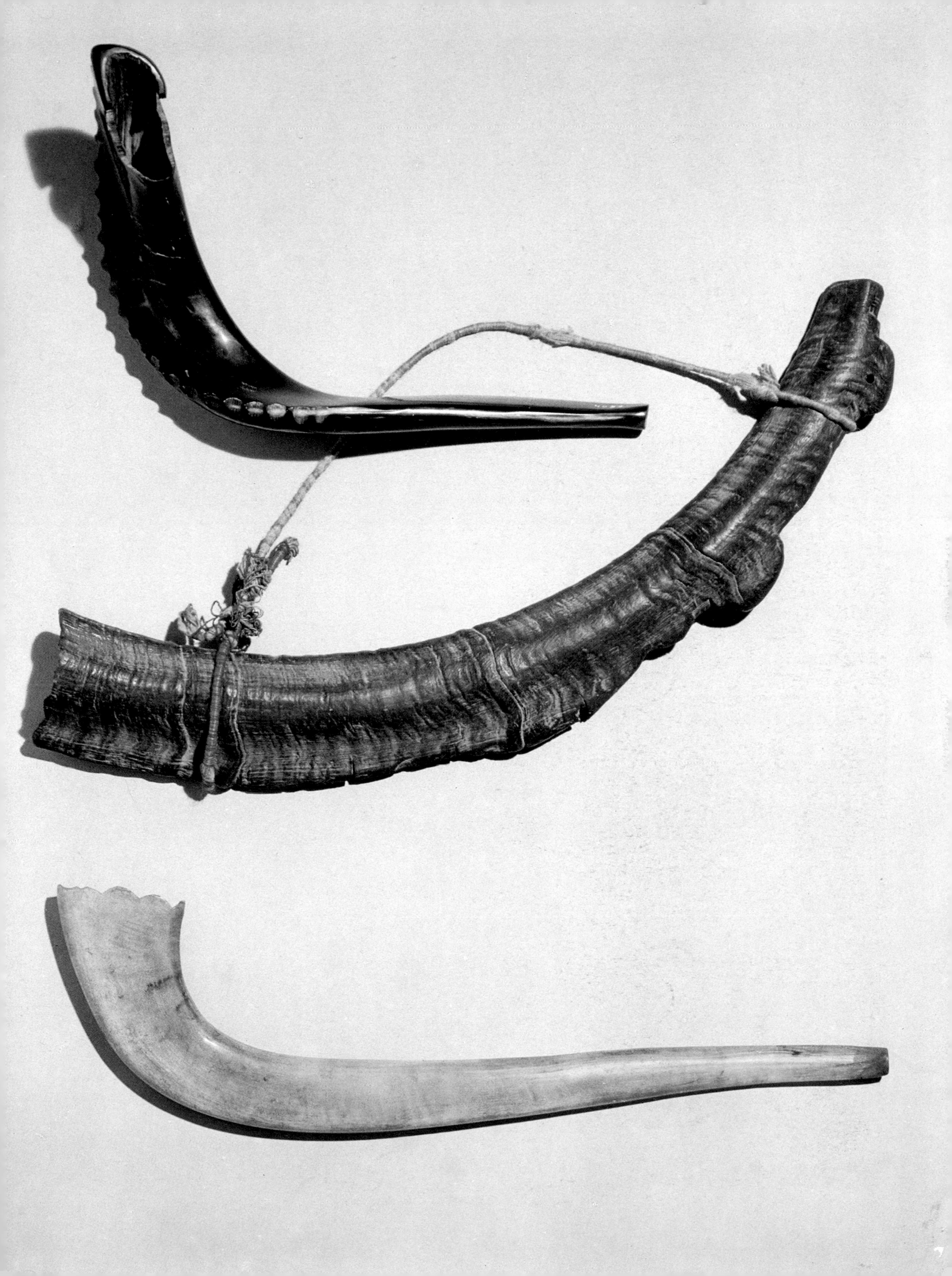

I. — 7. **Greek aulos and harp** (5th century B.C.)

I. — 8. **Roman tuba curva** (1st century B.C.) ▶

I. — 9. **Celtic carnyces** (1st century B.C.)

I. — 4.

Harp player (stele of the 12th dynasty — 2000-1785 B.C.). The player Neferhotep is blind, as was the god of the harpists. The harp in the picture is incomplete, lacking its base.
Rijksmuseum voor Oudheden, Leiden.

I. — 5.

Pair of Egyptian castanets of the New Empire. These castanets were either of ivory or of hard wood, and at this period were always in the form of forearms. The pair shown is of wood. Length: *c.* 14 ins.
Musées Royaux d'Art et d'Histoire, Brussels. No. E 5794 1 + 2.

I. — 6.

Three shofarim — Hebrew instruments of distant origin, but still used in worship. A shofar is the horn of a goat, without mouthpiece. According to *The Bible* the shofar was at that time used not only in worship but also in war. At present, the shofar is used in the synagogues for such ritual signals as the *th'kiah* and the *hi'ruah*. Two of the horns are of Persian origin; the white shofar was used by the Ashkenazim Jews. Length: *c.* 18⅛ ins., 21⅝ ins., 19¼ ins.
M.I., Brussels. Nos. 4056, 3858, 2015.

I. — 7.

Detail of a Greek vase from the 5th century B.C. The figure on the left is playing a double aulos of the type having divergent pipes. On the right a woman can be seen playing a harp in the form of a boat. Similar harps may still be found in Central Africa. Height of the figures: *c.* 5¾ ins.
Musées Royaux d'Art et d'Histoire, Brussels. No. 1020.

I. — 8.

Facsimile of a tuba curva discovered at Pompeï; this one, dating from the 1st century A.D., is at present in the National Museum of Naples. Its mouthpiece is unusual in that it may be separated from the body of the instrument. Diameter: *c.* 49½ ins.
M.I., Brussels. No. 464.

horses may be seen plucking the strings of harps while donkeys perform on lyres.

A very large harp has been found at Kul-i-Firâ (Persia). The Assyrians knew the instrument, and also played an instrument whose strings were placed at a slant, as in the present-day Burmese *tsaung*.

It was in Egypt, after 2500 B.C., that the most rapid development of the harp took place. At first it was still in arched form, as in Mesopotamia, but soon the *angular harp* made its appearance, and from then on one notices an increasing degree of discrimination between the status of the two instruments; the arched harp was gradually abandoned to be played only by mendicants, whereas the popularity of the angular harp — whose strings were augmented to the eventual total of ten — spread among the leisured classes and the nobility and finally established itself at the Pharaoh's court. Very large harps, with anthropomorphic bases, appear in pictures painted in the sepulchre of Ramasses III who reigned from about 1200 to 1168 B.C.

The lyre is another very ancient instrument. Lyres with silver and even gold plating have been discovered at Ur; these are many-stringed instruments. Later, the size of the instrument became smaller, and its shape finer and more elegant, as is shown by the lyres of about 2600 B.C. unearthed during excavations at Telloh.

It was under the New Empire (1580-1090 B.C.) that the lyre was introduced to Europe, through Asia Minor, and established itself there. It is interesting that the hieroglyphic writing **knr,** with which the Egyptians designated the lyre, is related to the word *kinnor*, a kind of lyre said to have been invented by the Phoenicians and widely known to the Syrians and the Hebrews. As the kinnor was used in the rites of Astarte, it is hardly surprising to find it subject to the maledictions of the Prophets, such as Isaiah and Ezekiel.

The *lute* probably originated in Babylon. One has been found shown on a relief of the time of Hammurabi (*c.* 1700 B.C.). It already has a long neck reminiscent of the type of lute still used in Central Asia. There were also lutes in the Assyrian civilization, and later the instrument appeared in Egypt, where it became very popular at the same time as the lyre. The oldest known lute was discovered intact in an Egyptian tomb, that of a musician called Harmosis (*c.* 1500 B.C.). Later, the Arabs disseminated the lute in the West as well as in the East, where it may be found even in China (*pi'pa'*) and Japan (*biwa*).

Wind Instruments

Bas-reliefs and other representations bear witness to the great variety of wind instruments used by the Eastern cultures – flutes and trumpets of different sizes, single– and double-reeded *shawms*, as well as *bagpipes*. However, they seem to have won neither the esteem nor the wide propagation enjoyed by the stringed instruments.

The *double-pipe shawms* were of two kinds. In the one, the pipes were mounted parallel, as is still the case in the Arabian *arghûl*, whilst in the other the pipes made an angle starting from between the player's lips; in Egypt, this latter, scorned by the men, was exclusively played by women.

The tomb of Tutankhamen (*c.* 1350 B.C.) contained gilded bronze trumpets besides silver ones. The Egyptian trumpets that we know are all short, and consequently produce a thin, harsh sound; it was perhaps for this reason that certain Greek authors likened their sound to that of an enraged donkey.

Like the other Eastern peoples, the Phoenicians and the Hebrews made little use of wind instruments. It is worth noting that the Hebrews attributed the invention of the flute to Jubal, and that trumpets are spoken of favourably in the *Old Testament*. Moses even goes so far as to give indications as to how they were made. The *shofar* differs from the metallic trumpet in that it was made from ram's horn (the Hebrews were a nation of shepherds), and therefore dates from an earlier age; according to the *Bible* it was to the sound of shofarim that the walls of Jericho crumbled. In spite of the advent of other materials, the shofar continued to be made of animal horn. It was, in fact, only later, when the Jews dispersed over the world, that the shofar, used in cultural ceremonies, differed in its shape and ornamentation according to the region in which it was used.

Percussion Instruments

There were a good number of these, and they were much used.

The *sistrum*, a metallic jingle, is not (as is often believed) of Egyptian origin, for some may be found already depicted on Mesopotamian reliefs. However, it was most used in Egypt, already existing there under the Middle Empire (2160-1750 B.C.) alongside a form of *castanets*, particularly in honour of Hathos, the goddess of music. It consisted of discs and rods mounted in such a way that they would rattle when shaken.

Very large *kettledrums* already appear on Babylonian reliefs (at Guda). Bronze bells have been found in Assyria, whereas *tambourines* (the Biblical *timbrels*), sometimes with quadrangular frames like the modern Arab *duff*, were in use over a very extensive area.

GREECE AND ROME

It is now known that in many fields, the Greek civilization from its earliest years underwent the influence of the Eastern peoples bordering on the Mediterranean, with whom Greeks from the islands and mainland were constantly in contact. This influence is particularly clear in the musical instruments they used, even including those, such as the *cithara* and the *lyra*, which they considered their national instruments.

A peculiarity of the Greeks was their distaste for loud music, and so they scarcely used metallic wind instruments and percussion instruments at all. But they had many instruments of other types as we shall shortly see, and these lend themselves readily to classification.

I. — 9.

Three carnyx players depicted on a silver cauldron found at Gundestrup (near Aalborg, Jutland). This cauldron, belonging to the Iron Age, dates back to about the 1st century B.C. This is one of the very few illustrations we have of the ancient Celtic instrument. Height of the cauldron: *c.* 8¼ ins.
Coll. *Nationalmuseet,* Copenhagen.

Our knowledge of the instruments of the Greco-Roman epoch is almost entirely drawn from literary works and writings on musical theory of the time, and from monuments and depictions, chiefly those painted on terracotta vases and utensils.

Stringed Instruments

It is, without doubt, to one or other of the Asian nations on the Mediterranean coastline that we can trace the origins of four Greek plucked string instruments; the *pectis*, the *magadis*, the *Phoenician lyre* (as Aristotle calls it) and the *sambuca*. The Greek writers' descriptions of these instruments show that their design was sufficiently similar to sometimes confuse those attempting to describe them. All we know of them is that all four had a large number of strings of high pitch.

To correspond to these, in the lower register the Greeks had the *barbiton* and the *trigonon*, the latter being none other than the harp of the Egyptians.

Because all these instruments had numerous strings, they could yield a sort of chromatic and voluptuous music which, more than anything, betrayed their oriental origins. The pectis was especially suitable for this music, and was played by the women of Lydia. The poetess Sappho (*c.* 610 B.C.) encouraged the playing of the instrument at Lesbos, where the magadis also was well known.

The Spartans and the Athenians, who took the greatest care in providing a balanced education for citizens and soldiers alike, were rather averse to the adoption of these instruments, whose sounds they may have thought likely to weaken moral strength; they preferred the lyra and the cithara to the extent of considering them their national instruments. The primitive simplicity of these instruments was more suited to their temperament, and being easy to play, they were popular amongst all classes of society. This is why they are so often depicted on monuments and other objects of the time (jewellery, paintings, vases, statues, etc.), unlike the four other instruments mentioned above. The many representations of the lyra and the cithara allow us to study in some detail their structure and evolution.

The Greek lyra and the cithara may have been taken over from the Egyptians at a time when those instruments used on the banks of the Nile were still fairly simple in structure.

The oldest cithara to have been found on Greek territory dates from the sixteenth century B.C., and was discovered in the palace of Hagia Triada (Crete).

At the same time, the Homeric poets referred to an instrument similar to the cithara by the name *phorminx*. Homer himself, in the ninth canto of *The Iliad*, speaks of a phorminx which was sonorous and had luxurious ornamentation and a silver crosspiece.

The lyra and the cithara differ in shape. They underwent different evolutions up to the point when, in Roman times, they gave birth to a hybrid instrument referred to either as the lyra or the cithara, or as the *lyra-cithara*.

Originally, the lyra had a body made from a tortoiseshell,

over which a skin was stretched. Later, when this shell was replaced by a wooden resonator, the original shape was preserved. Two graceful, slightly curved supports are attached to the sound-box. Finally, a bridge fixed on the latter serves to separate it from the strings.

The cithara, which may be considered as a sturdier type of lyra, was built on the same principles, except that the supports were thicker and straighter so that the tension of the strings could be made greater without bending or snapping them. So either the existing strings were tightened or a greater number of strings was used.

This explains why, although supplementary strings were later added to the lyra, it was denied the kind of evolution whereby the cithara gradually became transformed into an instrument like the large concert *zither*. By the same token, the lyra was more widely played since practically anyone could learn to play it; it was the only instrument permitted in primary musical education and in popular festivals, whereas in the course of time the cithara became more and more the speciality of virtuoso performers. As for the pectis, the magadis, the Phoenician lyre and the sambuca, they were only tolerated in orgiastic feasts and ceremonies.

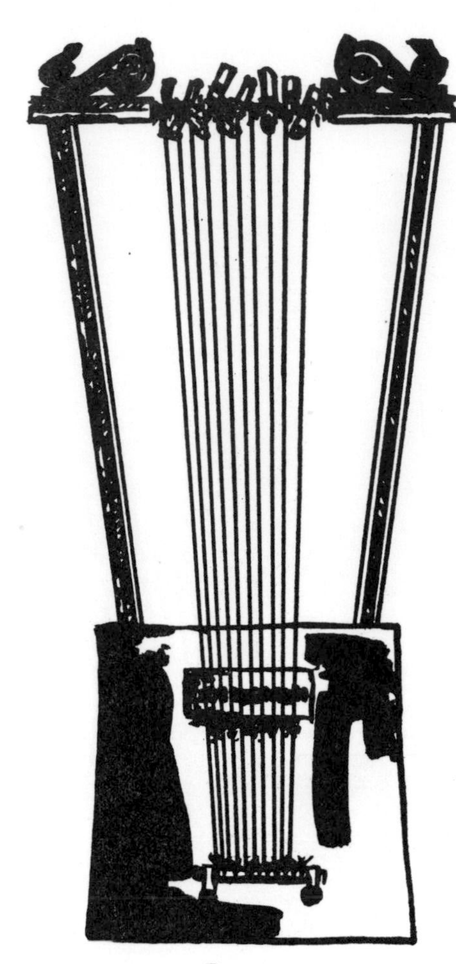

Baganna.

The Lesbian poet Terpander (*c.* 700 B.C.), who taught in Sparta, is credited with the invention of the seven-stringed lyra, but it was very probably known before his time. Later an eighth, and then a ninth string were added. Such was the lyra of about 500 B.C. — and such it was to remain.

On the other hand, the cithara, whose development up to this time seems to have been parallel with that of the lyra, had more strings added until, by about 420 B.C., it had twelve. These new strings were not added at the top or at the bottom of its range, but filled out those already present so as to give chromatic semitones, thus giving a new flavour to Greek instrumental music and allowing for niceties of playing impossible on the lyra.

We have noted the possibility of Egyptian influence on the lyra and the cithara. The contemporaneous evidence for this is supported by the fact that one meets with these instruments today in countries on the Egyptian border; the first is known by the name *kissar*, and may be found almost anywhere in East Africa, whilst the second is played in Ethiopia, where it is called the *baganna*.

For several centuries the Greeks retained the simplicity of form in the lyre and the harp which suited their mode of education. At first, the Romans took over these instruments from the Greeks without modification, but during Alexandrian times (about 200 B.C.), both Greeks and Romans underwent a marked influence from the East. This led to various modifications to musical instruments, including a further increase in the number of the cithara's strings — it now had fifteen — and the appearance of citharas of different registers. At this time, musicians cultivated extreme virtuosity. According to Livy, it was in 187 B.C. that the influence of Eastern music began to affect Rome, and Juvenal tells us that it was at this time that the sambuca was introduced. This instrument was played by the *ambubajae* of whom Horace speaks; women of easy virtue, of Syrian origin, who had banded together in a corporation in order to ply their trade.

The harp and the lute did not prove at all popular in Greece and Rome, where they encountered some scorn and were considered rather uncouth.

Wind Instruments

The name *auloi* was used by the Greeks as a generic term for all the wind instruments they allowed in their musical performances. Strictly speaking, in fact, the word *aulos* referred to a single- or double-reed instrument similar in type to our clarinet or oboe, whereas the word *syrinx* specifically referred to an instrument identical with our vertical flute. As for the instrument that corresponded to our transverse flute, although it existed in the East, it was spurned by the Greeks, and only later reached Rome through the Etruscans.

Hydraulus.

The aulos (in Latin, *tibia*), single- or double-reeded, had a cylindrical bore. It could be played in pairs, in which case the two pipes could be parallel or could diverge. Whilst playing, the instrumentalist would wear a sort of shield called the *phorbeia*, in order to conceal the swelling of his cheeks and to minimize facial fatigue. Today, players of the indigenous oboe of Indonesia do the same.

Aulos pipes might be made of reed, wood, bone, ivory or metal, without any change in their timbre. At first they were not very long and the few holes which could be drilled to shorten the column of air did not permit a great number of sounds to be played. However, their length increased gradually over the years, as did the number of holes, so that finally the instrument was able to yield a complete chromatic scale. After this, as soon as the spacing of the holes was such that the fingers could not block them all at the same time, moving keys were fitted to the instrument's body so as to perform this function, either in part or entirely.

Aristoxenes of Tarenta (about 350 B.C.) classified the auloi in five groups according to whether their register was higher or lower. The Romans attempted to extend the tibia's range towards the bass, and succeeded in making a tibia as low in register as our *bassoon*. Thus the first bassoon in fact dated from well before the sixteenth century A.D. to which it is commonly attributed. Examples of these *tibiae bassae* may be found in the Museum of Naples and in the British Museum.

The vertical flute (*syrinx monokalamos* in Greek, *fistula* in Latin) has little history. Its length, and therefore its register, remained limited. In all its forms, it remained in the soprano register.

The *syrinx polykalamos*, nowadays better known as the *panpipe*, goes back to very distant times. Depending on the period and the locality, it was made of from 5 to 13 pipes of increasing length placed alongside each other. The Greeks and Romans never used them in their recitals and concerts, for they were considered to be instruments with severe limitations; generally only the shepherds played them. Yet it was this syrinx polykalamos that fathered our king of instruments, the *organ*, said to have been the invention of Ktesibios — who lived in Alexandria in the third century B.C. — and which was at first called the *hydraulus*. This ingenious invention made use of a keyboard with sliders, each of which opened and shut a corresponding pipe or group of pipes; a volume of water in one or two tanks maintained the necessary air pressure.

Two different writers, Hero, a near-contemporary and probably a compatriot of Ktesibios, and Vitruvius, Augustus's architect, have left us fairly detailed descriptions of the hydraulus; it is also depicted on reliefs, coins and mosaics.

According to Vitruvius, the hydraulic organ could have as many as eight registration stops, but unlike the present-day organ these appear to have been intended solely to bring into play different combinations of registers, and today would be known as mixture stops. It is not known when keys began to replace the sliders.

The hydraulus had a range of three octaves and was in part chromatic. According to Suetonius, Nero never tired of hearing it, and was even responsible for adding more refinements to it. Septimus Severus also played it. In fact, under the Empire, the Romans became infatuated with it and brought it to all the territories they occupied. However, because it was an instrument capable of playing polyphonic music invented at a time when only monodic music was practised — a situation which held good for long afterwards — the hydraulus remained more of a curiosity than a concert instrument. It was displayed and heard in circuses and theatres, for its powerful sound could be heard by all at a large gathering.

Part of a hydraulus was found in 1931 near Budapest (Hungary) on the site of the ancient city of Aquincum. The city was built in the time of Septimus Severus, and the instrument must date from some time before A.D. 228, in which year Aquincum was destroyed by fire. Fragments of hydraulus have also been found at Pompeï.

Organs of this type continued to be made up to the eighth or ninth century, but in the third century the pneumatic organ appeared, and gradually supplanted the older type.

It was above all in the Eastern part of the Roman Empire that the pneumatic organ evolved to the detriment of the hydraulic organ, whose weight made it difficult to move from one place to another. At Byzantium, organs played an important part in ceremonies and were often transported to different parts of the town. There, the pneumatic organ underwent several improvements, the most important of these being the division of stops into one or more ranks of reed pipes and stopped pipes in addition to the mixture stops.

At Rome itself, it seems that the hydraulic organ was deemed sufficient. The early Christians rejected this instrument because of its associations with pagan ceremonies, but also because at the time of the persecutions its powerful sonority would have betrayed the clandestine meeting-places of the faithful.

Later, when their religion had become accepted, it is quite possible that they were not so strict in their avoidance of the organ, for one finds the Church Fathers, such as St. Ambrose and St. Augustine, protesting at the use of the instrument at certain meetings of the Christians.

The Greeks and Romans were familiar with some of the

instruments we now call "the brass", but they never used them in concerts because of their limitations. They were mainly called on for the fanfares which were a part of certain civic, military and religious ceremonies. Pollux (second century A.D.) gives interesting details of these instruments, and some specimens have been unearthed in excavations.

The *salpinx* (trumpet), traditionally of Etruscan origin, had a slightly conical bore. It might be straight or curved: straight, it corresponded to the Roman *tuba*; curved, it was identical with their *bucina*. The mouthpiece of these two types of salpinx was of bone, and the body of bronze or iron. The tuba could attain a length of about four feet; but the bucina, due to the curve of its body, might extend to eleven feet, so that the larger number of sounds it could produce enabled melodic lines to be played on it, whereas the tuba was confined to fanfares. Pollux gives the names of these different distinctive fanfares, each of which, like modern military trumpet-calls, had its own meaning.

It was not only in the army, but also in the temples that the tuba was used, and those whose lot it was to play the instrument held the rank of priest.

Another instrument, the *keras*, corresponding to the Roman *cornu* and to the mediaeval *cornett*, was, as its name suggests, made from animal horn, which, as Aristotle tells us, was sometimes heated over a fire to improve its sonority. It had a lustreless, muted sound, in contrast to the bright, sometimes painful sound of the salpinx or the tuba, which the ageing Ennius found terrifying: "... *at tuba terribili sonitu taratamtara dixit...*". The small size of the keras, or cornu, made it suitable only for signalling.

In their armies, the Romans used another instrument called the *lituus*, which had a straight, almost cylindrical body about 5ft. 4 ins. long, and a slightly flared bell in the form of a hook at the end. Again, it was from the Etruscans that the Romans took this instrument — the first in the history of wind instruments to possess an independent mouthpiece. There is an Etruscan bronze lituus (discovered at Cervetri in 1827) in the Vatican Museum, and the Saalburg Museum (in Homburg, Germany) has an exactly similar Roman lituus.

Before going on to the percussion instruments, it should be said that it was again to the Etruscans that the Romans owed the transverse flute, which the later Greeks called *plagiaulos* and the Alexandrians called *photinx*. In order to have the instrument played in their temples, the Romans employed Etruscan players, who seem to have formed a sort of trade union; for Livy reports that they would not hesitate to call a strike, and the Romans were obliged to ply them with wine before they would return to work.

Thus it may be seen that in general the Romans took over from the Greeks the instruments which played a part in their civilian life, and those intended for military use were largely taken from the Etruscans.

Percussion Instruments

By far the greatest number of the percussion instruments known to the Greeks and to the Romans were introduced from the East together with the rituals they accompanied. Examples are the *kymbala*, (small *cymbals*) used in the Phrygian cult of Cybelos, the *krotala*, (castanets), small bells, and finally a tambourine called the *tympanon*, of which the ambubajae, referred to above in connection with the sambuca, were particularly skilful players.

It is interesting to note that small metallic *gongs* have been found in Italy, mostly in central and northern regions, which date from the Villa Nova period, that is, about the beginning of the Iron Age.

Before closing this chapter, we must mention that the Celts at first were influenced by the Romans through the legions and colonial settlers scattered over all the Empire.

Tubae with sliding telescopic bodies (so that they could be made shorter when not in use) have been found at Neuvy-en-Sullas and at Saumur.

The *carnyx*, typically Celtic in that its bell is in the form of a dragon's head, recalls the shape of the lituus. Its mouthpiece was of lead. This type of instrument has also been found in Dacia (Rumania) and even in Paplagonia (Asia Minor) where we know many Celts settled. In Ireland, around 300 B.C., there were carnyces side by side with lurs. A Celtic bronze horn has been found at Nice, and clay horns of the Bronze Age have been unearthed at Numancia (Spain).

II - The Middle Ages

L'us menet arpa, l'autre viula
L'us flautella, l'autre situla
L'us mena giga, l'autre rota,
(Guiraud de Cabrera,
Roman de Flamenca, 1340)

HICPSALPROPRIE
SCRIBITURDDET
EXTRANUMERUM
PUSILLUSERAM
INTERFRATRESMEOS
ETADOLESCENTIORIN
DOMOPATRISMEIPAS
CEBAMOUESPATRISMEI
MANUSMEAEFECERUNT
ORGANUM ETDIGITIMEI
APTAUERUNTPSALTERIU
ETQUISADNUNTIAUIT

CUMPUGNAUIT
GOLIATHICPSLIN
EBREISCODICIBUS
DNOMEODEME
IPSEDNSIPSEOMNIUM
EXAUDIUIT
IPSEMISITANGELUMSUU
ETTULITMEDEOUIBUSPA
TRISMEIETUNXITMEIN
MISERICORDIAUNCTIO
NISSUAE
FRATRESMEIBONIETMAGNI

II. — 1. **Page from the Utrecht Psalter**

Historical Background

When, in A D. 395, Theodosius divided the vast Roman Empire between his two sons, he was in fact giving his blessing to its final collapse. The Eastern half, allotted to Arcadius, survived until 1453, but the Western part, with which we are more concerned here, was to last less than a century (until 476), torn apart by political conflicts which were to leave it in a state of indescribably chaotic disorder.

In the West, the natural boundaries of Rome and its provinces — the Rhine, the Danube, and the African deserts — which had from the time of Augustus been guarded by numerous legions, began to yield to the pressure of barbarian peoples mainly coming from the North, who were followed by others who gradually made their way towards the South. In this way, new empires were created in which natives and invaders had more or less intermingled.

Christianity bound together their disparities more and more firmly, replacing that which had been lost in terms of ethnical unity with a sense of spiritual community.

Christianity had gained tolerance with the Edict of Milan (313), under the Emperor Constantine, and was instituted as the national religion in 392 by the Emperor Theodosius; now it could and did spread freely wherever the Romans were in power. After the fall of the Empire it was to continue spreading and also reinforce its first footholds.

It was thus that out of a widespread chaos, the Catholic Church soon emerged as the only possible religious authority. The earliest missionaries who travelled first all over Italy and then to neighbouring countries, took care not to go too much against the grain of the religions and beliefs they found already in existence. They allowed certain compromises, not perhaps always in complete harmony with the spirit of Roman doctrines, but not in direct opposition to them either; however, we have no need to take these into account here.

Following the instructions of the Church, the missionaries and bishops prohibited the use of instruments in worship. However, they could not prevent their converts from playing instruments in the course of their secular activities. Unfortunately, these instruments, cheaply constructed and poorly maintained as they were, were not durable. For this reason, practically no instruments have survived from the Middle Ages before about A.D. 1000; exceptionally, a few ivory horns have survived the ravages of time because of the durability of the material itself.

Here and there in the writings of the Church Fathers we find descriptions of certain instruments, but these must be very carefully interpreted, since they are very often symbolic descriptions. They are certainly based on fact, but we cannot assert that the basic facts have not been twisted for the purpose of elucidating a symbol. This may be seen from a quotation from a letter (in any case apocryphal) from St. Jerome to a certain Dardanus, in which he describes various instruments such as the organ, the trumpet, the flute, etc. To take only one example, this is what we find with regard to the organ:

"Of all the instruments, the organ yields the most powerful sound; it is made of two concave elephant skins and twelve bellows to which correspond twelve brass pipes which produce a sound so powerful that it may be likened to the sound of thunder, to such an extent that it may be heard a mile and even further away."

Here the description of the organ ends, and the accompanying sketch is very rough giving barely any clues about the instrument. On the other hand, the text goes on to make various points about the organ which can hardly be said to shed much light on the instrument itself. The different parts of the organ just described are made to correspond with elements from the Holy Scriptures. The two rugged skins are said to represent the rigour of the two laws; the twelve bellows recall the Patriarchs and the Prophets; the twelve brass pipes represent the Apostles, whose immense voice fills the whole earth, etc. It is clear that such a text cannot give a reliable indication of the real nature of organs of that period.

As soon as our written sources become more numerous, that is to say for several centuries from the time of Charlemagne onwards, a number of instruments are mentioned in epics, romances and chronicles, without being more fully described. Most of these names, written in texts originating sometimes in very different regions, have features in common. However it would be rash to think that they always referred to the same instrument, for sometimes an instrument would be given different names in different regions. Here, then, we will only take into account those facts which appear to be well established.

We know for certain that the Greco-Roman instruments introduced to Roman occupied territories were used there to the same extent as instruments native to those areas during the first centuries of Christianity. The two sorts of instruments co-existed for a certain time, reciprocal influences playing a part in their development until finally they resulted in the creation of hybrid or, occasionally, new instruments. Again and again we shall be able to observe this phenomenon.

Stringed Instruments

The first instrument we have to deal with outside the Greco-Roman world is a kind of lyre; it consists of a sound-box with two supports joined together by a cross-piece. We must look for its origins in the North, for lyre-like instruments seem not to have been played in the South, where lute-like instruments (sound-box with an upright neck) appear to have been popular. In France, where North meets South, both types could be found.

This lyre-like instrument was called *harf* by the Germans, and the Romans in the same region coined the word *arpa* to refer to the instrument. They even went so far as to use the word arpa to designate all instruments with plucked strings. In so doing, they were merely reverting to the original Greek αρπαζειν meaning "to seize" or "to pluck".

That the Germanic word harf has nothing to do with what we nowadays call the harp is shown by the Greek historian Diodorus of Sicily, who lived in about 90 B.C., and who tells us in his monumental *Historical Library* that the Germanic harf was similar to the lyre (meaning the Greek lyra).

Only several centuries later do we find a text appearing to confirm this use of the word arpa to mean a kind of lyre. This text is part of a long poem by Venantius Fortunatus, who was Bishop of Poitiers from 597 to 600:

Romanusque lyra plaudat tibi, barbarus harpa
Graecus achiliaca, chrotta britannia canat.

In these two lines, four peoples or groups of peoples are named, and to each is assigned an instrument bearing a different name. But whether it is called the lyra, the arpa, the *achiliaca* or the *chrotta*, it is in fact one and the same instrument, in other words the lyre. The opening of each of the two lines names a Mediterranean people, whilst in the second halves we find respectively the *barbarus*, presumably including Franks and Alemanni, and the Britons. Since the Middle Ages, the Welsh word *crouth* or *crwth* has meant a type of lyre. This word is probably of Irish origin, and has an equivalent in the Latin *chrotta* or *rotta*.

There is already mention of this crwth in an Irish epic poem dating from pre-Christian times. The poet calls the instrument *coircethairchuir*, meaning "thou, who art quadrangular and harmonic". The crwth, which survived in Wales up to the eighteenth century, has the same shape. A letter from the English abbot Gutberg to his friend Lul, Bishop of Mainz, who lived from 705 to 786, provides further evidence that the crwth is a kind of lyre, for in it he asks to be sent a player of the cithara, which, he adds, "we call the rotta". So when the mediaeval Latin writers speak of *cithara teutonica,* they are referring to the lyre; and by *cithara anglica* they mean the Irish harp.

Clairsighe.

After about the tenth or eleventh century, the crwth or rotta became the bowed lyre, and may therefore be considered one of the ancestors of the *viol.*

The harp was another instrument with plucked strings. The oldest known mediaeval harp is of Irish provenance. At the beginning of the Middle Ages there were two versions of the instrument: one, smaller and older, appears to have had only one support, which also served as the sound-box; it was gradually supplanted by the other, larger model, which finally established itself in about the seventh century. In its turn, this was replaced in the ninth century by a third type, the *clairsighe,* more finely made, and notable for its gracefully curved anterior support; the upright rear support acted as the sound-box. The tenth-century Anglo-Saxon *Psalter* preserved at Berlin contains a miniature portrayal of King David playing an Irish harp.

In *The Bible* of Charles the Bald (823-877) we see for the first time a hybrid form taken from both the lute and the lyre: King David is shown holding a lyre, between whose two supports the miniaturist has painted a neck, over which only a small number of the strings are stretched.

At about the same date, the first illustration in the Lothar *Psalter* shows us the same instrument, but this time having more strings; here, King David is holding a bow, but it is obvious that this bow has nothing to do with the instrument depicted, whose structure is such that it could only be played by plucking the strings with the fingers or with a plectrum. Possibly the artist wanted to take the opportunity to show off the bow as a novelty of the time.

The biography of St. Dunstan, Bishop of Canterbury (d. 988), is the first to mention the *dulcimer*, another stringed instrument. In this instrument, which is in the shape of a trapezoid, the strings are struck in the manner of a percussion instrument.

The mediaeval dulcimer is of Asian origin. In fact it derives from the Persian *santûr,* whose strings were struck with two wooden beaters held between the player's thumb and index finger. Sometimes the word "psaltery" was used in mediaeval writings to refer to the dulcimer. This is clearly erroneous, since the word "psaltery" should refer only to plucked string instruments, deriving from the Arabian *q'anun.*

According to Isidore of Seville (*c.* 600) the psaltery was in the shape of a delta, in other words triangular, as was also the cithara barbarica; the difference between these two instruments was that in the psaltery the hollow sound-box was in the upper position and the strings were plucked lower down, whereas precisely the opposite was true of the cithara barbarica.

It is thought that the psaltery came from the East at the beginning of the twelfth century, and was particularly widespread in the West from the thirteenth century onwards. Already, in the twelfth century, it had a variable number of single or double strings, which were stretched by means of pegs across the body. At that time it had from six to ten strings. Some manuscripts of the twelfth century show us, besides the triangular psaltery, a ten-stringed psaltery shaped like a "square buckler" as one of the writers puts it.

In the course of the thirteenth century the number of strings increased, going from ten to fifteen or sixteen strings. Finally, in the fourteenth century, the psaltery was often built in a stylized T-shape; here the strings were parallel to the base, and were deployed in the same way as those found in the "square buckler" psaltery.

It is worth noting that the psaltery was mostly used in the South, whilst, at first at any rate, the dulcimer was more particularly to be found in the North. This is why the Italians called the dulcimer *salterio tedesco,* to distinguish it from the psaltery itself.

The final stage in the evolution of the psaltery was its adoption of the trapezoid shape; after that, only the addition of a keyboard was necessary for the instrument to be transformed, with a few modifications of details, into the *spinet* and the *virginal,* whilst the dulcimer, also given a keyboard during the second half of the fourteenth century, became the prototype of the *échiquier d'Angleterre,* then of the *clavichord.*

Another instrument with plucked strings found at this period was called the *micanon,* and was shaped like half of a T-shaped psaltery, in which the division went up the centre of the T. Its form recalls the Arabian q'anun, but sometimes it is found to have a hollowed-out side. When the time came to add a keyboard to it, as in the case of the psaltery, the instrument provided the basic shape of the harpsichord which likewise has a plucked-string action.

Q'anun.

After 1300, church and cathedral carvings often feature the psaltery and dulcimer, but they are portrayed with such imprecision of detail that it is not always possible to tell which of the two instruments is represented.

In about the ninth century, when there were the first signs of a tendency towards polyphonic music, a scale of fixed intervals became necessary. So as to calculate these intervals, mediaeval theorists had recourse to an instrument called the *monochord,* a description of which could be found in the *De Institutione Musica* of Boethius (d. 526), a treatise widely used in mediaeval musical education. This instrument consisted of a long calibrated sound-box, over which a string was stretched. Supporting the string, was a movable bridge, by means of which the string could be lengthened or shortened. Thanks to this movable bridge, the exact measurements of the intervals — concords and discords — could be precisely calculated. Incidentally, the monochord was used by the Greeks, who gave it the name *kanon.* The mediaeval monochord, originally intended for theoretical purposes, soon began to be used as a musical instrument in its own right. Rather than using the movable bridge to lengthen and shorten the one string so as to produce notes of different pitches, several strings of different lengths began to be used on the same sound-box; the lengths of these strings corresponded to those which could previously be obtained on the single string by moving the bridge.

Although now possessing more than one string, the instrument nevertheless continued to go under the name monochord. In the fourteenth century, monochords with fourteen strings were played.

The instrument was referred to in mediaeval treatises as the *monocordum*, but it might be popularly known as the *manicorde,* the *manicordion* or even the *manicorda.* Under this name it was usually a one-stringed monochord, used, not as a laboratory instrument, but as one which could take part in musical performances. It is as this type of instrument that we find it referred to by the famous musician and poet Guillaume de Machaut at the end of the fourteenth century; at that time it was played with a plectrum. It is rather curious that an instrument of the clavichord family was referred to as the manicordion in France at the end of the fifteenth century; in seventeenth-century Spain the *harpsichord* was known as the *monocordio.*

In the thirteenth century, and perhaps already in the twelfth, appeared a strange instrument called the *tromba marina* (in German, *Trumscheit*) which was mainly used in convents.

This instrument had a very long sound-box, in the shape of a narrow trapezoid, on the top of which was a neck. The tromba marina had only one string, which was of fairly thick catgut and passed over a bridge; the bridge was peculiar in that it had one leg against the sound-box and another, shorter one, which remained free. When the string was set in vibration, this free leg vibrated against an ivory or bone plate embedded in the sound-box. The string was played with a bow, but contrarily to the normal manner of playing bowed string instruments, the bow was placed on the string between the player's hand and the head or scroll of the instrument, rather than between the hand

and the bridge. Moreover, instead of pressing the string onto the neck, the player's hand only touched it lightly, in such a way that the vibrating string produced a harmonic rather than the fundamental note. The combination of the sound of the harmonic with that of the vibrating free leg of the bridge resulted in a bright and brassy sound which might recall that of the trumpet.

It is worth investigating the origin of the name tromba marina, a name as curious as the instrument itself. Beyond doubt, the sound of the instrument resembled that of the trumpet. This is confirmed by the opinion of Jean-Baptiste Prin, who lived in the second half of the eighteenth century and was one of the instrument's few virtuoso performers. Prin's intention had been to perfect this instrument, and he wrote a pamphlet on the subject called *Mémoire sur la trompette marine.* There he claimed to have invented a bridge which imparted to the instrument "the strength of a trumpet, the sweetness of a flute and the harmoniousness of a harpsichord". Extravagant claims, one might think, but the important thing is that Prin gives pride of place to the instrument's really characteristic sound-quality — that of the trumpet. As for the qualifying adjective *marina,* we have here a distortion of the German word *marieken,* often found in conjunction with the name *Trumscheit,* meaning "trumpet of the Daughters of Mary", in other words: a trumpet used by nuns. The tromba marina was played up till the seventeenth century and even the start of the eighteenth, for they were still featured in Louis XIV's *Grande Ecurie du Roy.*

The lute is an extremely ancient instrument. Its origins in the East go back to the most distant times. [1]

Often shown in old Psalters, such as that of Utrecht (832), the lute, with its long neck and pear-shaped body, had three strings; it resembled its Asian ancestor the *tanbûr* rather than the Arabian lute *(al'ûd)* which the Moors introduced in Spain and which spread through France to Germany and Italy (being mentioned by Boccaccio in the *Decameron* and by Dante in the *Divine Comedy).*

II. — 2.

Manuscript of the 10th century containing the *De Institutione Musica* of Boethius preceded by an apocryphal letter of St. Jerome to Dardanus and a fragment of the *Etymologiae* of Isidore of Seville. This letter and fragment, which deal with musical instruments, are followed (fol. 51 *v*° and 52 *r*°) by the illustrations reproduced here.

Staatsbibliothek, Munich.
Cod. 13523, fol. 51 *v*°, 52 *r*°.

II. — 3.

Miniature from The Bible of Charles the Bald (823-877). In the centre, King David is holding a triangular harp; above him, to the left and to the right, musicians are holding a sort of shofar and castanets. At the bottom, a crwth player can be seen on the left and a lituus player on the right.

Bibliothèque Nationale, Paris.

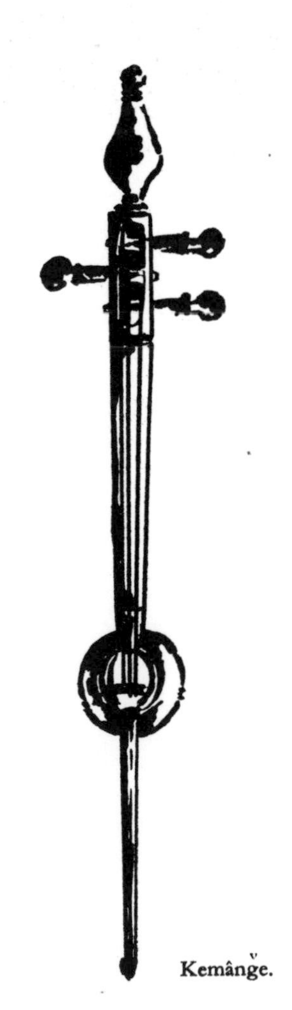

Kemânǧe.

1 *We have called "lute-like" any stringed instrument in which the sound-box is surmounted by a neck, however embryonic; "lyre-like" has been used for any stringed instrument in which two upright arms, joined towards the top by a cross-piece, are attached to the sound-box. The difference between these two types is immediately obvious; in lute-like instruments any string placed over the neck can be shortened by the pressure of a finger, and is thus able to give sounds of several different pitches. On the other hand, in lyre-like instruments, the string, only able to vibrate down its full length, can only produce one note. It follows that to produce the same number of notes of different pitch, lyre-like instruments would need many more strings than those of the lute family.*
In dealing with these two types of instrument, a variety of instruments will be encountered bearing different names, but which may be classed in general as belonging to one or the other of the two types.

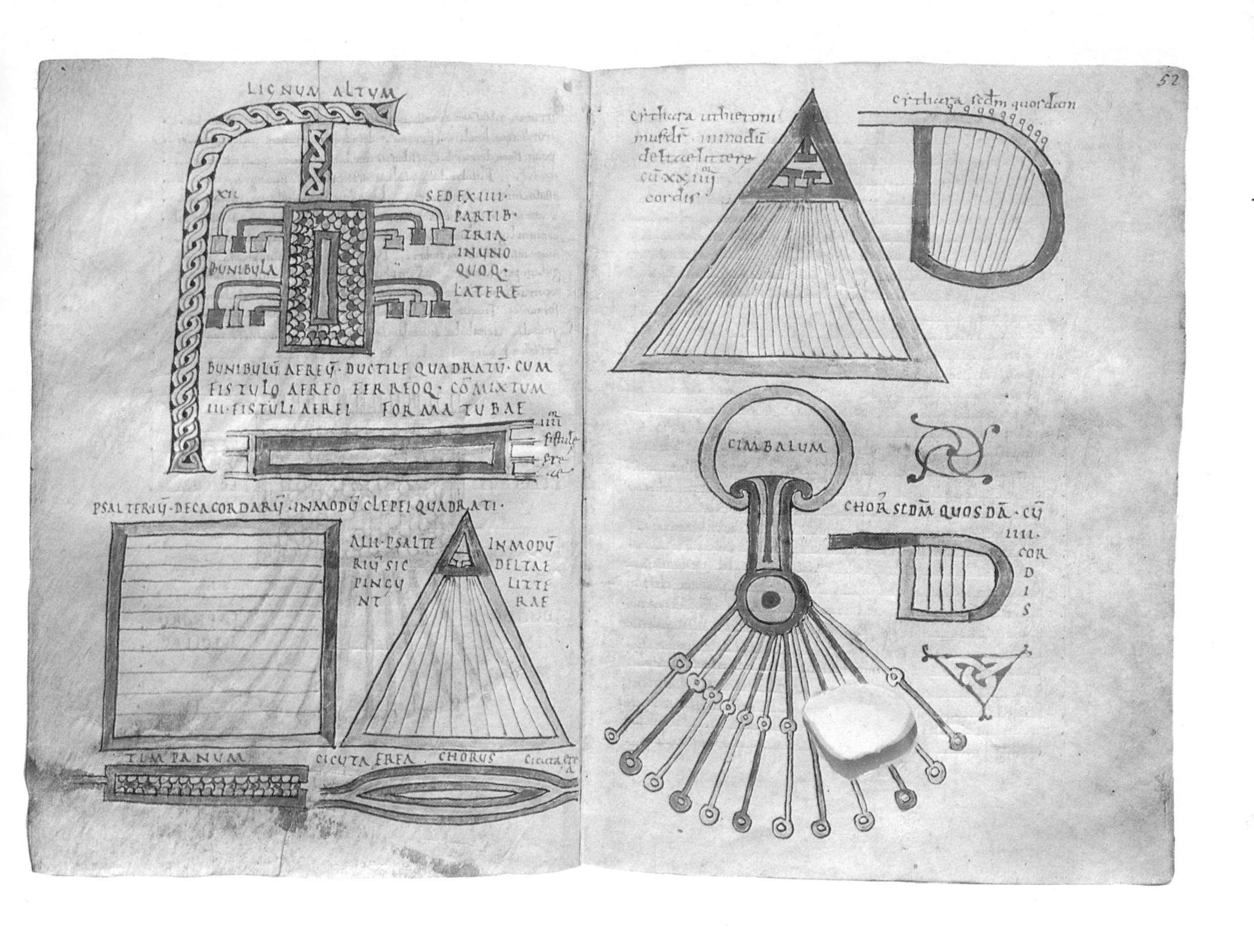

II. — 2. **Apocryphal letter of St. Jerome** (10th century)

PRUDENTIA
IUSTITIA
ASAPH
AEMAN
DAUID REX ET PROPH
CERETHI
ET PHE LETHI
AETHAN
IDITHUN
FORTITUDO

◀ II. — 3. **Bible of Charles the Bald** (823-877)

II. — 4. **Utrecht Psalter** (*c.* 850)

CXLVIIII ALLELUIA
CANTATEDNO
CANTICUMNOUUM LAUS
EIUSINECCLESIASCORUM,
LAETETURISRAHELINEOQUI
FECITEUM ETFILIISIONEX
SULTENTINREGESUO;
LAUDENTNOMENEIUSIN
CHORO·INTYMPANO
ETPSALTERIOPSALLANTEI;
QUIABENEPLACITUMEST

ALLELUIA
DNOINPOPULOSUO ETEX
ALTABITMANSUETOSIN
SALUTE,
EXSULTABUNTSCIINGLORI
A LAETABUNTURINCUBI
LIBUSSUIS,
EXSULTATIONESDIINGUT
TUREEORUM· ETGLADII
ANCIPITESINMANIB;EOR
ADFACIENDAMUINDICTĀ

INNATIONIBUS· INCRE
PATIONESINPOPULIS
ADALLIGANDOSREGESEORŪ
INCOMPEDIBUS· ETNO
BILESEORUMINMANICIS
FERREIS;
UTFACIANTINEISIUDICIŪ
CONSCRIPTUM· GLORIA
HAECESTOMNIBUSSCIS
EIUS

◀ II. — 5. **Utrecht Psalter** (*c.* 850)

II. — 6. **"Angels Making Music" by Hans Memling** (*c.* 1480)

◄ II. — 7. **Two fiddles** (11th and 12th century)

II. — 8. **Oliphant** (16th century)

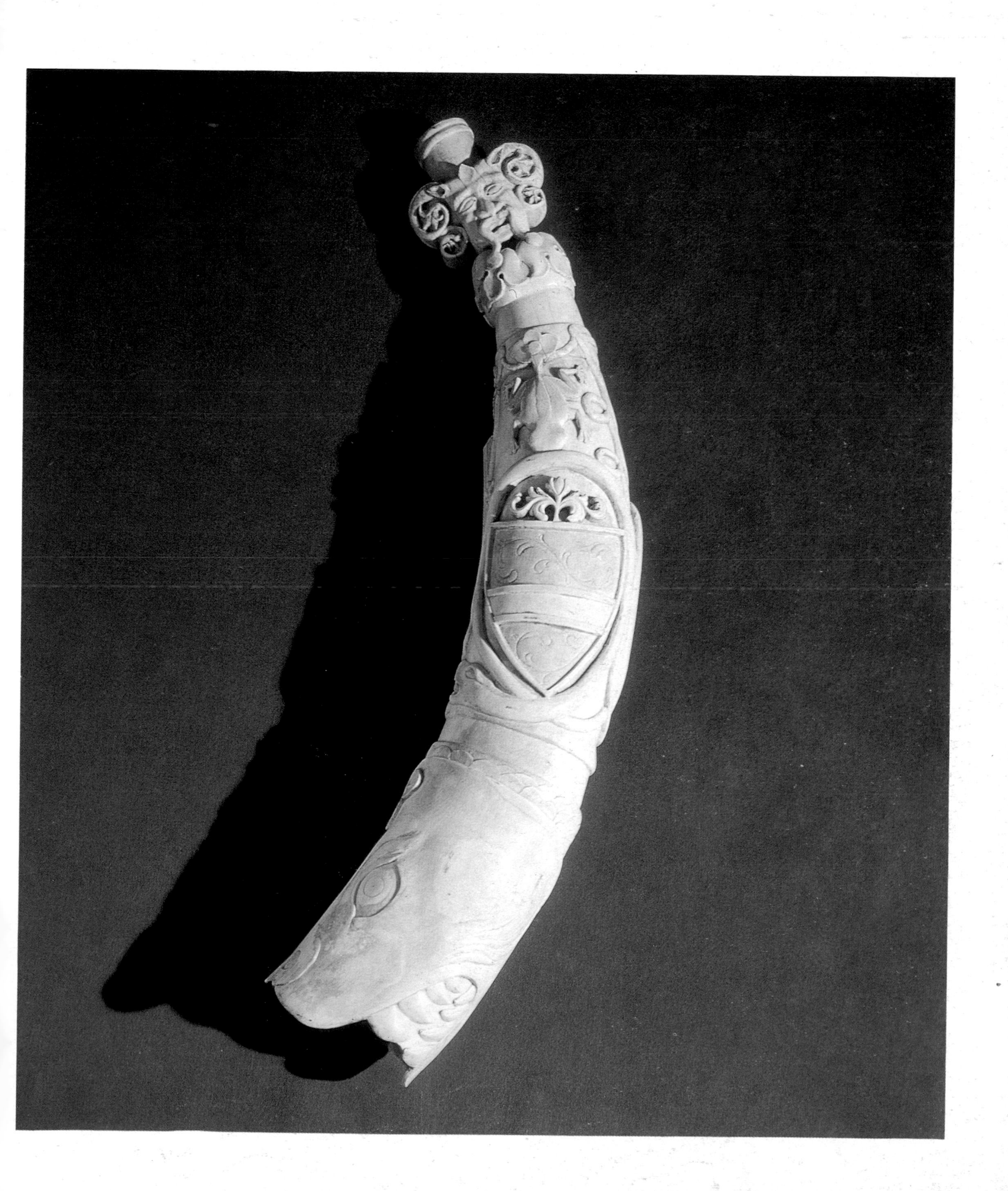

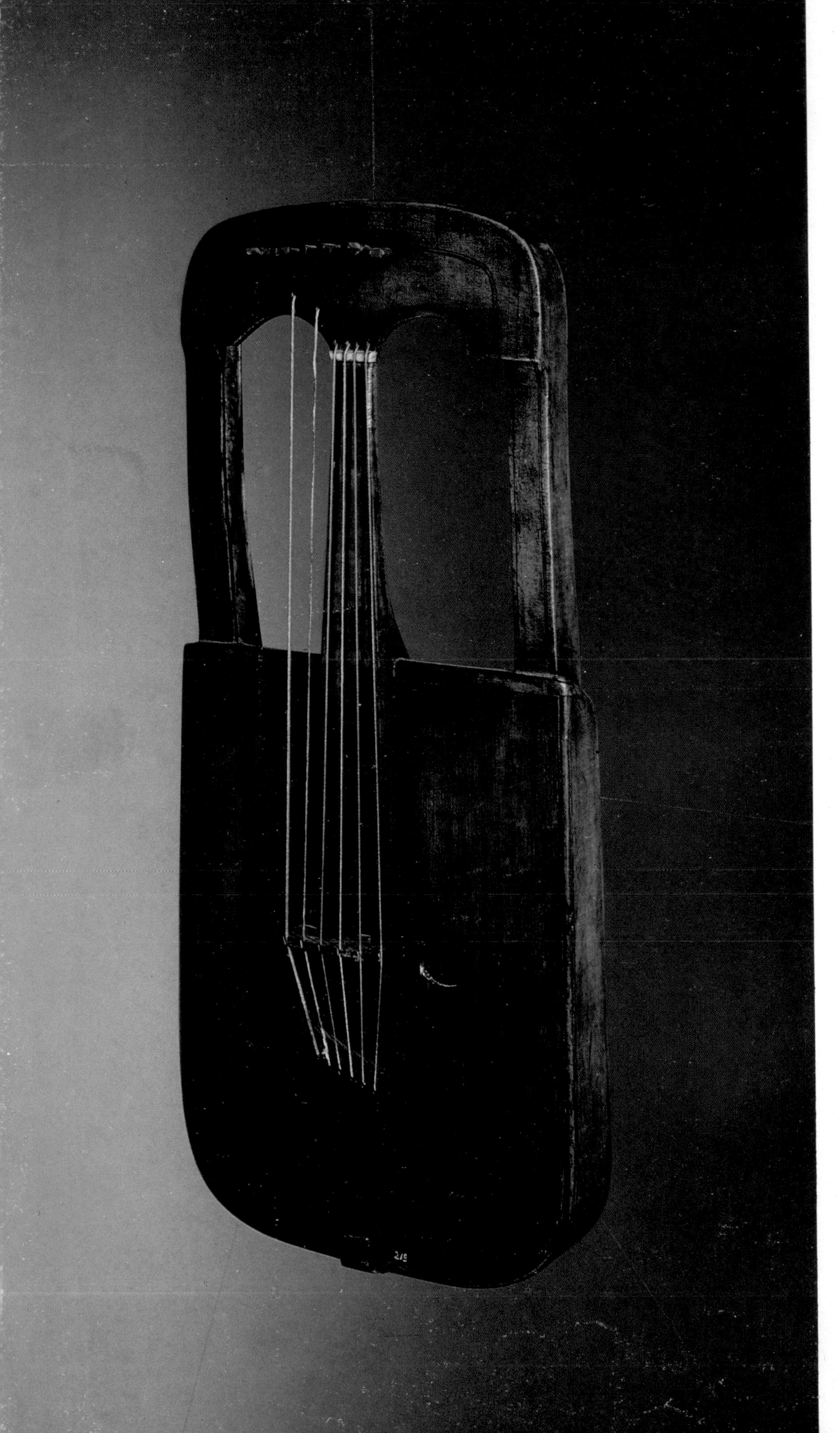

II. — 9. **Welsh crwth**

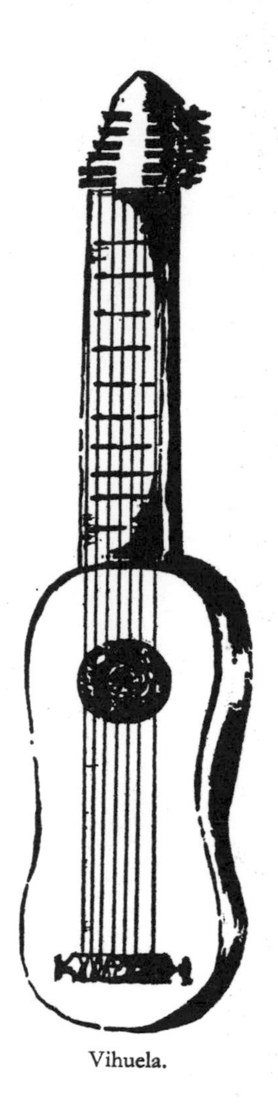

Vihuela.

II. — 4.
The so-called Utrecht Psalter, written after 850 and probably originating in the Benedictine Abbey of Saint-Pierre de Altumvillare (Hautevilliers). Folio 63 *v*⁰, reproduced here, bears an illustration of Psalm 107. To the left of the picture is shown a musician carrying a triangular harp on his shoulder and a lute in his left hand; in his right hand he holds a stick which many have thought to represent a bow.
Universiteitsbibliotheek, Utrecht.

II. — 5.
Utrecht Psalter, folio 83 *r*⁰. At the top of the page are depicted a lyre player and a harpist; at the bottom, to the right and to the left, there are players of horns and lyres; the central position is taken up by a pneumatic organ; its bellows are operated by four men and its keyboard by two players. The instrument has two rows of pipes.
Universiteitsbibliotheek, Utrecht.

At first, the lute had pegs placed in arrowhead formation in a flared pegbox. Towards the ninth century, the lateral placing of the pegs on both sides of a narrower and deeper pegbox appeared, betraying the influence of Arabian instruments. Later still, in addition to this change in the position of the pegs, the pegbox itself was altered, now bent backwards to permit a greater tension of the strings.

The strings of the lute were plucked with a plectrum, and, in contrast to present-day practice, the instrument was held on the knees.

The first bowed string instruments in Europe were related to the Arabian *rabâb* or to the Persian *kemânǧe,* each of which had only two strings, placed on the same level, which could be set in vibration separately by a slight inclination of the bow. The problem really arose when a third, and sometimes a fourth, string was added to the first two, it was no longer possible to keep the strings at the same level, since the middle strings — the second and third — could only be set in vibration if the bow was already touching one of the outside strings, and even perhaps all the strings at once. At this juncture in the development of the instrument, a number of modifications gradually came into being, and we can easily trace their introduction with the help of carvings and paintings of that time. Firstly, the bridge, which had originally been flat, became arched; then the middle of the sound-box developed an inward curve on each side. Broadly, we may say that in the thirteenth century a new form of bowed stringed instrument, a form of the kind such as we see in the present-day violin, took shape. Furthermore, the one or more rose-type sound-holes were replaced by C-shaped sound-holes, which in their turn were supplanted, also in the thirteenth century, by sound-holes shaped in the following form : ꞔ. This latter shape is the prototype for modern violin sound-holes, which are in the form of an *f*.

Before continuing consideration of bowed string instruments, two more lute-like instruments should be mentioned.

One of these is the *guitar*, different from the lute in that its back is generally flat and attached to the belly by splints. It is believed that the instrument is of Eastern origin and that it was introduced to Europe from Arabia, through Spain. It is to be found portrayed on the Portico de la Gloria at Santiago de Compostela and appears in several miniatures in the manuscript of the *Cantigas* of Alfonso X (the Wise), dating from the thirteenth century. There was already in the twelfth century a distinction between the *guitarra morisca* and the *guitarra latina*, two instruments which were each to follow a quite distinct evolution. In fact the guitarra morisca was to develop a more and more pronouncedly arched back, gradually coming to closely resemble that of the lute, until it finally (in the fifteenth century) became the *mandola*, or *mandora*, an instrument with four double strings, whose flat, ovoid belly developed towards a point at the top; the guitarra latina, for its part, gave rise in the thirteenth century to the *vihuela,* an instrument that was to remain typically Spanish, with a flat sound-box, a short neck that was bent backwards, and a pegbox mounted at an angle. From the thirteenth to the sixteenth century, the vihuela itself was of three types; one sort was played with a plectrum, another was bowed, and the third was played with the fingers.

Instruments of the guitar family, with arched or flat backs, were given the names *guiterne* or *quinterne* in thirteenth- and fifteenth-century France. (*Cf.* the English *gittern.*)

Likewise, the name *fiddle* was used in the Middle Ages to designate any bowed string instrument, whatever its shape or the number of its strings. For this reason, one may classify the bowed crwth of which we have spoken as a fiddle, as well as those bowed instruments whose body is surmounted by a neck (in the manner of a lute), even if this is only rudimentary, as in the *gigue* and the *rebec.*

To return to the crwth, we have said that this became a bowed instrument in about the eleventh or twelfth century. At that time, the crwth had a fairly long flat sound-box, rounded at both ends; towards the top there were two holes so that the fingers of the left hand could easily pass through in order to stop the strings. Seen another way, the crwth had taken over from the lute the neck upon which its strings could be shortened by the player's hand. This instrument was the three-stringed crwth and was played with a pronouncedly curved bow in arch-form. Since it possessed a flat bridge, the middle string could not be set in vibration without one or even both of the outer strings sounding at the same time. The Welsh crwth proper was an improvement on the three-stringed crwth. A fourth string was added to double the upper of the three existing ones, whilst two more strings were placed away from the neck, which, played in open position, acted as bourdons (drones); a further improvement was the lengthening of one leg of the flat bridge, which now passed through a sound-hole to rest on the back of the instrument so that the sonority of the sound-box was amplified. We quoted above the text which dates back to pre-Christian times, "thou, who art quadrangular and harmonic", which seemed to apply to the crwth and to bestow on that instrument a putatively very ancient origin. However that may be, we may be more certain in asserting that the crwth was well known in Britain from the sixth century onwards. At that period, the ancient bards used it to accompany their songs, until such time as they abandoned it in favour of the harp, and particularly the so-called Welsh harp, an instrument we have so far not dealt with, which was a chromatic harp on a small scale, already known in the Middle Ages, having three ranks of strings, the middle rank of which contained the chromatically tuned strings; this Welsh harp was still in use right up to the nineteenth century.

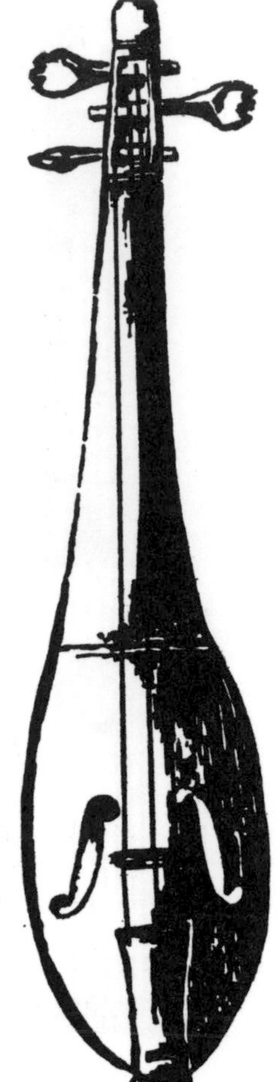

Rebec.

Another kind of fiddle was the *lyra* (not to be confused with the Greek lyre of the same name), which had three strings. This name was used for a long time, especially in Italy, to refer to a similar type of instrument.

Yet another sort of fiddle was the gigue, which usually had only one string, and whose shape was rather peculiar, since, having no lateral indentations and being somewhat elongated, it looked something like a leg of ham. The instrument's name might derive from the words *gigot* and *gigue* (leg of mutton, and haunch of venison). The name gigue appears for the first time in the *Dictionarium* of Jean de Garlande, a musical theoretician who lived in the first part of the thirteenth century.

The rebec, generally having three strings, was also used

II. — 6.

"Angels Making Music" by Hans Memling (1435-1494). The left-hand panel, reproduced here, is part of a great triptych, painted in about 1480 and intended for the church at Najera (Spain). This panel shows angels playing the following instruments (reading from left to right): a psaltery, a tromba marina — note that the bow is placed not between the lower bridge and the hand touching the string but well above the hand, and thus producing harmonics — a lute, a trombone — it is assumed that it had a sliding mouthpiece — and a pommer. Size of panel: *c.* 7½ ft. × 5½ ft.

Kon. Museum v. Schone Kunsten, Antwerp. Cat. 779.

II. — 7.

Two fiddles. Copies by Auguste Telbecque. On the left, a three-stringed fiddle after a portal sculpture of the Cathedral of Amiens (11th century). On the right a gigue (other authorities would say a lira) after a portal sculpture of the Abbey of Moissac (12th century). The backs and bellies of these two instruments are slightly rounded.
Length: *c.* 22 ins and 19¾ ins.

M.I., Brussels.
Nos. 1330 & 1327.

II. — 8.

Oliphant (horn) of ivory from the sixteenth century. The two flat sides, in high relief, bear escutcheons enclosed by serpents and surmounted by a toad. On the far side may be distinguished two lions rampant and a crocodile. The instrument's heterogeneous embellishments make it impossible to precisely determine its origins. Length: *c.* 28½ ins.

M.I., Brussels.
No 3153.

II. — 9.

Welsh crwth. The body, except for the sound-board, is cut and hollowed from a single piece of wood. Of the six gut strings, four are played with a bow and placed over the neck, whilst the other two are plucked. The bridge has one foot resting on the sound-board and the other, passing through the left sound-hole, on the back. It is conjectured that the instrument was always played with two strings tuned at the octave.
Length: *c.* 22 ins.

M.I., Brussels.
No. 218.

in the Middle Ages, before disappearing in the seventeenth century. It was very similar in form to the Arabian rabâb, except that its belly, instead of being a stretched skin, was made of light wood. It was played with a very short arch-shaped bow, and was principally used by minstrels, as its harsh and penetrating sound had rapidly made it popular as an instrument on which the music for village dances could be played in the open air.

The only mediaeval author to give us precise details about the bowed string instruments is Jerome of Moravia, who lived in Paris, and who speaks of the *rubebe* and the fiddle in the last chapter of his important treatise on music, written in about 1260.

He says of the rubebe that it is an instrument of two strings, tuned at the fifth, which, like the fiddle, is played with a bow. It is not too difficult to establish the fact that this rubebe is related to the Arabian *rabâb el-mughannî* (singer's rabâb), which also had only two strings.

As for the fiddle, Jerome of Moravia tells us that it has and "should have" five strings. This number of strings is confirmed by Elias of Salomon who, in his *Scientia artis musicae* (1274), attempts to convince his interlocutor of what great things can be achieved by modest means by giving as an example the fiddle and "suchlike instruments", which, with their five strings, can cover all the notes of the vocal range.

Thus a type of fiddle — the *troubadour fiddle* — existed in the Middle Ages which was quite distinct from all the other instruments generically referred to by the name fiddle.

Moreover, Jerome of Moravia tells us that the fiddle could be tuned in three different ways, depending on the positioning of the strings on the instrument. In the first method, one of the strings was placed away from the neck and could therefore produce only one note, acting as a drone, while the fourth and fifth strings — the highest — were tuned in unison. In the case of the second method, the five strings were all placed over the neck and tuned at different pitches, so that each string consequently had a role of its own. In the final case, the five strings were placed over the neck, and the first and second were tuned in unison as well as the fourth and fifth.

We learn from this text that at least two types of troubadour fiddle existed, the one with and the other without a drone. Also, if we bear in mind the methods of tuning the strings, we can see that in the case of the first and third methods, where certain strings are doubled at the unison to strengthen their sonority, the fiddle once more became, in effect, an instrument in which three strings, placed over the neck, were tuned at different pitches.

Wind Instruments

Two kinds of flute were known in the Middle Ages: "*flaustes traversaines et flautes dont droit joues quand tu flaustes*" ("transverse flutes and flutes you play upright when you are fluting"), as Guillaume de Machaut put it.

The vertical flute, also called *recorder*, was very popular. In Latin texts it is referred to as *fistula anglica* (English flute), which might point to the possibility that the instrument originated in

Britain; the first known mention of it is to be found in a twelfth-century English manuscript now in the library of Glasgow University.

On the authority of *Li Contes des Hiraus* (thirteenth century), which speaks of "*flajos doubliers*", vertical flutes may sometimes have been played in pairs; they would then have been held by the player at an angle as was the case with the double aulos of the Greeks.

As opposed to the fistula anglica, the *fistula germanica* or *helvetica* was quite simply the transverse flute, which, Eastern in origin, had reached Europe by way of Byzantium. The oldest representation of this instrument on European soil is on an ivory carving of the tenth or eleventh century now in the National Museum at Florence. The instrument is also depicted in an eleventh-century picture in Kiev Cathedral, and is also shown in illuminations on the manuscript of the *Hortus Deliciarum* of the abbess Herrade of Landsberg, who died in 1195. (The autograph manuscript of the *Hortus Deliciarum* was destroyed at Strasbourg in the course of hostilities in 1875.) The transverse flute was soon adopted as the instrument of Swiss and German peasants, and was often given the name *Swiss pipe*, or *fife*.

Reed instruments such as the shawm, the bagpipe and the *bladder-pipe* are often mentioned by chroniclers and poets in their descriptions of open-air or martial music.

In French, the name *chalumeau* (shawm) was very widespread, but was not used before the twelfth century, when it began to appear in the form *chalemie* or *chalemèle*. As the word derives from the Latin word *calamus* (meaning a reed), it could apply to any instrument made of reed, including the seven-piped panpipe, whose ancestor was the syrinx polykalamos of the Ancients.

The shawm was an oboe-like instrument, of conical bore and with a double reed; it had from two to five holes, and sometimes had a characteristic bulge near the mouthpiece and near the bell; in other examples it had no bell.

Two types of shawm are known. In the one, the bore was very narrow and gave a rather sweet sound, whilst the other had a wide bore giving a harsher sound. This distinction will be touched on in the next chapter when we go on to look at the *pommer* and the *dulzian* types of shawm.

The word chalemie may also have applied to a primitive form of *clarinet* (with single reed and cylindrical bore), but we have no authority for this assumption.

An instrument of reputedly Moslem origin, resembling the shawm, is met with in Sicily. The shawm is another of the many instruments depicted in the miniatures found in the *Cantigas* of Alfonso X, and here it is played by two instrumentalists.

The bagpipe, still known the world over today, is particularly prevalent in Europe, where in the various regions it bears different names, and there are divergences in the form of some of its component parts (bag, single- or double-reeded pipes, drone-pipes). The instrument's history can be traced back to the *tibia utricularis* of the Romans, and even to a certain degree to the Greek aulos with its phorbeia.

However, it was not until the ninth century that it appeared

Bladder-pipe.

on Western European statuary. From that time it could be found particularly often in Ireland. Three centuries later, the bagpipe was to become the national instrument of Scotland.

The first portrayal of the instrument in Britain was found at Richborough (Kent). This was undoubtedly the kind of instrument of which Suetonius (*c.* A.D. 75 - *c.* 160) tells us when he writes of the Emperor Nero's predilection for this sort of instrument.

At first, the bagpipe had no drones, and the instrument Jean de Meung tells us of in the second part of the *Roman de la Rose* (*c.* 1276) is indeed a fairly simple one:

> *Puis prent sa muse et puis travaille*
> *Aux estives de Cornewaille.*

The first drone only made its appearance in about 1350, followed by a second which was added some time after 1400. The number increased, for we find in the sixteenth century bagpipes with a number of large drones.

Up to that time, the bagpipe was as popular among the aristocratic classes as with the common people, who were to continue to play the instrument right up to the present day — in some regions, at any rate — whilst after the sixteenth century, the upper classes preferred the smaller *musette.* We shall be meeting this instrument again later.

The bladder-pipe, still played in Poitou, was a mediaeval variant of the bagpipe. This instrument consisted of a blowpipe leading into a bladder, on another part of which were two reed-pipes, one being the chanter, the other the drone. In the fifteenth century the chanter had a curved shape.

Between the thirteenth and seventeenth centuries there are many representations of the bladder-pipe, often side by side with the bagpipe proper; to judge by a portrayal in the already oft-cited *Cantigas,* the two instruments seem to have often been played together.

The most obvious marks of the influence of the Romans on the musical instruments of the territories they conquered are to be found in the military instruments introduced and disseminated by the Roman legionaries. So it is hardly surprising that a Roman lituus appears in *The Bible* of Charles the Bald that we have already mentioned.

The French word *cor* was used in mediaeval texts to designate various instruments of quite different types. It could refer to the cowhorn, the cornett, or even the *oliphant.* The commonest type of horn was certainly that made of an animal's horn, for the material was easy to come by. It was used to give out martial or hunting calls, as was the oliphant, which, made from the more expensive elephant's tusk, was more an instrument reserved for the nobility.

Nafîr.

The Cathedral at Aachen has a tenth-century oliphant, and the Cathedral of St. Vitus at Prague possesses the one said to have been used by Roland, the nephew of Charlemagne. The instrument was widespread in the Middle Ages, but because of its costliness, a number of oliphants were made from horns or teeth belonging to animals other than elephants. Quite a lot of oliphants have been recovered from the site of the battlefield at Agincourt, thus dating them from 1415. Soldiers generally used only a large metal horn, circular in shape, which, judging by an illustration in the choir of Worcester Cathedral (fourteenth century), was carried around the player's body. Horns of English origin must have had a considerable reputation, since in 1375 the Duke of Burgundy eagerly placed an order for several of them.

Trumpets were not so common. It is in a ninth-century manuscript from the Abbey of Saint-Gall that we find the first picture of one; the colours the miniaturist used are sufficiently exact for us to be able to see that this trumpet was of metal. At the same abbey lived Eckhard (tenth to eleventh centuries) who mentions the *Alpine horn* as a "tuba".

From the eleventh century onwards, the trumpets, which had till then been modelled on the Roman tubae with their straightforward and somewhat rough sound, began to grow longer and thinner as their bells widened. Undoubtedly, this was a result of the influence of Moslem trumpets which militant Christians must have noticed on battlefields in Spain and meridional Italy. In France, these new trumpets were called *cors sarrazinois* (Saracens' horns), whilst in Spain the Arabian name *nafîr* was taken over for the instrument, becoming *añafil.* Two and a half centuries later, Joinville (1224-1319), the chronicler of St. Louis, wrote of the cor sarrazinois as an instrument giving out sounds like those of "a fairly loud bagpipe".

The French nobility preferred to call this trumpet the *buisine* (in English, busine), derived from the Latin word *bucina*, which in Roman times, however, had referred to a hooked instrument. In the *Chanson de Roland* (eleventh century), we read: "*... mit à sa buche une clère buisine*", whilst an equivalent term in German can be found in the epic of Parzival: "*die hellen Businen mit Krach vor im gâben dôz*". There is also a similar word (*pusûne*) in the *Nibelungenlied:* "*... manec pusûne lûte vil kreftliclîch erdôz...*".

These busines were fairly expensive, and thus were more an instrument of the nobility, also figuring on royal coats-of-arms. They nearly always appear on mediaeval representations of the three Magi. Angels also appear to have favoured them. On the other hand, they never appear in pictures of popular or country life.

As the busine was reserved for players who were in the service of a king, a prince or a lord, it was decorated with a cloth bearing a coat-of-arms. Before long, the towns themselves began to imitate the nobility and started to employ busine players, displaying the communal coat-of-arms on the instrument. In thirteenth-century France, the town musicians, freemen, formed guilds, and it became an offence punishable by fines for any unauthorised person, especially mendicants, to play the instrument. Soon afterwards, the German townships followed suit.

We learn from an order laid down for the townsfolk of Arezzo, by the Emperor Frederick II, that there were already two kinds of trumpet in 1240: one, which the Italians called the *trombetta,* was smaller than the other and made in wood; the other, larger and made of metal, was the busine itself, and was known as such.

The busine was to retain the long, straight shape of the

nafîr for more than three centuries. Only in the fifteenth century, to make it easier to manipulate, was it folded back on itself.

The busine was, in fact, a natural trumpet; in other words, having no way of shortening or lengthening the tube, it could only give the fundamental note which corresponded to the length of its tube and the harmonics of that note. Since it is unlikely that many trumpet players of the time were capable of producing the tube's upper harmonics, the repertoire of the instrument was limited to signals and fanfares.

The painting "Angels Making Music" by Hans Memling, now in the Museum of Antwerp, shows an angel playing a trumpet whilst holding its mouthpiece. From this we may deduce that while playing, the trumpeter could adjust the length of the instrument by sliding the mouthpiece in and out of the tube, thus changing the fundamental note and consequently also the harmonic. This being the case, we are dealing with an early example of the *tromba di tirarsi* (the slide-trumpet), the distant ancestor in fact of our *slide-trombone.*

Percussion Instruments

Percussion instruments were very numerous in the Middle Ages, and were of Roman or Eastern origin. Isidore of Seville tells us of the *tympanum,* made of a skin stretched over a wooden frame, in the shape of a seive; this was identical with the tympanum of the Romans. He goes on to say that it was a half of the *symphonia,* which was made of a hollow wooden body over each end of which was stretched a skin; when the skins were beaten with drumsticks, the resultant concomitance between the higher and the lower pitches produced the most agreeable music.

This text, to which perhaps too little attention has so far been accorded, presents us with a genuine drum whose two skins yielded differently pitched sounds in *concordia* — in consonance. Now, the only *concordiae* — in Greek, *symphoniae* — admitted by the Greek and Latin theoreticians, and consequently by the musicians of the Middle Ages, were, in order of importance, the octave, the fifth and the fourth. And since the text speaks of "*suavissimus cantus*", it appears likely that these two skins were tuned an octave apart.

If the tympanum was half of a symphonia, the *margaretum* (still according to Isidore of Seville) was half the size of the tympanum and, like it, had a skin which was struck with a beater; the name itself tells us that the instrument had small bells attached to its frame, and was thus similar to the instrument which today goes by the somewhat dubious name of tambourine, which was known in the Middle Ages as the timbrel.

The instrument was of Asian origin, and had spread along the shores of the Mediterranean — an interesting example is shown on a Greek mosaic at Pompeï. As the timbrel was of very simple structure and has hardly changed to this day, it will be sufficient to point out here that in some cases small cymbals took the place of bells. This is the form in which we now know it. It was, and has remained, very popular in Spain, the South of France, and the meridional regions of Italy, and before long, instead of

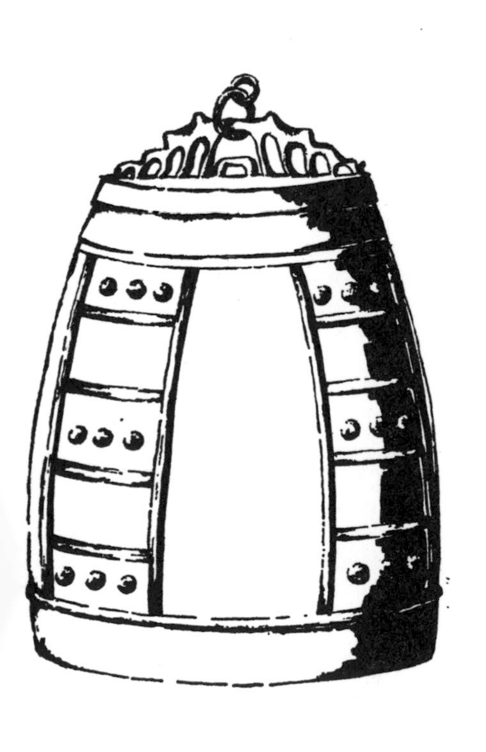

Chinese bell.

being played with a drumstick, it was struck by the hands or knuckles of dancers who used it to provide a rhythmic accompaniment to their movements. If played by lightly rubbing the skin rather than striking it, the instrument gives a gently rolling sound accompanied by the shimmering of its cymbals; if, however, it is merely shaken in the air, the instrument produces a joyful and variegated jingling of its metal parts.

Naturally, with such versatility, this instrument, simple though it is, has remained popular throughout the ages. As an open-air instrument, in the hands of many young dancing girls, the timbrel made its contribution to the brilliance of Charles V's reception at San Vincente de la Barquera in 1517, as well as that of Charles IX at Saint-Jean-de-Luz in 1564.

The *tambourin* in fact was a kind of drum, and it and other drums, such as the similar *tabor*, first appeared in Europe towards the end of the Middle Ages. The tambourin was a fairly long, narrow drum, and was struck with one or two sticks. The sound it made was "jarring and quivering".

The *nakers* were small kettledrums, worn on the belt; they were of Eastern origin, and we have evidence of their presence in the West during the fourteenth if not the thirteenth century.

Of the mediaeval percussion instruments already mentioned, the symphonia and the naker were the only ones to produce clearly determined sounds. Other percussion instruments of the period were the *bell*, the *metal* or *glass plate*, and the *wood block*.

The bell dates from prehistoric times, and its chief function was to disperse evil spirits; it was used especially in primitive forms of ritual worship. It was Gregory of Tours who, in the sixth century, is said to have adopted the use of the bell to summon the faithful, although he apparently had a precedent in the case of St. Paulinus, who is said to have used for the church at Nola in Campania, in the fifth century, a group of several bells of different sizes and distinct pitches which were struck with small hammers. (For this reason it seems that bells were often referred to in the Middle Ages by the word *nola* or *campana*.)

In the twelfth century, we hear of sets of at least seven bells struck with hammers. These sets generally belonged to monasteries, and it was not until the thirteenth century that they were installed in church towers and belfries.

Soon, these bells were sounded mechanically by means of a cylinder which was set in motion at fixed hours. Pins fixed on the cylinder released the hammers which in turn struck the corresponding bells, and thus the sound of a brief musical motif coming from a bell-tower might be heard in towns and the neighbouring countryside. Here we have a rudimentary form of the *carillon*, one which has not yet acquired a keyboard.

This short musical motif, which the Flemish (who first thought of the idea) called the *voorslag,* sounded immediately before the striking of the hour. Such *voorslagen* are known to have existed in the fourteenth century in many parts of the Low Countries: at Mons, in 1328; at Malines, in 1372; and at Tournai, in 1392.

Two ways of manufacturing bells were known in the late Middle Ages; they could be either forged or cast. One of the early Belgian foundries was that of Albert, "*fusor campanorum*"

II. — 10.

French psaltery. Copy of an instrument depicted on the portal of the Church of Saint-Pierre de Saintes (Lower Charente). This instrument has 32 strings tuned in pairs. The ridges of the case function as bridges. Height: *c.* 26¾ ins.

M.I., Brussels.
No. 1490.

II. — 11.

Plan of harpsichord, shown in fol. 128 r⁰ of the manuscript treatise of "*maistre Henry Arnault de Zuuolis, maistre en médecine et en astrologie demeurant à Dijon...*" who died of the plague in 1466. One the one hand we can find here four systems of attacking the strings, and on the other hand, in the main drawing, the internal structure.

Bibl. Nat., Paris.
Cod. Lat. 7295.

II. — 12.

Woodcut forming part of the *Theorica Musice* of Franchino Gaffori, published in Milan in 1496. Gaffori was singing master at the Cathedral of Milan. He was born in 1451 and died in 1522. The woodcut shows Jubal, Pythagoras and Phylolaus, who, according to a mediaeval tradition, were the first musical practitioners. The instruments appearing on this woodcut are: a set of bells, musical glasses, a monochord and a number of wind instruments. Height: *c.* 9⅞ ins.

Bibliothèque Royale, Brussels.
F. Fétis No. 5278.

II. — 13.

Copy of a miniature from an Italian manuscript dating from the early years of the 11th century: *De Universo Libri XXII* by Hrabanus Maurus. The three musicians are playing a pair of cymbals, a sort of triangular harp *(cithara)* and a three-stringed lute. In the foreground may be seen a six-stringed lyre.

Abbazia, Montecassino.
MS 1896. Lib. XVIII, cap. IV, 444.

II. — 14.

Ivory bas-relief dating from the fourteenth century, depicting two lute players. The instrument on the left is of the cittern type, that on the right an ordinary lute. The cittern here has seven strings.

Musée Cluny, Paris.

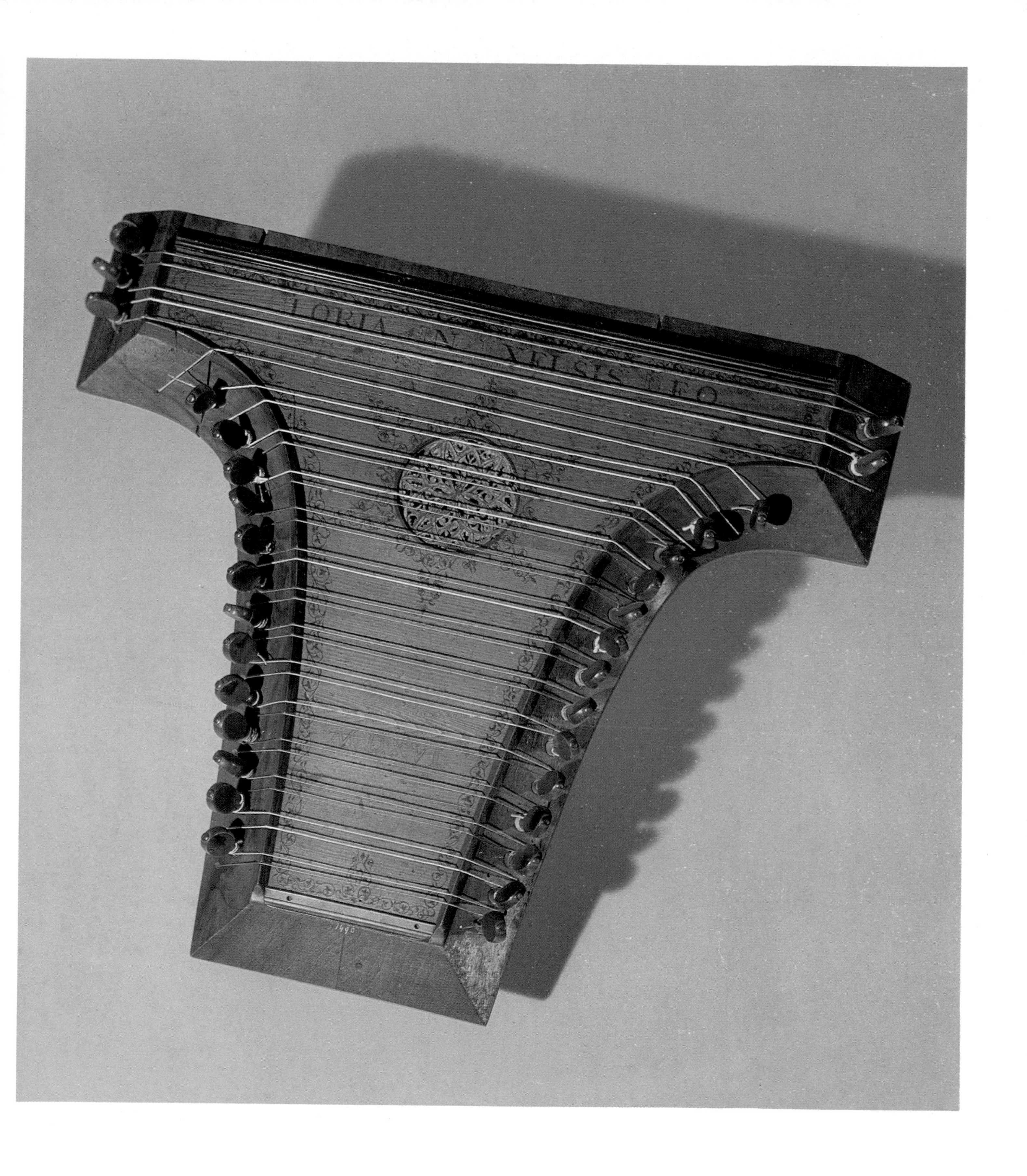

II. — 10. **French psaltery**

II. — 11. **Plan of a harpsichord** (14th century) ▶

II. — 12. **Illustration from "Theorica Musice"** (1496) ▶ ▶

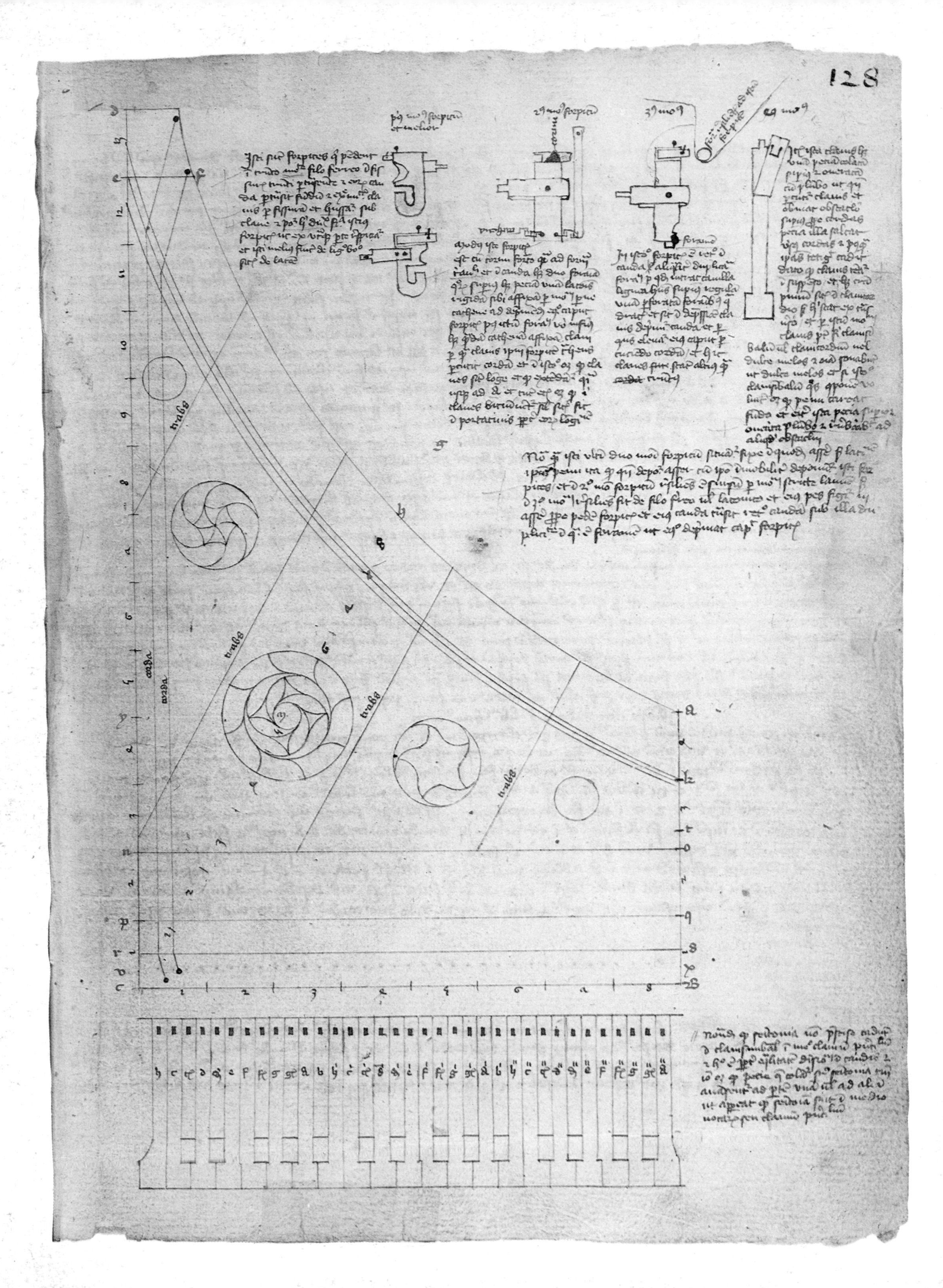
128
trabs
trabs
trabs
trabs
corda
corda

IVBAL
PYTACORA
PITAGORAS
PYTACORA
PHYLOLAVS

II. — 13. **Italian miniature** (11th century)

II. — 14. **French bas-relief** (14th century) ►

II. — 15. **Details of a Flemish painting** (14th century)

II. — 16. **Catalan painting** (15th century) ▶

II. — 17. **Catalan painti**
(14th century)

Hurdy-gurdy.

at Louvain in 1340; in the same town in 1380, we find also the founder Maistre Jehan le Clocghieteur.

Up to the thirteenth century, bells generally preserved the shape of their Asian ancestors, in other words, they were hive-shaped; they were also struck on the outside. But, from the fourteenth century on, they underwent the influence of Gothic design, taking on the shape they still have today, and were usually struck by a mobile beater attached on the inside.

The size, and consequently the weight, of these bells was constantly increasing. That of Ratisbon, cast in 1325, already weighed about five tons.

Metal is not alone in being able to produce a definite note; wood also yields distinct notes if cut up into suitable blocks or cylindrical shapes. In order to give a musical sound in this way wood, like metal, must be able to vibrate freely, and thus must either be suspended on a string or placed on an isolating structure.

It was on such a basis that the mediaeval *xylophone* was constructed. The first type of xylophone was the *échelette* (French for small ladder), made by tying together with cord a number of wooden blades in a strict order of diminishing sizes and at a certain distance from each other. The instrument could be held at its upper end (in other words, where the blades are smaller) by the left hand, or could be fixed to a stick, also held in the left hand; the right hand used a beater to strike the blades.

This was a kind of portable xylophone, used in parades and processions. Otherwise, the instrument was placed horizontally on a table, and its blades were separated from the surface by beds of straw. Thus it was possible to use two beaters with which to play the instrument.

Keyboard Instruments

Keyboard instruments were to assume such historical significance that although they tend to belong to one or other of the categories we have already dealt with (strings, wind, percussion), it will be preferable to treat them separately so as to avoid unnecessary reduplications about the keyboard which is their common feature and about the more and more complex mechanisms it entailed.

The *harpsichord*, an instrument with plucked strings and keyboard, is named for the first time in 1404 as the *clavicembalo* and appears in a miniature from the *Très riches heures du duc de Berry* (1485). The instrument was described in about 1440 by Henri Arnault of Zwolle. As we have said, it is in fact a larger version of the micanon to which has been added a keyboard and a mechanism for setting the strings in vibration. This mechanism consists of a small piece of wood, called a jack, whose base rests on the farther end of the key, and whose head is provided with a plectrum which plucks the string when the leverage exerted by the player's finger depressing the key causes the jack to rise to the string.

From the beginning of the fifteenth century, the harpsichord already had quite a considerable range, since its keyboard contained forty-five keys — that is, nearly four octaves. Its exterior shape was similar to that of a micanon or a harp placed on its side. Its strings, single or double, decrease in size from left to right and lie parallel to the keyboard.

We shall deal with the virginal and the spinet — two other instruments with plucked strings and a keyboard — in the following chapter, where we shall also examine improvements in the design of the harpsichord.

We know that the clavichord, an instrument with struck strings and keyboard, was in existence at the end of the Middle Ages; a keyed dulcimer is also described by Arnault of Zwolle.

The clavichord is mentioned for the first time in 1405, in a poem of Eberhard Cersne, *Der Minne Regel,* and the first known picture of it dates back to the fifteenth century (in a church at Shrewsbury).

In the clavichord, the string is not struck by a hammer, but by a small blade (or tangent) of brass fixed perpendicularly at the farther end of the key, and thus forming a right-angle with it. Because it is thus fixed, the tangent continues to touch the string for as long as the player holds the key in the depressed position.

It is probable that the échiquier d'Angleterre, first mentioned in 1360, and whose name was to disappear in the course of the fifteenth century, was an instrument with struck strings and a keyboard, serving as an intermediary in the development of the dulcimer into the clavichord. Its rather unusual name has given rise to a number of interpretations which, though interesting, are not necessarily valid. It has been suggested, notably, that the name *échiquier* was used because the box framing the instrument resembled that used for playing chess, or that the succession of black and white keys suggested the squares on a chess-board itself.

The *hurdy-gurdy*, an instrument with rubbed strings and a keyboard, was in mediaeval times sometimes given the Latin name *organistrum* or *symphonia,* or in French *chifonie*. It seems to have been a European invention, and in the following centuries constantly occupied the imagination of inventors who tried to find more satisfactory ways of making an instrument in which a keyboard could be combined with rubbed strings.

The instrument is portrayed on the twelfth-century carvings from the Abbey of Bocherville, now in the Museum of Rouen. The hurdy-gurdy, in its popular and traditional form, could have a flat sound-box like the guitar's, or a rounded one like the lute's. Hence, it is referred to as guitar-like or as lute-like, as the case may be. (On the above-mentioned carvings, the hurdy-gurdy's sound-box is more or less rectangular.) A case was fixed along the length of the sound-box, at the top end of which was a pegbox. This case contained the tangents which, operated by keys on the outside of the case, shortened by different degrees the strings which, starting from a tail-piece, passed through the case to end in the pegbox. These melodic strings, of which there were generally two tuned in unison, were set in vibration by a rosin-coated wheel; this was placed at the base of the case and keyboard, and its upper half projected from the sound-box. It was rotated by means of a crank at the lower end of the sound-box. Four larger strings, two on each side of the case, acted as drones. It was not obligatory to play all strings at once, for it was possible to separate

II. — 15.

Two details from a painting by an old master of the Netherlands (14th century). One depicts an angel playing the positive organ (note the lay-out of the chromatic and diatonic keys in superposed rows), the other shows angels playing the cornett, the mandora and the fiddle.

Musées Royaux des Beaux-Arts, Brussels. No. 999.

II. — 16.

Catalan painting (early fifteenth century) in the Byzantine style, showing the Virgin and Child surrounded by angels making music: on the left an angel playing the shawm and another a fiddle in the form of a mandora; on the right two other angels, one playing the shawm, the other the lute.

Musées Royaux des Beaux-Arts, Brussels. No. 707.

II. — 17.

Painting by the Catalan artist Pere Sera (Barcelona, 14th century), forming part of the altarpiece in the Church of St. Clara at Tortosa. The Virgin and Child are surrounded by music-making angels playing the recorder, the lute, the portative, the psaltery, the mandora and the triangular harp. It is interesting that the angel playing the portative uses only her right hand whilst the left is operating the bellows; this involved a special fingering which was later to influence — at least at the very first — the fingering of the virginalists.

Museo de Arte Cataluña, Barcelona.

the strings from the rosin-coated wheel severally or even all at once.

Unlike the other three, one of the drone strings was not placed on an ordinary bridge, but, as in the case of the tromba marina, on a bridge one of whose feet, shorter than the other, came into contact with the instrument's belly. In France, this string became known as the *mouche* (fly) or *trompette* (trumpet), the former because its buzzing sound resembled that of the insect, and the latter apparently by analogy with the mechanics of the bridge of the tromba marina.

There is reason to believe that at first the organistrum had only one melody string and one drone. Some have tried to show that the organistrum already existed in the tenth century, basing their case on a mention made of it in a brief text by Odo, Abbot of Cluny (878-942). But this text, like others attributed to him, was not written by this abbot, who was first and foremost a reformer of monastic regulations, but partly by a namesake, and partly by an anonymous hand; it might date from any time up to the thirteenth century, since it is only in manuscripts of that time that we find the text in question.

The existence of the organistrum at this time, already proved by the twelfth-century carvings of Bocherville, is confirmed by certain miniatures in the thirteenth-century *Cantigas de Santa Maria* of Alfonso X, where a number of chifonies, some in fact quite large and probably attaining a length of more than six feet, are shown being played by one or two men; in the latter case, one man turns the crank while his partner operates the keys.

The sound of the hurdy-gurdy, like that of the rebec, was harsh and squeaky. It was above all an instrument played by the strolling fiddlers, even if it could sometimes be found in the hands of people of higher standing; but it was chiefly in the eighteenth century, as we shall see later, that it was played in high society. Today, it is hardly met with outside certain regions in France, such as the Auvergne, Béarn and north Brittany, whereas it was once met with in districts scattered all over Western Europe.

The organ was the only wind instrument with keyboard of any interest. The hydraulus became obsolete at the time of the fall of the Roman Empire. So it was a pneumatic organ rather than a hydraulus that the Byzantine Emperor Constantine Copronymos VI sent to Pepin in 757. On the other hand, the organ the Venetian priest Georgius built in Aachen for Louis the Pious in 826 was still a hydraulus.

There would be little point in quoting all the texts written between the ninth century and the beginning of the thirteenth which mention the existence of an organ in such and such a church. From being an essentially profane instrument, the organ was in fact becoming one which was a useful, if not indispensable, element in Christian worship, and the chroniclers do not neglect to mention its presence here and there without, however, giving adequate details about its construction and evolution. Even when information is given, this very often more properly belongs to the domain of legend. Thus an organ is described as having been built at Winchester Abbey in 980 which is said to have had "400 pipes, 40 keys and 26 bellows". Two players were needed at the manuals.

More than sixty strong men were needed to operate the bellows, and the keys were so huge (about 5 ft. 9 ins by 6 ins) that they had to be struck with the clenched fist or with the foot.

What is more certain is that the same priest Georgius, who had built the hydraulus for the palace at Aachen, later became the Abbot of Saint-Savin in Poitou, and in 827 built an organ there (whether hydraulic or pneumatic, we do not know) which was in fact the first of all *church organs*. In Belgium, this example was not followed until towards the end of the tenth century, when Folcuin, the Abbot of Lobbes, took the idea up; the organ of Saint-Hubert at Bruges is of a later date, having been built only in the eleventh century.

The noise made by the bellows in ancient organs was so loud that some organ builders placed the bellows on the outside of the building. The sounds themselves were extremely powerful and even provoked the clergy to protests, such as those of Aelred, Priyor of Rievaulx.

Subsequent to the development of vocal polyphony — a type of music ill-suited to being accompanied by too great a volume of sound — the organ was constructed, after the thirteenth century, in three different models: the *ninfali,* or *portative,* used in processions, the *positive,* placed in the choir, and finally the larger church organ, in the loft itself.

In the thirteenth century, the keys as we know them today, the modern system of transmission, the different registrations and their separation into ranks all made their appearance. The first manuals were incomplete, as they did not have all or sometimes any of the chromatic sliders — or, later, keys — and of course also lacked the corresponding pipes. During the thirteenth century, the number of chromatic keys tended to increase, even though a portative of the fourteenth century, belonging to the Cistercian monastery of Nuestra Señora de Piedra (in Aragon, Spain) has only one chromatic key.

Finally, the first pedal-board was built in 1306 by Lodewijk van Valbeke of Louvain.

III - The Renaissance

III. — 1. **Detail of a Flemish tapestry** (16th century)

Historical Background

If not absolutely impossible, it is certainly extremely difficult to give an exact date for the beginning of the literary and artistic period commonly known as the Renaissance, for the first signs of the movement appeared in fourteenth-century Italy, whereas in the other central and western European countries they were not to make an appearance until the sixteenth century.

During this period, the mediaeval Christian ideal which, in the form of dogma, had been imposed on all intellectual and artistic aspiration became progressively weaker. The classical Greco-Roman culture was once again admired; its notion of the world, of man and of beauty was studied and rediscovered in its entirety, and was to become the starting-point for original and individual creation in all the spheres. The artisan made way for the artist, the compiler for the inventor.

From the point of view of musical instruments, the Renaissance was a point of departure. Mediaeval treatises spoke only very rarely of the instruments and simply listed them, sometimes classifying them, and very rarely describing any — those they did describe were always the same ones. What is more often found in these treatises, or in the few anonymous texts of the time, is a description of how to make a monochord, with one or more strings, or a series of pipes, without any mention of the nature of these strings or of the alloy from which the pipes are constructed, etc.

It is really only after the beginning of the sixteenth century that, apparently as a result of the influence of the humanist philologists who had been studying and publishing critical editions of the Greek and Latin writers, the systematic study of musical instruments was launched. The first known author of such a work was Jean Mauburnus (1460-1503), a native of Brussels; the second edition of his *Rosetum exercitiorum spiritualium* (1510), published after his death, contains a chapter called "*De pictura et musicis instrumentis*", not found in the first edition (1494), and includes illustrations of instruments.

More important is the work *Musica getutscht* (in other words, written in German), published in 1511 by Sebastian Virdung. This short treatise, in which the keyboard instruments, and others in current use, were illustrated and described, was only the first part of a large treatise on music which the author was preparing, and which never got further than this preliminary publication.

In the same year was published a very important work on organ-building, *Spiegel der Orgelmacher und Organisten,* by the blind organist Arnold Schlick. This work also contained some pieces written for the instrument, songs for voice and lute, and pieces for lute solo. In 1529, the book *Musica instrumentalis deudsch,* by Martin Agricola (1486-1556) in its turn made an important contribution to knowledge of intruments and of their technique. *Musica teusch* (1532), by the famous lutenist Hans Gerle was devoted entirely to the viols and lutes, and above all their technique; Gerle was an expert on the subject, for he manufactured viols and lutes himself. *Fontegara* (1535), by Sylvestre Ganassi gives interesting details about various kinds of flutes, whilst the same author's *Regola rubertina* (1542-43), tells us of the viols and of their outstanding performers.

In his turn, Othmar Luscinius (his real name being Nachtigall), who pursued various studies at Louvain, published in 1536 a *Musurgia, seu praxis musicae*, which deserves mention as containing several illustrations of instruments that were in use at the end of the fifteenth and the beginning of the sixteenth centuries. In some of its sections, this book owes much to Virdung's *Musica getutscht,* and sometimes even follows it word for word.

Finally, after the publication of the *Declaración de instrumentos* (1549 and 1555) of Juan Bermudo, there is a gap of more than half a century before the publication of a second volume of the *Syntagma musicum* (1614-19) by Michael Praetorius (1571-1621) called *De organographia* (1619) which is a mine of valuable information about ancient and contemporary musical instruments and is enhanced by illustrations. Even more valuable and detailed is the *Traité des instruments,* covering seven books, which constitutes a part of a considerable work by Père Marin Mersenne (1588-1648), the *Harmonie universelle* (1636-37).

These works of Praetorius and Mersenne are already outside the period we are dealing with in this chapter. However, it was relevant to mention them, since they still contain information about instruments in use at the time of the Renaissance.

The invention of the printing press at the end of the fifteenth century had given rise to a greater dissemination of thought in all the fields to which it was applied. Thus the Renaissance developed a tendency towards universalism without, for all that, forsaking any of its manifestations of personal or ethnic individualism; but in the end, these strains of individualism often became reciprocally influential.

It is impossible to deny the existence in sixteenth-century music of a Roman school, a Venetian school, a Spanish school, etc., each having different aesthetic identities and different techniques of musical craftsmanship. Yet, especially in the realm of technique, all these schools show an identical evolution, starting in the last years of the fifteenth century and finally resulting in the *a cappella* style.

Whereas in previous centuries polyphony only occurred in music where the upper voices alone were melodic whilst the others, often given to instruments, gave support in notes of more or less long values, now all the voices had been given an equal importance; from the highest to the lowest, all became melodic, and as a result of this equality, the musical theme was able to travel from one voice to another, extending itself into a polyphonic texture composed of more or less strict imitations. Such a construction led quite naturally to the desire for a homogeneity of timbre in the music's performance; for this reason, from that time, performances of such music were entrusted to the human voice, unaccompanied by any musical instrument, and composers started to write those famous *a cappella* compositions for four, five, six, or even more voices. These works were always firmly founded on a vocal quartet (soprano, alto, tenor and bass), and composers wishing to write for a greater number of voices added a second soprano, a second alto, etc.

In the fifteenth century, works were written for at the most three or four voices, and one or two of these were given to some instrument or other, without regard for their timbre; any instrument that could be found conveniently at hand was used, provided its register corresponded to that of the voice it was replacing. Furthermore, with the exception of dances, works had never before been composed specially for a group of monodic instruments, so that when, having been successful in their original form, vocal polyphonic compositions were to be played in the form of instrumental transcriptions, no indications were ever given as to which monodic instrument should take the part of which voice. In this respect, a very typical example is the *Harmonice Musices Odhecaton* (1501) of Ottaviano Petrucci, the first man to print music. This book, which happens also to be the first one Petrucci printed, is a collection of vocal compositions by the most famous French and Flemish masters of the time; but, whilst he prints the music in its entirety, Petrucci gives against each of the voices or parts only the first words of the song. So these must be instrumental transcriptions in which no indication is given of which instruments are to be used. Therefore, when nowadays an instrumental group whose aim it is to revive this ancient music uses a flute where another group would have a viol or a small harp (played monodically), both groups are in fact doing exactly what ensembles of around the year 1500 would do, either by using the only instruments they had at hand, or, given the possibility of a free choice from among different instruments, by allowing their preference for one or other of these instruments to influence their choice.

In the course of the sixteenth century, the situation was to change. At the same time as *a cappella* performance had resulted in homogeneity of timbre or colour in vocal music, there was also a tendency in instrumental music to make families of instruments, each having the same type of instrument in all registers from the highest to the lowest. From that time each instrument of a family underwent developments in the register to which it was best suited. The more this register was restricted, the more numerous did the family become, for the instruments were supposed to link up with one another to cover the largest possible continuous pitch-range between them. To give just one example, this is why the recorder family soon included treble, descant, alto, tenor, basset, bass and contrabass models. Thus, the timbre remained the same from the lowest pitches to the highest, and a composition written for an ensemble of recorders would have a similar sound in all its registers.

Obviously, whether the instruments were single-reed, double-reed, brass, bowed string instruments, etc., they did not suddenly appear as complete families and it was necessary to create the missing instruments for each of them so that there would no longer be any gaps in the musical range of each family. This was one of the tasks that the Renaissance set itself.

The appearance of the various families of instruments was to enable composers, after the end of the sixteenth century, to establish the tone colour of their works in accordance with a consistent notion of timbre. From this time on, each family was used according to the effect it was called on to make, and once the composition was of suitable dimensions, two or more families could be used at different times, and might sometimes join forces in a large and powerful ensemble. At the same time, it should be noted that it was still a question of contrasting one group with another, in other words, one timbre with another. Moreover, when the groups were combined, each of their members lost its independence, since instruments of the same pitch were nearly always doubled, whatever group they belonged to. Thus, if it is still impossible to speak of orchestration in the modern sense of the word, the fact that the instruments had been categorized into families indicates that a first step had been taken towards such a concept. However, strictly speaking, this was not to take place until the end of the sixteenth and the beginning of the seventeenth centuries, notably in the Ricercari and Sonatas for several instrumental parts by Andrea and Giovanni Gabrieli, whilst, in the earliest years of opera, Monteverdi, in his *Orfeo* (1607), very successfully used the various families of instruments according to the character of the dramatic scene he wished to provide with musical emphasis.

As in the previous centuries, monodic instruments continued to be used in transcriptions of vocal works, but now they were grouped in families. For the performance of dances, a family of loud-toned *(haut)* instruments or one of only moderately loud *(bas)* instruments was chosen, according to whether they were to accompany *hautes danses* (dances with leaping steps, therefore fairly boisterous) or *basses danses* (dances with gliding steps).

In another field, the polyphonic instruments, in other words those capable of yielding several simultaneous sounds, such as the organ, the harpsichord and the lute, underwent a very rapid development during the sixteenth century, for they met the needs of every musician or dilettante who wished to be able to perform by himself not only the transcriptions of vocal works, but also compositions which were not simply transcriptions with ornamentations but works in their own right, specially written for performance on the organ, the harpsichord or the lute.

For these three instruments, a particular sort of notation called tablature was used. Instead of the normal notes, this sort of notation used letters or figures. The oldest tablatures date from the fourteenth century and were intended for the organ and, to a lesser extent, the harpsichord; the letters or figures represented the notes to be played. The same was not true of the lute tablature: this, making its appearance at the beginning of the sixteenth century, principally comprised as many horizontal lines as the lute had strings — generally five or six; the letters or signs, placed on or above each of these lines, denoted the placing or position each of the fingers should occupy on the corresponding strings of the instrument to produce the desired sounds.

In Germany, the method of organ tablature was firmly established by the well-known *Fundamentum organisandi* (1452) of Conrad Paumann, and was maintained, with few variants, right up to the eighteenth century. On the other hand, in Italy, France and England, for the harpsichord as well as for the organ, letters and figures came to be replaced by normal notes appearing on staves, the number of whose lines varied. Thus, what the Italians, French and English at the time called harpsichord or organ tablature was in fact none other than a score of the type we have today.

If, in comparison with previous centuries, the sixteenth

III. — 2.

Detail of a Flemish tapestry of the beginning of the 16th century. A number of instruments may be identified in the lower plane, notably: on the left, a keyboard instrument — probably a clavichord — placed on a table and played in a standing position, as was the general practice at the time, and a recorder; in the centre, a recorder and a lute; on the right, a recorder, a tabor, a harp, a positive organ and, at the extreme right, a recorder.

M.R.A.H., Brussels.
No. 9923.

III. — 3.

Two lutes. An Italian lute from the beginning of the 17th century, made by Giovanni Hieber, who, though of German origin, lived and worked in Venice. Apart from the finely wrought rose-hole in the sound-board, this lute is not embellished. Its shell consists of broad pieces of wood. This lute has six double strings and a melody string. Also a German lute by an unknown maker, its shell consisting of ivory ribs. It has six double strings.
Length (without pegbox) : *c.* 26½ ins. and 25¾ ins.

M.I., Brussels.
Nos. 1561 & 1557.

III. — 4.

Italian chitarrone or archlute by an unknown maker and dating from the 17th century. This instrument has five double strings and a melody string for the lower pegbox and six deep strings for the upper pegbox. The rose-hole is edged with ebony and surrounded by discs of mother-of-pearl and precious stones.
Length : *c.* 6¼ ft.

M.I., Brussels.
No. 1576.

III. — 5.

Mezzo-colascione, or small colascione, of Italian origin (17th century). It is the work of an unknown maker. The shell, edged with two tortoise-shell bands, is in ivory threaded with ebony. The neck is of hard wood and the fingerboard of ebony incrusted with ivory. The pegbox is surmounted by a dog's head sculpted in ivory. The instrument has three strings and nine frets.
Length: *c.* 37 ins.

M.I., Brussels.
No. 1567.

III. — 2. **Flemish tapestry** (16th century)

◀ III. — 3. **Italian and German lutes** (17th century)

III. — 4. **Italian chitarrone** (17th century)

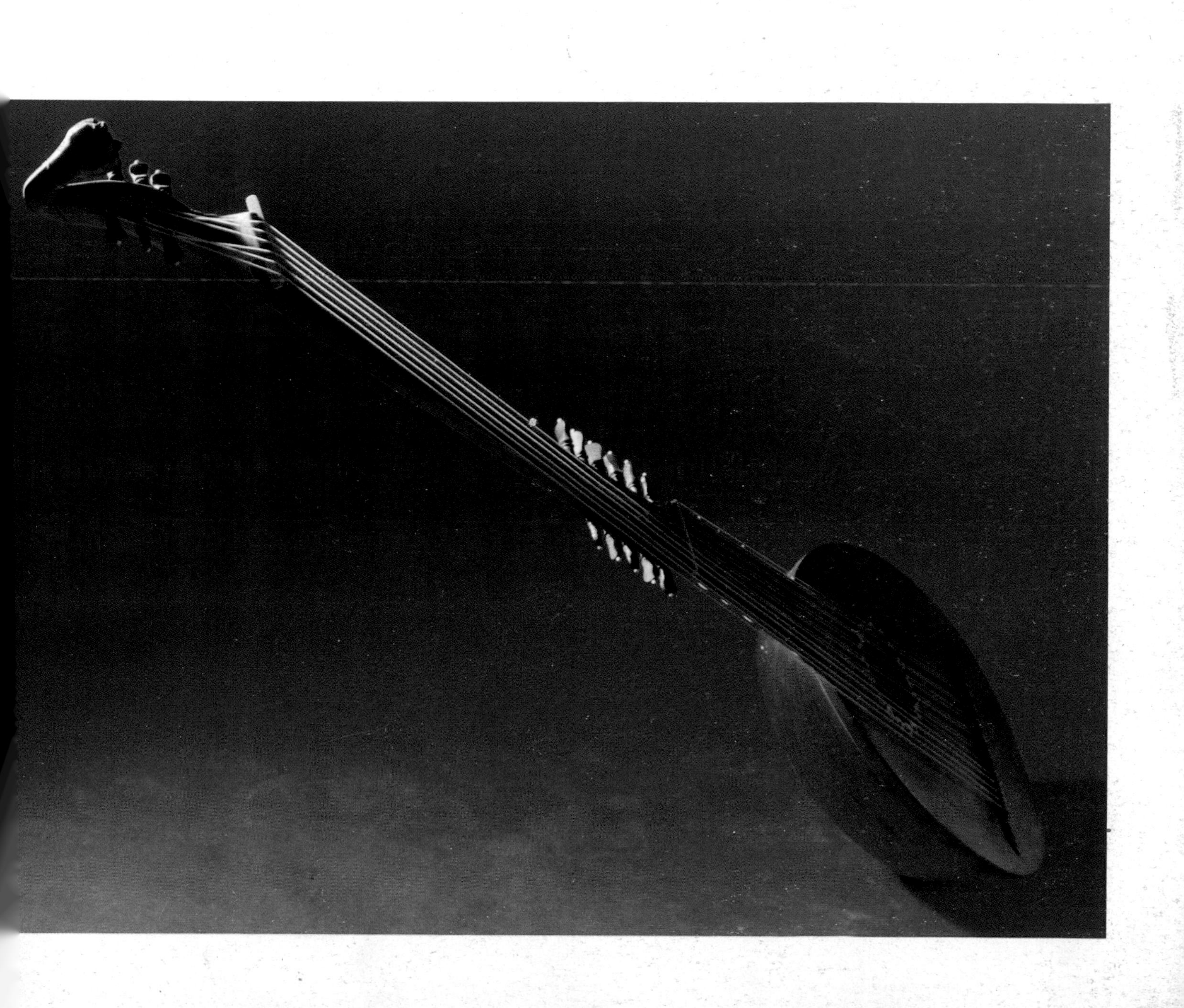

◀ III. — 5. **Italian mezzo-colascione** (17th century)

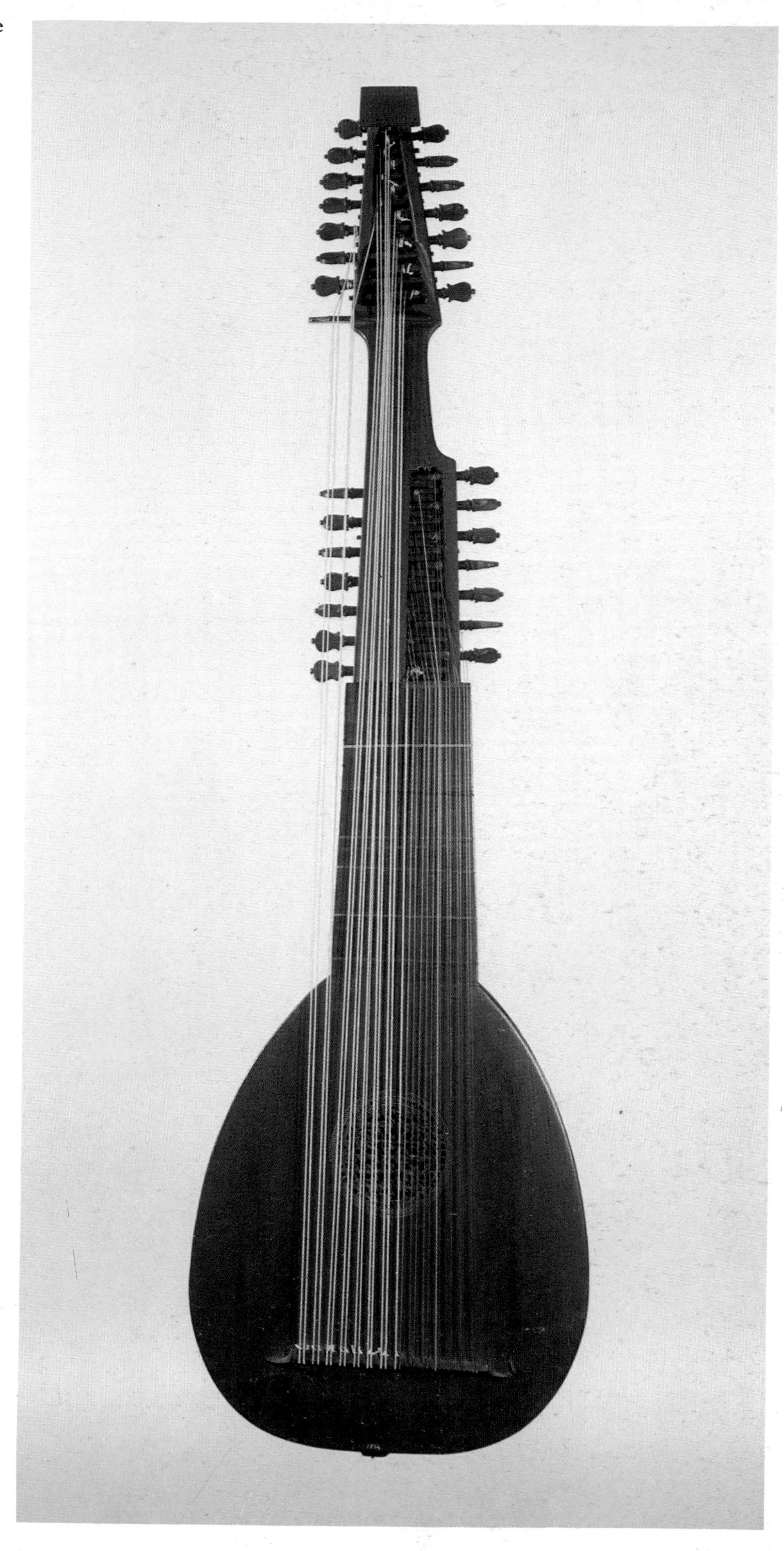

III. — 6. **Italian theorbo** (*c.* 1600)

III. — 7. **Italian guitar**
(16th century)

III. — 8. **French cittern** (17th century) ▶

III. — 9. **Italian viola bastard**

III. — 6.

Italian theorbo, not bearing the maker's name but attributable to Wendelio Venere, the Italianized name of Wendelin Tieffenbrücker who lived in Padua from 1551 to 1611. The instrument has two pegboxes each having seven double strings tuned, in the one case, in fourths and thirds as in the lute, and in the other diatonically.
Length: *c.* 3¾ ft.

M.I., Brussels.
No. 1564.

III. — 7.

Italian guitar, bearing the mark of Matteo Sellas, who lived in the first half of the sixteenth century. Its back consists of lengths of Brazilian rosewood separated by ivory threads. The belly has a rose-hole in gilded lead surrounded by incrusted ivory and ebony. The fingerboard and pegs are embellished with carved ivory plates illustrating fables of Aesop. There are ten ivory pegs and five double strings.
Length: *c.* 34 ins.

M.I., Brussels.
No. 550.

III. — 8.

French cittern of the 16th century, by an unknown maker. The instrument's body is made of different materials: the belly, flat, is of deal, the back, equally flat, is of maplewood and ebony. It has a double thread. The pegbox ends in a woman's head sculpted in wood. This cittern has ten strings tuned in two groups of two and two of three. Not all the brass frets cross its entire breadth, so that a variety of chords may be played.
Length: *c.* 28 ins.

M.I., Brussels.
No. 1524.

III. — 9.

Viola bastarda by the Venetian maker Antonio Ciciliano, dated 1660. The famous maker is thought to have been born in Bologna at about the beginning of the 17th century and to have died after 1660. This instrument is thought to be the last he built. Praetorius says of the viola bastarda: "*... wird ein Tenor von Violn de gamba gestimmet... aber das Corpus ist etwas länger und grösser.*" (It is tuned like a tenor viol... but its sound-box is a little longer and larger.) Length *c.* 43½ ins.

M.I., Brussels.
No. 1424.

century has left us many more instruments, and if these include a large number whose quality is luxurious, this is due not simply to the Renaissance infatuation with music, but also to the fact that collections of instruments, belonging both to the nobility and to the rich bourgeoisie, have come to light; but it is interesting that the choice of these collectors was determined more by the instruments' decorative value than by interest in their handicraft. This is why we have from this period instruments which are genuine *objets d'art*, made in costly materials, coated with mother-of-pearl or ivory, even embellished with precious stones or rare variegated woods worked in marquetry.

It is also at this time that we find instruments, and particularly keyboard instruments, with inscriptions such as the following: "*Rendo lieti in tempo gli occhi el core*" (I give pleasure at the same time to the eyes and to the heart), which was painted on a harpsichord made by Trasontino in 1560. However, some collections did not always correspond to this desire to amass works of art, but were rather designed to form a musical ensemble which could be used for collective musical performances.

Several inventories of such collections of the one sort or the other have come down to us. Of these, a notable example is that of Queen Isabella of Castile, drawn up in 1503. The collection of Henry VIII of England had no less than 381 instruments; its inventory, dated 1547, tells us that it included, amongst other things, organs, regals and recorders ("viii Recorders greate and smale in a Case couered with blacke Leather and lined with clothe and one great base Recorder of woode in a Case of Woode"). [1] Another inventory is that, drawn up in 1596, of Raymund Fugger the Younger, an Augsburg banker; there is also that of Ferdinand, Duke of Tyrol, dating from 1596. Subsequently, further inventories throw light on the contents of more or less ancient collections, and though it lies outside the scope of the present chapter, we may mention the important collection of Ferdinand de Medici, Grand Duke of Tuscany, of which we have an inventory as recent as 1716, for the reason that for a time it was in the care of Bartolomeo Cristofori (1655/5-1731), the inventor of the piano.

The inventories show us that, though at first wind instruments were collected in preference to stringed instruments, this state of affairs was not long maintained.

Stringed Instruments

The most widespread plucked stringed instrument in the last two centuries of the Middle Ages and during the period of the Renaissance was undoubtedly the lute, derived from the Arabian instrument al'ûd, which the Moors had brought to Spain but which travelled no further until the tenth century, whereas the lute previously used in Western Europe and discussed in the preceding chapter rather recalls, with its long neck and three strings, the Asian tanbûr.

[1] *This collection included the following instruments: 78 transverse flutes, 77 recorders, 30 shawms, 28 organs, 25 crumhorns, 21 horns, 5 cornetts, 5 bagpipes, 32 virginals, 26 lutes, 25 viols, 21 guitars, 2 clavichords and 3 claviorganums.*

The lute proper, as we still know it today, has a sound-box in the shape of half of a pear which is prolonged by a neck, at the end of which is a pegbox placed at a right-angle. Though at first the instrument's shape varied a little, by the fourteenth century it began to settle down. On the other hand, the number of strings increased over the centuries, bringing with it the necessity for a corresponding increase in the breadth of the neck.

Originally having four single strings that were tuned in a pair of fourths separated by a third, in about 1350 the lute's strings began to be doubled at the unison so as to increase their sonority (we have already met with such double strings in certain types of mediaeval fiddle). Half a century later, the fifth string appeared, a single one added to the upper register and serving as a melody string. Finally, shortly before 1500, a sixth string was added, this time a double one in the lower register. With this last addition, the classical lute, for which so much music was to be written, was born. It now had eleven strings, making as many as five double-string courses surmounted by the high melody string. From then on the strings were tuned as follows (reading from the lowest string): *G*, *c*, *f*, *a*, *d*, *g* — in other words, two fourths followed by a third, followed in turn by two more fourths. This is the normal tuning and it came to be called the "old tune" by lutenists of later generations when they came to introduce new and equally important ways of tuning the instrument. By that time (the seventeenth century), the number of lower courses had again increased. Finally, it should be mentioned that the neck of the lute is provided at each semitone step with a thin gut string tied and knotted round it. These ligaments, called frets, served to indicate the place on the neck where the finger should be applied to the string in order to give it the required length in vibration; in fact, the finger is placed not on the fret but immediately behind it, in such a way that the sonority produced will be that of an open string. If the sounds produced gain in homogeneity in this way, it also becomes impossible, on the other hand, to use a vibrato tone. The frets, numbering four in about 1400, ran to eight in about 1520, and a few years later increased to ten. One snag arose from the use of gut frets tied and tightened round the neck: if they became loosened, they would travel along the neck of their own accord, and would thus no longer occupy the exact place given them so as to obtain the required note. The use of a plectrum to pluck the strings was abandoned in favour of the fingers, with which a sweeter and more delicate sonority could be produced.

Although the lute appears fairly large, it is extremely light, for its sound-box, made with ribs usually of sycamore and numbering between nine and about forty depending on the quality of the craftsmanship, is very thin. Sycamore is sometimes replaced by ebony, rosewood, cypress, sandalwood, or even ivory. As a special refinement, one even comes across lute ribs made alternately of two different kinds of wood, whilst the neck and the edging of the belly, as well as that of the rose-type sound-hole are inlaid with mother-of-pearl or ivory.

During the sixteenth century, the lute played as important a role as did the piano in the romantic era. It might be played by any music lover who enjoyed performing pieces written specially for the lute, but also he could turn to transcriptions of dance music or of songs for several voices. If the same music lover could sing at all, he could draw on transcriptions of polyphonic vocal works in arrangements for solo voice with lute accompaniment, and such arrangements were to be one of the factors which contributed to the transition from polyphonic to harmonic music whose first important manifestations appeared in the first decades of the seventeenth century. To this we shall return later, but for the moment it is tempting to draw a comparison between these transcriptions for voice and lute of the sixteenth century and those of operas, then in vogue, made in great number for the piano in the Romantic era. At that time too, fantasias were written, based on the principal airs of these operas, but also every middle-class young lady who could tap out a few notes on the *piano* and had the semblance of a voice would have piano reductions of the orchestral accompaniment; in this way she could identify herself with the heroines of her dreams and show off her talents, whilst around her, young guests would accompany her, humming, as Massenet would have it, like "honey-bees".

The lute became so widely known that in France the name *luthier*, given to lute manufacturers, is still used to designate any maker of stringed instruments, of whatever kind these may be.

The first books of lute tablature were printed in Italy at the beginning of the sixteenth century. Germany, then France soon followed; England had to wait longer. To be aware of the role the lute played in those times it is only necessary to know that in about 1546 forty or so books were published for the instrument in Venice alone, and that once the lute repertoire had become international lutenists such as the Italian Francesco da Milano (1497-1573), also called *Il Divino*, and the Hungarian Valentin Bakfark, as well as a number of others, were having their works printed in several countries at the same time. To enumerate the anthologies of pieces for solo lute or for voice and lute which were at the time appearing in many different places would be a lengthy task; instead, let us take at random the example of the Louvain editor Pierre Phalèse, who in the one year 1545 published five books of *Chansons reduicts en tabulature de luc*, or that of the French lutenist Jean-Baptiste Besard, also a consultant jurist and doctor, who in 1603 published in Cologne his *Thesaurus harmonicus*, a vast anthology of more than 400 pieces for the lute, some of which were of his own composition, the others forming a very interesting selection of what was played in different parts of Europe during the last years of the sixteenth century.

The vihuela, which, as we saw in the previous chapter, was a plucked stringed instrument with a typically Spanish flat back and played with either a plectrum, a bow, or the fingers, was generally only plucked with the fingers from the sixteenth century on. At that time, like the contemporary lute, it had five double strings and one single string, tuned in a similar way. The majority of the vihuela tablatures were published between 1535 and 1578, and their chief authors were the performers Luis Milan, Pisador and Fuenllana. After 1580, this instrument, which had been treated as a national instrument, disappeared to be superseded by the so-called *Spanish guitar*.

In order to know what distinguished the guitar of the first half of the sixteenth century from the vihuela of the same period, one needs simply to know what Bermudo tells us about it in his *Declaraciòn de instrumentos*: "If you wish to alter a vihuela into a guitar, take away its first and sixth strings". This was the form in which the guitar appeared in other countries — with four strings. Although Bermudo does also mention a five-stringed guitar, this did not replace the other, and only spread during the second half of the century, coming to be known as the Spanish guitar in order to distinguish it from the four-stringed model the other countries continued to use. After that time, the popularity of the vihuela waned; from then on, it was rather for the *guitarra española* that composers wrote their works. The first treatise on this new guitar was written in 1586, calling the instrument the "*guitarra Castellana y Cathalana*" (guitar of Castille and Catalania). Moreover, it was in Barcelona that its author, Juan Carlos Amat, also a doctor, published it. It is curious that one chapter of this treatise — the ninth — deals with the four-stringed guitar, which must still have had its devotees, whilst the tenth and last chapter is concerned with the method of tuning a six-stringed instrument called the *vandola*.

It is not only in its number of strings and the flat back of its sound-box that the guitar differs from the lute, but also in its slightly waisted sound-box (even though, unlike the viol, the reason for this cannot be that the instrument was played with a bow) and by its tuning pegs, which are placed in arrowhead formation in a pegbox that is bent slightly backwards.

Though the guitar was played in other countries, it was in Spain that it was most played, and that, moreover, to the detriment of the lute, which was hardly used at all there.

Another plucked stringed instrument, which appeared in the sixteenth century only to die out after the seventeenth century, was the *cittern*, having a flat back, a fairly elongated neck, and metallic double strings which, instead of being attached to a tailpiece fixed to the belly, were joined to the lower end of the soundbox; also, probably in order to diminish the instrument's weight, the pegs became thinner towards the base, whilst in general, so as to restore the balance that had been upset by this narrowing, the neck was lightened by a groove cut along its whole length on the side held by the player's thumb. The cittern was a favourite instrument with the upper middle classes.

During the Renaissance, the harp, as it was known on the Continent, remained diatonic, and thus differed from the small Welsh harp which, as we have seen, was already in the Middle Ages a chromatic instrument. The Continental harp received a greater number of strings in the course of the sixteenth century. For this reason, the instrument's frame had to be strengthened to withstand the greater tension of the strings it carried; thus it increased in both size and weight.

The mediaeval fiddle had above all been played by minstrels, who were at the same time poets and itinerant musicians, and who used the instrument to accompany their own prose or verse recitations. These minstrels had gradually united in a sort of confraternity, whose importance was such that after 1338 they adopted a single leader, R. Caveron, known as *Roy des Ménestrels du Royaume de France*. This title, and the responsibilities it entailed, survived until 1773, and the statutes of the *ménestrandie*, as the minstrelsy was known, were endorsed by all the successive kings of France up to Louis XIV, who granted them new rulings in 1658.

The statutes of the year 1407 contained very strict rules, and they tell us that in order to be accepted as a fully-fledged master, every minstrel had first to undergo an apprenticeship lasting six years; no one could open a school for the demonstration and teaching of minstrelsy without the authorisation of the *Roy des Ménestrels*, and so on. Such was the power of this corporation that in 1620 it authorised Richomme to use the title *Roi des violons*.

Outside France, similar bodies existed. A corporation of Saint Nicholas was in existence, in Vienna, as early as 1288, whereas London had to wait until 1381 before having a confraternity of minstrels.

Without doubt, the rigorousness of the rules found in the 1407 statutes hastened and perhaps even provoked the modification of the bowed fiddle, which developed during the fifteenth century into the viol. Indeed, six years of schooling in order to attain mastery would provide the successful minstrels with the sort of technique that would not rest at such a rudimentary instrument as the fiddle; besides, the masters, being the only performers privileged to play at weddings or at important social functions, would feel the need for a more refined instrument whose richer possibilities and nobler sonorities would distinguish them from the minstrels to the sound of whose fiddles the common folk would make merry.

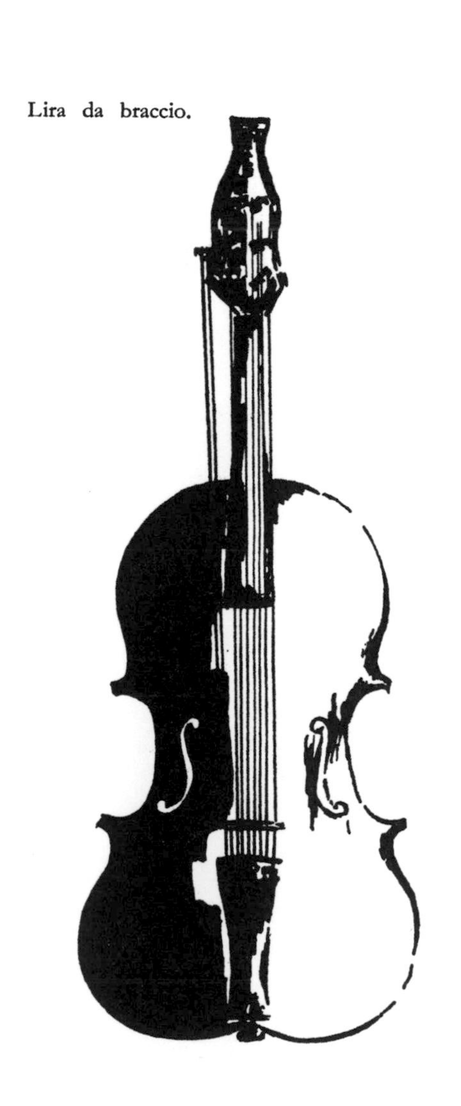
Lira da braccio.

We have seen that according to Jerome of Moravia one of the three types of mediaeval fiddle had five strings, placed over the neck and tuned to different pitches; these were: *G*, *c*, *g*, d^1, g^1. This fiddle provided the basis for the *tenor viol*, the standard model of the viol family. In fact, its tuning covered the same range (from *G* to g^1), though so as to avoid difficult positions on the neck, a sixth string was added to the others and the tuning was identical with that we have given for the lute; consequently any lutenist could learn to play the viol without much difficulty, as the technique for the left hand remained the same. Agricola (1529) gives this tuning for the tenor viol, but later we come across different versions.

The tenor viol had a number of other characteristics in common with all the other instruments of the same family: the soundbox, generally having a flat back, often terminated in a point at the top and had lateral curves of almost semicircular shape, giving the impression that the instrument's body was made in two distinct parts. The C-shaped sound-holes were taken over from the fiddle, but now, placed symmetrically on each side of the bridge, they took on a more elongated, sometimes flamboyant shape. As for the neck, it followed the lead of the lute in having frets and in ending in a backward-bending pegbox to facilitate resistance to string tension.

The same structure holds good for all the viols, from the smallest, the *pardessus de viole*, about two feet long, to the double-bass viol (Praetorius's *gar gross Bass* measured seven feet). These instruments make up the family of *viola da gamba*, so called because they were all held between the legs or supported on a cushion, whereas in the Middle Ages the fiddler had held his instrument either in front of his body or against his shoulder.

In the Middle Ages, the fiddle existed in two different forms, large and small, the former of which was held in front of the player, parallel to his body, a mode of playing which resembled that used by the Orientals for a similar instrument, by which one may assume a close relationship to have existed between these instruments. In about the fourteenth century, the small fiddle overtook the larger one in popularity, and it was usual to hold this instrument against the shoulder. However, in the course of the fifteenth century, the large fiddle again became more popular, apparently because of the beauty and richness of its timbre which made quite a contrast with the harsh, thin sounds of the other, and, as we have seen, it was this model that gave birth to the tenor viol, the standard model of the viola da gamba family.

Nevertheless, the small fiddle had not disappeared; it had itself been developed and transformed into a different type of viol, the *viola da braccio*, which, like the viola da gamba, also had semicircular curves which appeared to divide the body into two parts, and a bent-back pegbox. However, its belly and back were slightly humped, and were edged round with inlaid threads; the upper part of the sound-box was rounded, rather than pointed, and each end of the semicircular curves was extended to a point. When we add that the viola da braccio was not fretted along the neck, had only four strings, and took over from an older instrument, the *lira da braccio* (which we shall be dealing with soon), sound-holes in the shape of two superposed and reversed C's (Ͻ C) which have already been met with in the thirteenth century, it will be seen that we have here an instrument whose significance is vast, for it was to become the modern violin.

Thus, the viola da braccio family included the four-stringed instruments which extended from the violin down to the cello. Because they had fewer strings than did the viola da gamba, in order to cover a sufficiently wide range, they had to be tuned in fifths, rather than in fourths and thirds. The wider spacing of this tuning could hardly be a great disadvantage to the violinist, for, since the violin's neck was more slender than that of the viol, the player's hand could stretch further along it. It should be noted that although it belonged to the viola da braccio family, an instrument like the cello, by reason of its large size, could not be held between the hand and the shoulder, but, like the viola da gamba, was held upright between the legs.

As often happens, a newcomer can be treated with suspicion in an already fairly full field, and to provide reasons for its rejection faults may be found with it that often are not in fact faults at all. This is what befell the violin, which soon found itself treated as *vacarmini* by the well-established viol players who formed a sort of aristocratic society of those who played those noble instruments, the viols, "with which gentlemen, merchants and other men of worth pass their time" as opposed to the violins "used in communal dancing ... at some wedding or mummery", as Philibert, known as Jambe de Fer, wrote in his *Epitome musical* (1556). It was for this reason that, at least throughout the sixteenth and the first

III. — 10.

Pegbox of a bass viol attributed to Gaspard Duiffoprugcar (or Tieffenbrücker), born in about 1514 and died in about 1570. On its back, the instrument has a map of 16th-century Paris in marquetry as well as a depiction of Saint Luke. The back of the pegbox, which ends in an unidentified animal's head, is sculpted in wood and shows, notably, the god Pan playing his flute as well as a number of musical instruments. This instrument has seven gut strings.
Length: *c.* 49½ ins.

M.I., Brussels.
No. 1427.

III. — 11.

Viola da spalla, or tenor viol, of the 17th century, bearing on its label the inscription of the maker Iseppo Merfeotto of Rovigo (near Padua). He was most likely the same man as the Guiseppe Mafeotto one of whose instruments may be found in the collection of the Copenhagen Instrumental Museum. The instrument shown here is varnished with albumin. Unlike the viola da gamba, the viola da spalla has only four strings.
Length: *c.* 27½ ins.

M.I., Brussels.
No. 1439.

years of the seventeenth centuries, viol players belonged to a higher intellectual and artistic class than did violinists, who were disdained by lutenists, harpsichord players and organists alike, and were not admitted to musical chapels either religious or secular.

The lira da braccio was another bowed string instrument, played especially in fourteenth- to sixteenth-century Italy, which provided some of the elements of the violin. This lira da braccio preserved the straight pegbox of the old fiddle; the pegbox was in fact in the shape of a heart pierced by the pegs. There were five strings of which the lowest two were placed off the neck and served as drones. The tuning was in fifths.

Painters of the time often depicted angels playing the lira da braccio, and it is also ideally portrayed in Tintoretto's famous "Women making music".

The bass version of this instrument, the *lira da gamba*, or *lirone*, took over elements from various instruments: the body resembled that of the lira da braccio, but the rose-type sound-hole added to the two others was taken over from the lute; like the fiddle and the viola da gamba, the lira da gamba was provided with frets. The number of its strings could vary between nine and thirteen, to which were added two lower strings; in Germany there was even a sixteen-stringed lirone, whilst in Italy, the maximum known number is fifteen, three of which were the double-strings of the drone. Since the bridge was very flat, it was only possible to sound the outer strings on their own; as a result, the instrument served mainly to provide chords which could support a melody played on a different instrument, notably the lira da braccio.

Some of the bowed string instruments that were already used in the Middle Ages survived without major modifications into the Renaissance era. The rebec, still just as shrill as it always had been, was heard by an ever more plebeian audience and before it disappeared in the seventeenth century was relegated by civil laws to use in low public houses and other equally ill-famed establishments; the gigue was to be more lucky, for over the years it had developed from the single-stringed instrument it had originally been into a more useful three-stringed instrument, and had acquired a family, having, in the sixteenth century, four members — treble, alto, tenor and bass — which provided a homogeneous quartet on which transcriptions of polyphonic vocal quartets could be played (in the same period we find also gigues with 4 or more strings); finally, the tromba marina, which in about 1500 adopted a lateral instead of a frontal peg, had, over the years, a more and more asymmetrical bridge with unequal feet, and it was doubtless as a consequence of the beating of the longer foot on the wooden sound-box that the Germans customarily called this instrument the trumscheit (drum-log).

As for struck stringed instruments without keyboard, their sole representative was in fact the dulcimer, still retaining its mediaeval shape and structure, and without the addition of any new elements.

Wind Instruments

Wind instruments too played a vital role during the Renaissance period. Like the stringed instruments, they too tended to be grouped into families.

The recorder, though threatened by the growing popularity of the transverse flute, was made in various sizes, corresponding to different registers. Whereas in 1500 only four sizes were known, Praetorius, at the beginning of the seventeenth century, mentions nine; the smallest was barely 8 inches long, whilst the great bass was more than 6ft. 6ins. long. The Museum Vleeshuis at Antwerp even has a double-bass model about 8ft. 6ins. long, on which one could play notes as low as *D*. This gigantic instrument came from the Hanseatic House in Antwerp, where it was particularly noticed by Charles Burney on one of his musical journeys to the Continent in 1772; he also tells us that this Hanseatic House possessed about thirty recorders.

In the larger of the recorders, to facilitate the blocking of those holes farthest away from the player, a lever attached to a leather stopper was used for this purpose. This type of key was known as an open key to distinguish it from another type in use around that time, the closed key (open, because the hole remained open when the key was at rest); it was first mentioned in a Netherlands text of 1413. The use of these keys did not always make for very satisfactory results, since sometimes the blocking was incomplete and allowed a passage of air into the hole, thus weakening the tone. In his *Syntagma musicum* Praetorius draws attention to this drawback in the larger recorders which made itself felt all the more plainly when the larger models were used in consort with smaller flutes, whose sonority, in the absence of such keys, remained full-toned.

On the other hand, since the size of these bass recorders was such that the lower keys on the instrument were out of reach of the player's hand while he was using a mouthpiece at the upper end of the instrument, a brass tube curved in an S-shape was fitted at this end so as to bring the mouthpiece lower.

Several other types of recorder existed, such as the *double recorder*, a somewhat rare instrument that has now almost disappeared, the *tabor-pipe* and the *flageolets*. These instruments were very small and had an extremely narrow bore, thus were able to play only harmonics. They were given at least three holes.

The Basque tabor-pipe, like that found in the Béarn and in Gascony, was played with the left hand while the right hand, holding a drumstick, was playing a tambourine, or tabor. These instruments were used for country dances. Tabor-pipes of different sizes could be found in the above-named regions as well as in Northern Italy and in England.

The flageolet, an instrument as popular with the nobility and the bourgeoisie as with the common folk, was invented in Paris by Juvigny in 1581; it had six holes, four in front and two at the back. Soon it came to be called the *flauto piccolo* and became the highest instrument of the orchestra; later it was ousted by the highest of the transverse flutes, which also adopted the name *piccolo*.

We are told very little of the transverse flute during the Renaissance, and what we do know of it, whether from Virdung, from Agricola, or even from Praetorius, is vague and insufficient

III. — 12.

Italian lirone perfetto or lira da gamba, also known as accordo. This very old instrument has nine strings. It does not have the doubled lower strings that are normally to be found on lire da gamba. The back is flat. The very short fingerboard has 5 frets. Besides the rose-hole, the sound-board has two sound-holes. As with the lira da braccio, the pegs are in arrowhead formation. The almost straight ridge of the bridge shows that several strings were bowed simultaneously. According to Mersenne the sound of the lirone was very languorous and might inspire one to devotion.

Length: *c.* 43½ ins.

M.I., Brussels.
No. 1444.

III. — 13.

Three German recorders of the 17th century. The first is a basset recorder, provided with a bilobate key. The maker of this instrument is unknown. The second recorder is a soprano whose untypical form is extremely rare; its mouthhole and key are hidden in cages of engraved brass in the form of grilles. The last recorder is a tenor; it bears the mark Ṿ Ṿ branded near the base of the pipe.

Length: *c.* 37 ins., 20 ins. and 24¾ ins.

M.I., Brussels.
Nos. 1031, 189 & 1025.

III. — 14.

French transverse flute by the famous maker Claude Rafi, who died in 1553. In his day, poets wrote lines in honour of Rafi, who worked in Lyons at the beginning of the 16th century; Claude Marot, in his *Eloge sur Mme Loyse de Savoye:* " *De moy auras un double chalumeau - Faict de la main de Raffy Lyonnois* " (I shall give you a double shawm made by the hand of Raffy of Lyons), and A. de Baïf in *Les Jeux:* " *Après tous ces propos j'apporte une musette - Que Rafi Lyonnois à Marot avait faite* " (After all this I bring a musette made for Marot by Rafi of Lyons); also Fr. de La Salla, in his *Epistre de l'Asne au Coq:* " *Si vous avez coupfé le doy... - La bonne fleuste de Raffi* " (If you have cut your finger.. the good flute of Raffi).

Length: *c.* 28¼ ins.

M.I., Brussels.
No. 1066.

◄◄ III. — 10. **Pegbox of a French bass vi**
(16th century)

III. — 11. **Italian viola da spall**
(17th century)

III. — 12. **Italian lirone perfetto**
(17th century)

◀ Ill. — 13. **Three German recorders**
(17th century)

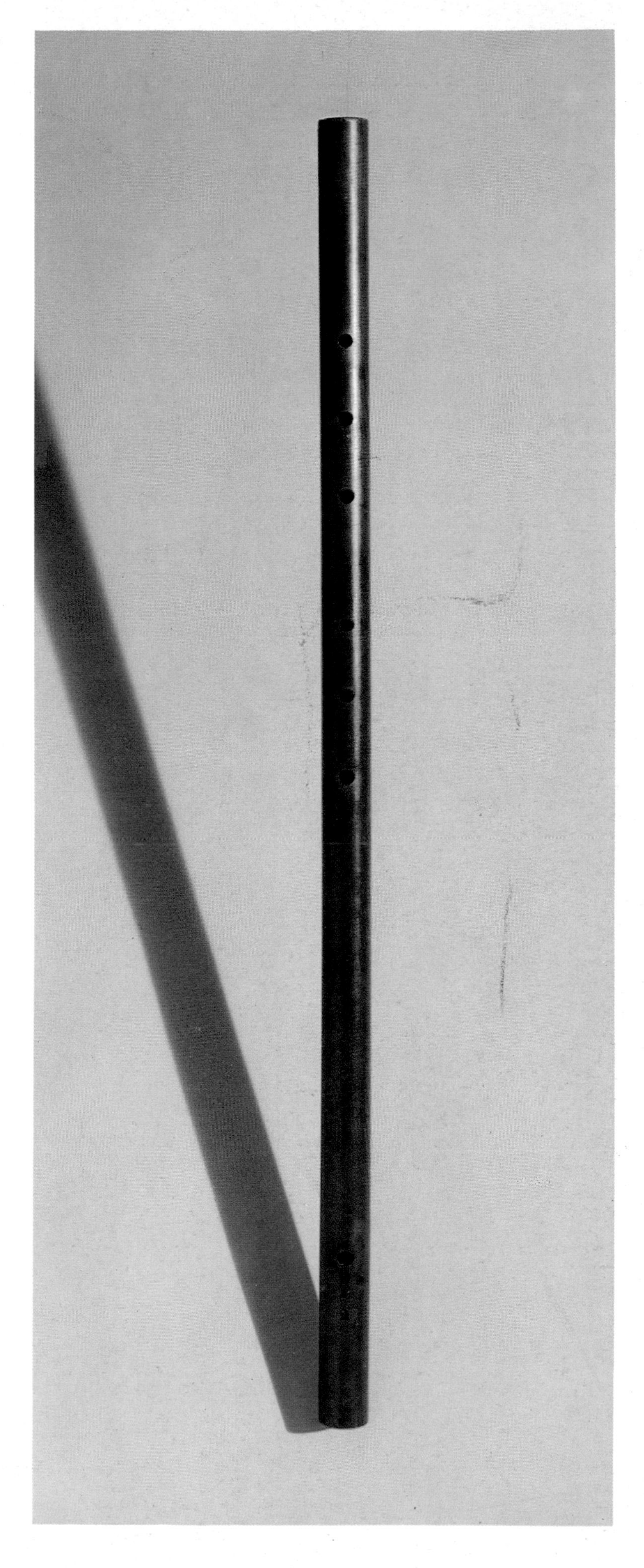

Ill. — 14. **French transverse flute**
(16th century)

III. — 16. **Two shawms** (17th century) ▶

III. — 15. **French serpent** (17th century)

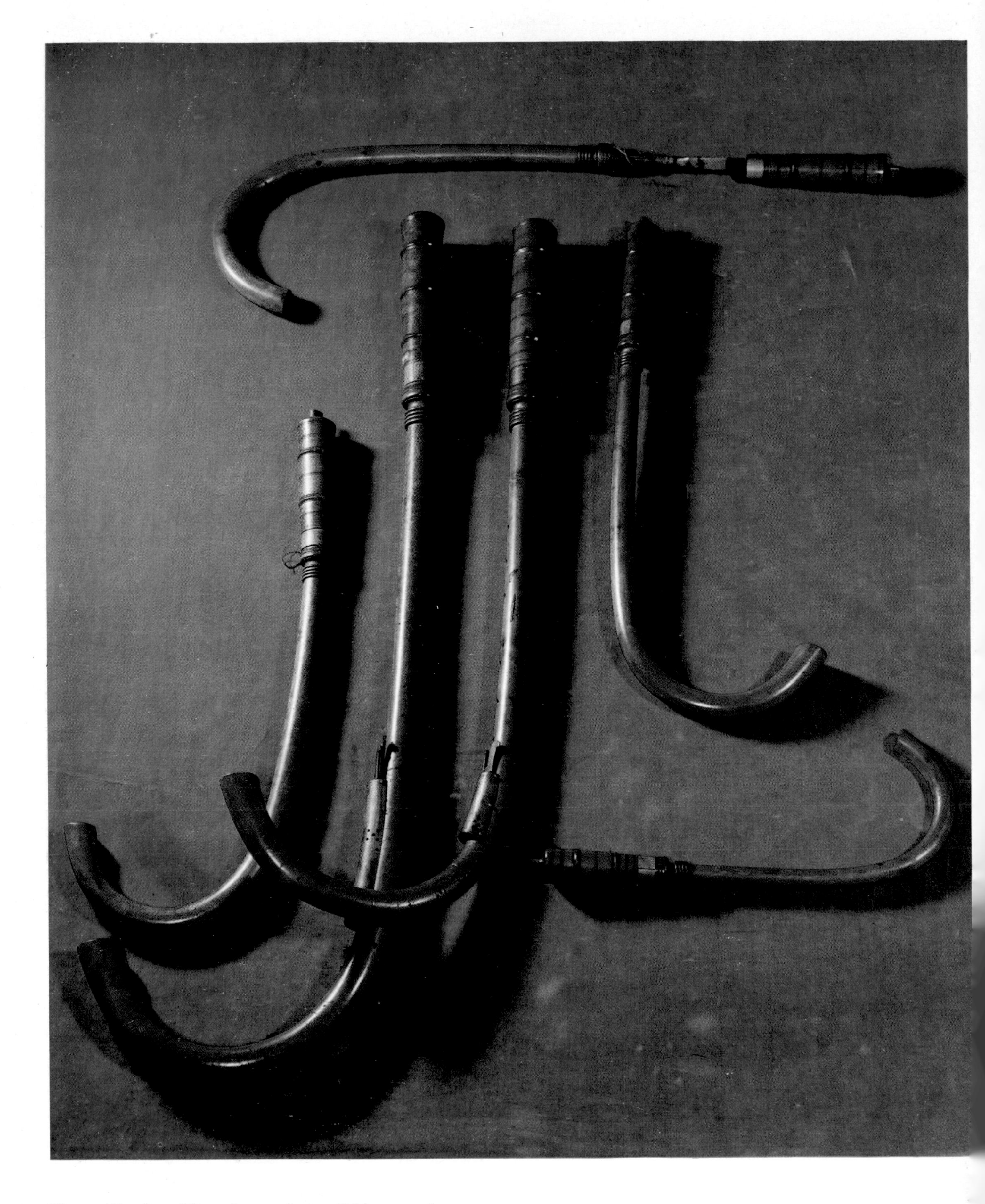

III. — 17. **Set of French crumhorns** (16th century)

Dulzian.

Racket.

Tournebout.

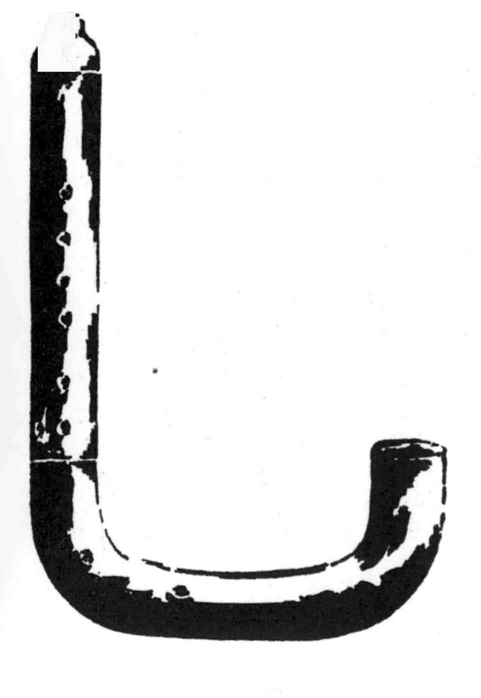

to serve as a firm basis for working out any precise details of how it was made. All we can say is that it continued to have a cylindrical bore, as it still has today, and that in accordance with the contemporary tendencies it was represented by a family of four differently pitched instruments.

The principal reed instruments used in the sixteenth century were those with double reeds. They derived from the mediaeval shawm, whose bass offspring was the *curtal*. These new arrivals, some of which had already appeared at the end of the fifteenth century, can be divided into those having a cylindrical bore and those with a conical bore, but in each case the means of sound production remains the same — that is, all have double reeds which activate the vibration of the column of air inside the instrument, and this double reed is either in direct contact with the player's lips as in the shawm or enclosed in a wooden cap as in the *crumhorn*. The names of some of these instruments are the shawm, or *hautbois*, the pommer, or *grosbois*, the *piffera*, the dulzian, the *sordone*, the *racket*, the crumhorn, the curtal, the *cornamusa*, and the *schryari*.

Obviously, there is not room here to go into the details of all these instruments, particularly as some of them can only be identified by details which are of no interest to the non-specialist. Instead, we shall simply describe the more important of them, and it should also be pointed out that, as was common at the time, most of them were made in various sizes.

The most widespread of the higher-pitched double-reed instruments were represented by the shawm (in French *chalumeau*) family, and these were extended to the lower registers in the pommer (in French, *bombarde*). Both of these had a narrow and slightly conical bore, and their double reed remained uncovered.

Both the shawm and the pommer had seven holes, the last of which was fitted with an open key. Again, since the pommer was fairly long, it was given an S-shaped tube like that of the bass recorder so as to facilitate handling; this tube was called a crook, and the double reed was fixed to the end of it. The pommer could be in up to seven sizes.

The curtal was also a double-reed instrument, but in this case the reed was sometimes enclosed in a cap, and the bore was cylindrical rather than conical. In spite of its length, it was easier to handle than the pommer, for it was bent back in the shape of a "U" at its lower end; it terminated in a flared bell.

The name, hautbois (which, in modern French, means oboe) occurred sporadically in texts written towards the end of the fourteenth century; the name in fact refers to the shawm, and only gradually in the course of the seventeenth century did this name replace the older one, and at the same time the instrument underwent palpable improvements. It should be noted that at the end of the fifteenth century, and still later, the names hautbois and shawm were sometimes used to designate any double-reed instrument, whatever its shape or size.

We do not know the date of the first appearance of the bassoon, which was to become to the oboe what the pommer was to the shawm. However, it is possible to say that it appeared, or rather reappeared — for a similar instrument was already known to the Romans — before 1574, for we know that in that year Philippe van Ranst was nominated bassoonist at the Court of Brussels.

The construction of the bassoon was clearly superior to that of the pommer, for it took over from the curtal its U-shaped bottom end, with the difference that now the returning tube continued upwards past the top of the first tube, to which was fitted a crook. In fact, it was now no longer a case of one tube bending back on itself but rather two adjacent tubes coupled at the bottom to form, in effect, a single tube of double length. In this way, the bassoon was half as long as it would have been if, like the pommer, it had remained as a single tube stretched out over its full length, which might reach ten feet or so.

The bassoon was also known by the names *bajon* (Spain), *Fagott* (Germany), *dulzian* (England), or *douçaine* (France). The instrument acquired the names dulzian and douçaine on account of the softness of its tone, which contrasted with the more forthright sound of the pommer.

Since the bassoon had its own family, we need not be surprised to find it appearing in various sizes, each of which might have its own name, such as the *Quint-*, *Quart-*, *Chorist-* and *Discant-Fagott*, or might be designated by a diminutive, like the *fagottino* or the *bajoncillo*, referring to the instrument's register.

The Brussels Instrumental Museum has some examples of such bajoncillos of various registers, Spanish instruments which, together with the *bajones* and the *chirimias* (a fairly crude type of shawm), made up the popular orchestras which doubled the voices in religious services. Chirimias may also be found in Mexico, used in small indigenous ensembles. Finally, it is worth mentioning a further instrument with conical bore, the Italian piffera, a simply-made shawm found in three sizes and mainly played by itinerant musicians of the Abruzzi in village festivals.

We shall now go on to consider some of the double-reed instruments with, cylindrical bore. The sordone, in five different sizes, and low in pitch like the pommer, was bored in a single piece of wood and provided with a hole in the side which served as a bell.

The racket, also called the *Wurst-Fagott* or *Faust-Fagott* in Germany and *cervelas* in France, consisted of a short, squat, ivory cylinder in which were bored parallel channels that were joined in such a fashion as to make one continuous tube. A crook, into which was fitted the double reed, was attached to the top of the first channel; this crook and part of the reed were covered in an ivory protective shield; Mersenne calls this shield a *pirouette*. Around the instrument's body were twelve holes which connected with one or other of the channels at different levels. The sound made by the racket resembled that of the sordone and of the crumhorn; it was very sweet, but also very weak. This curious instrument also had its own family.

The crumhorn was an instrument of far greater importance. It was made of a wooden tube that was relatively thin and bent downwards. Its shape was elegant, but when later it was thickened so as to widen the cylindrical bore, it was also known in France as the *tournebout*.

As was also the case with some curtals, the crumhorn's double reed was enclosed in a cap which prevented it from coming

Cornett.

III. — 1

French serpent, by an unknown maker. It is made of two hollowed-out pieces of wood glued together and then covered in leather. The tube has 6 lateral holes. The crook, on which is fitted the bone mouthpiece, is of brass.
Length of the tube: *c.* $7\frac{1}{4}$ ft.
M.I., Brussels.
No. 475.

III. — 16.

Two shawms, one a descant, the other an alto, by the Spanish maker Melchior R.S., whose name as well as his mark and a crown are engraved on the wood. These conical bore instruments date from the beginning of the seventeenth century.
Length: *c.* $25\frac{5}{8}$ ins. and $32\frac{3}{4}$ ins.
M.I., Brussels.
Nos. 2323 & 2326.

III. — 17.

Set of crumhorns, in boxwood, of French origin but from the court of Ferrara. This set dates from the end of the sixteenth century. It consists of a soprano, three altos, a tenor and a bass. The tenor and bass have bilobate keys. On the other instruments the first and second holes are set at the same height, at some distance from each other. One of these holes would be blocked with wax depending on whether the player was right-handed or left-handed.
Length: bass: *c.* $38\frac{1}{4}$ ins; soprano: *c.* 17 ins.
M.I., Brussels.
Nos. 610 - 615.

into contact with the player's lips. As there was also a family of crumhorns, they were made in various sizes; depending on which size the instrument was, the opening in the cap was either made in mouthpiece-shape at the top, or as a rectangular opening in the side of the cap. Like all instruments whose reed was covered, the crumhorn could only play the fundamental sounds, for harmonic sounds can only be produced when the lips are pressed fairly firmly against the reed.

The origins of the crumhorn in particular, and of all instruments with similar caps in general, is obscure. It might be possible to trace it back to the Orient. If one examines the German name of the instrument, *Krummhorn* (curved horn), one might come to the conclusion that it was simply a horn, a word used in the Middle Ages to designate certain popular double-reed instruments whose bell and mouthpiece were made of animal horn, the adjective "curved" pointing to one of the instrument's characteristics.

The complete family of the crumhorns was already known in France in the fifteenth century. In 1459, this name appeared in a document to designate an organ voice. In the sixteenth century it was still in France, as well as in the Low Countries and in Germany, that the instrument seems to have been something of a favourite, whereas in Italy it seems to have been rather ignored.

Other instruments of the period are known, such as the Italian *bassanelli* and the schryari, which was of Oriental origin, and found principally in Germany; these were fairly rudimentary types of bassoon. The same is true of an instrument which resembled the crumhorn called the cornamusa, which was in a number of sizes and consisted of a single tube blocked at its lower end; near this end, holes were bored in the side to allow the air to escape.

In about 1500, the *hornpipe*, or *pibgorn*, an instrument of Oriental origin, was introduced to Germany; of cylindrical bore, this was one of the few instruments of the Renaissance to have a single reed. The *tenoroon* also had a single reed, but its bore was conical. Instruments of conical bore whose air-column is activated by a single reed are indeed rarities; not until the nineteenth century did another instrument possessing the same characteristics, the saxophone, achieve a popularity which is still with us today.

During the sixteenth century, the bagpipe acquired more drone-pipes and was made in five sizes. It was less popular with the aristocracy, but the common people continued to favour it, as is shown by its inclusion in the numerous village festivals depicted by painters like the elder Breughel.

Before leaving the instruments we have just been studying, it needs to be said that for nearly all of them the fingering had not been finally established. In fact, the player could operate the open keys just as well with his left hand as with his right; this explains why the keys had two wings at the upper end. If the instrument maker had not thought it necessary to provide keys for some of the end holes, he took care to bore two holes there, one to the left and one to the right, instead of a single one; it was left to the player to block up with wax the hole he did not intend to use.

We now pass on from the reed instruments to those having a reedless mouthpiece, some of which we have already dealt with at length since they date back to the earliest antiquity.

An instrument which, if not altogether a new one, became very widespread during the sixteenth and seventeenth centuries was the *cornett*. This was made of an animal horn, and was also called a *zink*; in French it was the *cornet à bouquin*, meaning, roughly, horn with mouthpiece.

Instruments made of horn with holes to be stopped with the fingers go back to very ancient times and may still be found in certain districts, as for example the Norwegian *bukkehorn*.

When it took its place among the European musical instruments favoured by the upper classes, the cornett was no longer made of horn, but of ivory or wood. We can see an example depicted in a miniature belonging to a manuscript of the early eleventh century, now at Cambridge University. From the twelfth century on, the exterior of the pipe was cut in an octagonal shape, though at the same time, and later, we can find other examples with a straight or more or less curved pipe whose exterior has remained rounded. As the cornetts were yet another family, it was obviously the smallest of them, and consequently the highest-pitched, which had a straight tube, whilst the others took on a curved form, and when the instrument was very large it even had a double curve so that the player's fingers could reach to the farthest holes. A tapestry of Notre-Dame de Nantilly, dating from the fifteenth century, already shows two of these cornetts bent in the form called *cornetto torto* to distinguish it from the single-curved *cornetto curvo*.

The cornett's timbre was much appreciated. By reason of its sweetness, it blended well with the human voice. We know that early in the sixteenth century Augustine of Verona, a cornett player in the service of Charles V and later of the King of France, was much sought after, not only for his participation in chamber music, but also in the chapel, where he played "with the singers". In 1532, François I had among his musicians several cornett players, both from France and from abroad, and one of these was a certain Marc, also a native of Verona. Better still, in view of the quality of their timbre, one could find three descant cornetts not simply doubling the higher voices, but actually replacing them in concert performances. At the end of the century, there were many concerts given just by five of these instruments, and at the beginning of the next century they were immediately taken up by the opera orchestra, for they were given an important role in the first opera to use an orchestra, Monteverdi's *Orfeo* (1607). Moreover, the fact that Count Eitel-Friedrich IV of Hechingen sent his "*Zinkhenblaser*" Johannes de Fossa to Königsegg to perfect his technique shows how much interest was taken in the quality of performances on this instrument.

For their part, the trumpets, which had been bent back on themselves at the end of the Middle Ages so as to be less awkward to handle, could thereby also increase the length of their tube and produce harmonics which had previously been out of their range. In a general way, the trumpet of the sixteenth century was very much like that of modern times. Thanks to its narrower bell and deeper mouthpiece, it now had a softer sound than that of the busine and therefore could participate in chamber music as well as, at the beginning of the seventeenth century, in opera — the orchestra of Monteverdi's *Orfeo* included trumpets of five sizes. It seems that it was in *Orfeo* that the mute was used for the first time; this was a sort of small cardboard or wooden cone with a hole in its base which was placed in the instrument's bell in order to muffle its sonority.

In *Orfeo*, the members of the trumpet family are designated as follows: *Clarino*, *Quinto*, *Alto*, *Vulgaro* and *Basso*. In fact, a professional hierarchy was established between the musicians who played them, for greater skill and a more developed technique were required to play the higher instruments, to which the melodic line was given — a line often scattered with ornaments and difficult passage-work. For this reason, the Germans made a distinction between the *Feldtrumpeter* and the *Kammertrumpeter*. The former could only play trumpets of the middle or lower registers. If they contravened this regulation, they could be subject to severe forfeits, and might even be tortured. On the other hand, the *clarini*, or high trumpets, were reserved for the *Kammertrumpeter*, who formed a noble guild of veritable virtuosos; this is why present-day trumpeters, trained to play in all the registers, experience such difficulties when faced with high-pitched music of these ancient times, for the classical and romantic eras tended to neglect such sounds, and only with the advent of jazz did anything similar again come into being. Although they were cut off from the privileged circles of the *Kammertrumpeter*, the *Feldtrumpeter* swelled the ranks of the corporations of royal or municipal performers as had the players of the busine before them. The custom of making public announcements of official acts with the help of trumpet calls persisted in certain towns, and particularly in France, up till the eighteenth century. Today, it is still possible to encounter in certain villages such an echo of the distant past as a town crier warning people of his presence with the sound of a horn or a bell.

The name *sackbut*, mentioned by the theoretician Tinctoris in 1494, was used in the fifteenth and sixteenth centuries to denote the bass trumpet, which the Italians called *trombone*, a name which later became more usual and has continued to be used to this day.

The form of the sackbut (sometimes known as *tuba ductilis*) was of two straight tubes, parallel and joined to each other by a third tube which was bent double and could slide along the first two. The use of this sliding tube, which when joined to the other tubes made up a single tube of variable length, made it possible to produce seven fundamental sounds in a chromatic series, corresponding to the seven positions in which the slide could be held, and also the harmonics of these notes; it also made possible the playing of a glissando. In Germany, the trombone was called *Posaune*, a word derived from the mediaeval busine or buisine.

In 1503, sackbuts were played during a celebration of Mass at Innsbruck, whilst in 1520 those of François I were heard with the singers during an open-air mass at the *Camp du Drap d'Or*. In 1607, the orchestra of Monteverdi's *Orfeo* included five trombones of different registers.

Soon, the town of Nuremberg became the main centre for

manufacturers of brass instruments. However, there were also famous instrument-makers in Flanders, of whom one might mention from the second half of the fifteenth century, Pieter Bogaerts of Antwerp and Henry van der Moer of Malines; but later, the art of making brass instruments died out in the Low Countries, and after the beginning of the sixteenth century, Malines was ordering its trumpets from Nuremberg.

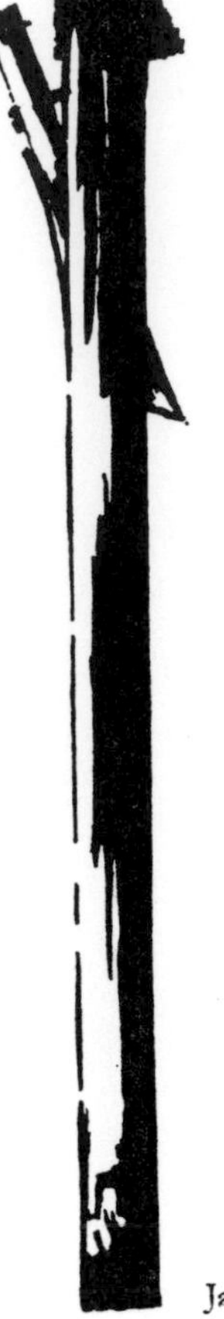
Jack.

Percussion Instruments

Like the trumpeters, the timpani players formed guilds among themselves. The timpani were large nakers (from the Persian *naqqâra*) and, like them, had been introduced into western and central Europe apparently during the years of the Crusades. Their origins continued to be well known, for in 1588 Thoinot Arbeau still called them "the drum of the Persians".

The *timpanum*, or kettledrum, was a large-sized instrument in the form of a hemispherical metal bowl covered with a stretched skin, which when struck gave a sound of definite pitch; according to whether the skin was more firmly or more loosely stretched, the sound produced would be higher or lower. Though today the kettledrum has keys around its circumference whose function it is to vary the tension of the skin, this does not seem to have been the case with the earliest models. Since the instrument was quite heavy, it was not carried in the player's hands, but was generally mounted in counterbalanced pairs, one on each side of a horse upon which the player rode.

Its use did not spread at all rapidly, for in 1457 Père Benoit, describing the procession of King Ladislas of Hungary in Paris, tells us: "*on n'avoit ni mi oncques veu des tambourins comme de gros chaudrons qu'ils faisaient porter sur des chevaux*". (No one there, including myself, had ever seen such drums, like great cauldrons, which their horses carried.) Yet already, Philip III (the Bold — 1245-1285) had sent his kettledrum players to Germany, "*aux escoles de leur métier*", to perfect their technique. The instruments were still objects of curiosity even in 1559, for when she married Philip II of Spain, Elisabeth of France was received at the frontiers of her new kingdom with the sound of the "*...tabartz, qui sont tabourins à cheval, à la moresque*". Kettledrums, played on horseback, became one of the symbols of power, and in northern Europe in the seventeenth century, no one under the rank of baron was allowed to possess them.

The xylophone, or the old mediaeval échelette, was already renowned for its lugubrious dry and sharp sounds. It is often to be found depicted in paintings of dances of death, as, for instance, in certain pictures by Hans Holbein. Thus when Saint-Saëns came to use the instrument in his *Danse Macabre*, the idea was far from new.

We have seen that hand-operated chime-bells were used in the Middle Ages, and that the use of a cylinder to replace manual operation originated shortly after the installation of such bells in church towers and belfries. The manually operated chime-bells survived into the fifteenth century, for they may be found in pictures by Memling. They could, above all, be found in French and Belgian Flanders.

A cylinder was probably used as soon as *voorslagen* began to be played. A little later, improving on the few notes that went to make a *voorslag*, real melodies began to be played, and these were called *voorspelen* (preludes). From 1501 on, we hear of these being played at Audenarde, and, after 1520, at Ath. Since the drum mechanism was no longer sufficient to play these more extended melodies, the chime-bells were given a keyboard, thus becoming the instrument known as the *carillon*, and now the player could perform a piece which had not been determined by the form of the cylinder. The keyboard was first installed at Audenarde in 1510, but the drum mechanism continued to be used in that town, playing as *voorslagen* parts of the *Veni Sancte Spiritus* and the *Salve Regina*.

The Flemish clock towers and belfries included more and more bells after this time. We know that the belfry of Dendermonde, which had six bells in 1526, contained twenty-one in 1549, and that the steeple had been given sound-holes, so that the sound would carry further. The important towns were not satisfied with just one carillon, and in Brabant — for the art of bell ringing had spread from Flanders into neighbouring regions — Brussels was known in 1541 as the "Town with seven Carillons". In the same year we hear of a carillon at Antwerp, and in 1583 of another at Malines, the town in which a pedal-board was first used in connection with the instrument in around 1600.

Due to this diffusion, Swertius was able to declare in 1603 that "in our country, one can hear almost every day a great concert of bells, in which there is such art and harmony that one would think one was hearing an organ".

Keyboard Instruments

In the previous chapter, we have already described in general terms the mechanism of the harpsichord. To this we should add that each jack was provided with a small piece of felt over its plectrum, to damp the sound when the jack returned to its normal position. This return was facilitated by a transverse bar of wood covered in felt, against which the jack struck after having plucked the string, thus hastening its fall back into position. So that on returning the plectrum should not again pluck the string, it was mounted on a wooden tongue, a moving part of the jack which was placed at a slant and tilted when the plectrum touched the string; thus, because of this tilting movement, the plectrum on its return journey barely touched the string and avoided setting it in vibration. A small metal blade, or a supple hog's bristle — used above all from the seventeenth century on — acted as a spring which brought the tongue, and consequently the plectrum, back into position after its return.

Clearly, this was an ingenious mechanism; it was also a satisfactory one, for it remained in use without modification up to the end of the eighteenth century, at which time the harpsichord gave way to the piano.

At first, each string corresponded to a key, but before long double strings tuned in unison were used in order to strengthen the sonority, and consequently jacks had to be used which could pluck both strings at the same time.

Having taken this first step towards increasing the number of strings, the harpsichord did not stop there, but went on to have several strings for each key, but these differed as to the pitch and the timbre of the notes they produced. In this way, for example, two jacks, activated by one and the same key, might pluck a 4-foot string and an 8-foot string simultaneously, so that a note would be heard doubled at the lower octave. Later, a third jack would be added to the same key, and would activate a third string, longer still since it would be a 16-foot string and would sound a double octave below the original note; or instead of being longer, the third string might be plucked in a different way so as to produce a different timbre rather than a different pitch.

As can be seen, the harpsichord was an instrument of great potential, as long as that potential was harnessed so that the instrument's capabilities could be fully exploited. For it would not serve much purpose when the instrument had two, three or four strings to each key if they always had to be used all at once; the effect produced would always be the same. On the other hand, if it were possible to sound each string on its own in turn, and better still to combine them in twos or in threes, one would make of the harpsichord an instrument of many sonorities in the same way as was the organ.

It was this problem which the instrument-makers faced at the beginning of the sixteenth century; they resolved it in the following way. They made as many holes as there were keys in a wooden slide, and planted the jacks in these holes so that they rested on the far end of their corresponding keys. If, for example, this slide held the jacks which played on the 4-foot strings, it only had to be pulled slightly to one side for the jacks to be deflected from their original course. Thus, the plectra would pass by the 4-foot strings without touching them, and the instrument would remain silent. As similar slides existed for the 8-foot, the 16-foot strings etc., they could be brought into play or not as the player wished. From then on all the combinations of stops (a term used for strings of similar pitch and also for those of similar timbre) became possible, and these combinations became more and more numerous as the number of stops increased.

Thus, in the same way as the organ, with its stops using rows of pipes of different registers or timbres, the harpsichord continued to enrich its palette over the years. If both instruments could strengthen their sonority by coupling several stops, they nevertheless lacked the ability to produce crescendi and decrescendi, which were only within the reach of those keyboard instruments with struck strings like the clavichord and, later, the piano, on which they could be achieved by varying the touch on keys which operated a tangent (also called a jack) or a hammer.

Certainly, much later, the harpsichord and the organ were to use a further device in the form of shutters made of planks which could be opened to a greater or lesser degree and would thus vary the volume of the sound emitted; but this invention was

III. — 18.

Large bass slide trombone by the maker Hans Hainlein, who sometimes called himself Hans Hainee, and who lived in Nuremberg from 1596 to 1671. He was one of this town's first great makers of brass instruments. The edge of the bell is decorated with engravings and angel's heads in relief. In the centre an inscription reads: "*Macht Hanns Hainee in Nurnberg* 1668". The narrower bore and more rounded mouthpiece give this instrument a softer timbre than that of present-day trombones. Length: *c.* 11½ ft.

M.I., Brussels.
No. 1265.

III. — 19.

Harpsichord, dated 1619, by Giovanni Battista Boni of Cortona; no other instrument by this maker is known. The present one is provided with a keyboard spanning four octaves the first of which is short. A number of "broken" black keys make it possible to sound different chromatic semitones (e.g. *Eb* and *D*). Length: *c.* 3½ ft.

M.I., Brussels.
No. 1603.

III. — 20.

Spinet of Venetian style by the maker Antonius Patavinus of Padua and dated 1550. The diatonic keys are of boxwood; the chromatic keys, of ebony, are embellished with ivory open-work ornaments. The escutcheon on the face is also of ivory and is that of the Venetian Bembo family. The Gothic rose-hole is of vellum. The case containing the instrument dates from about a century later. The keyboard encompasses four octaves and a fourth; the first octave is short.
Length: *c.* 60½ ins.

M.I., Brussels
No. 272

III. — 21.

Virginal by the Antwerp make Grauwels, built in about 1580. Th interior of the lid has a tint drawing attributed to Breughel the Elder. The range of the keyboard is thre octaves and a sixth, and the lowe octave is short. The paper use for the decoration of the face i similar to that of the instrument by Ruckers. Length: *c.* 5 ft.

M.I., Brussel
No. 292

III. — 18. **German bass trombone** (1668)

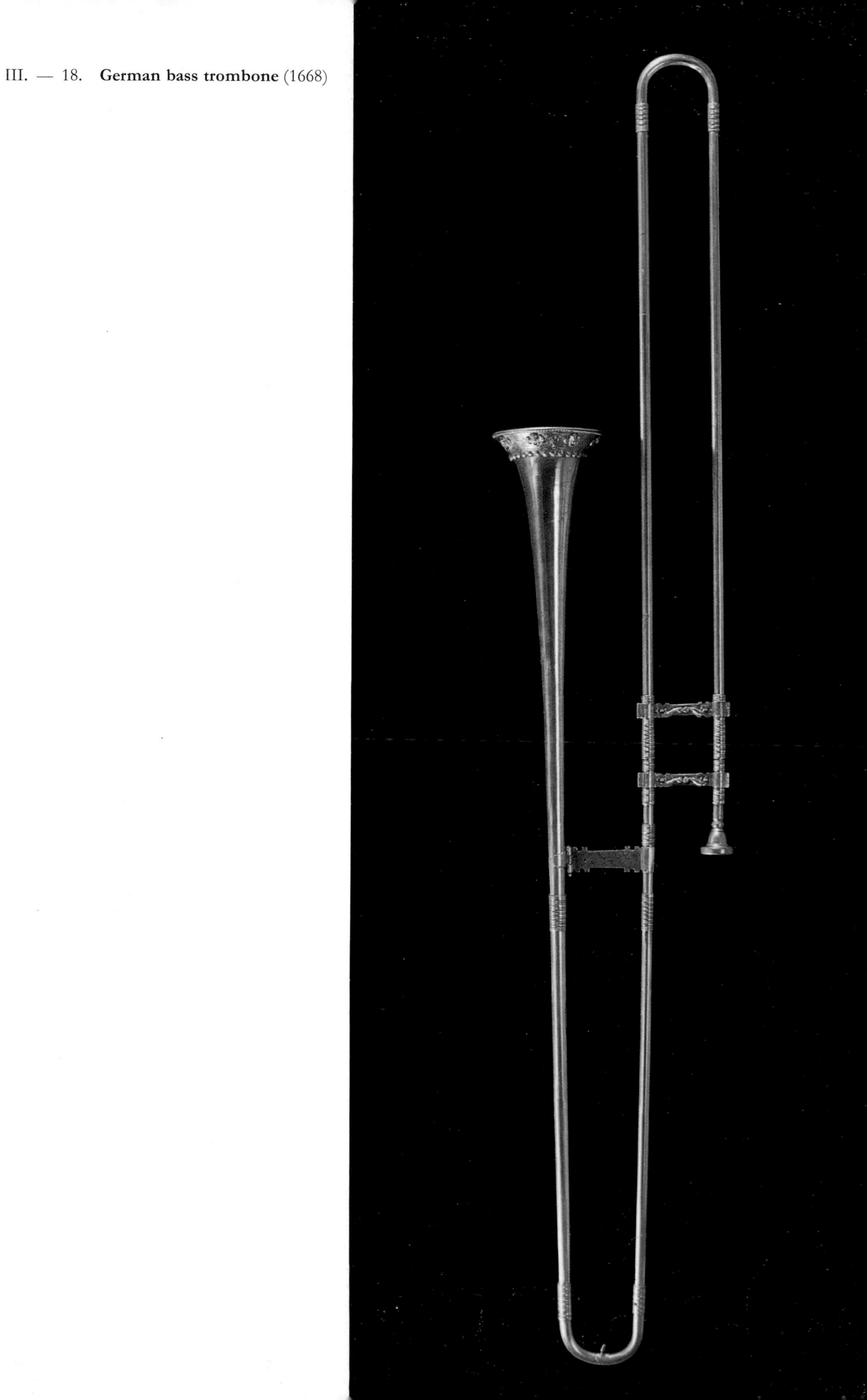

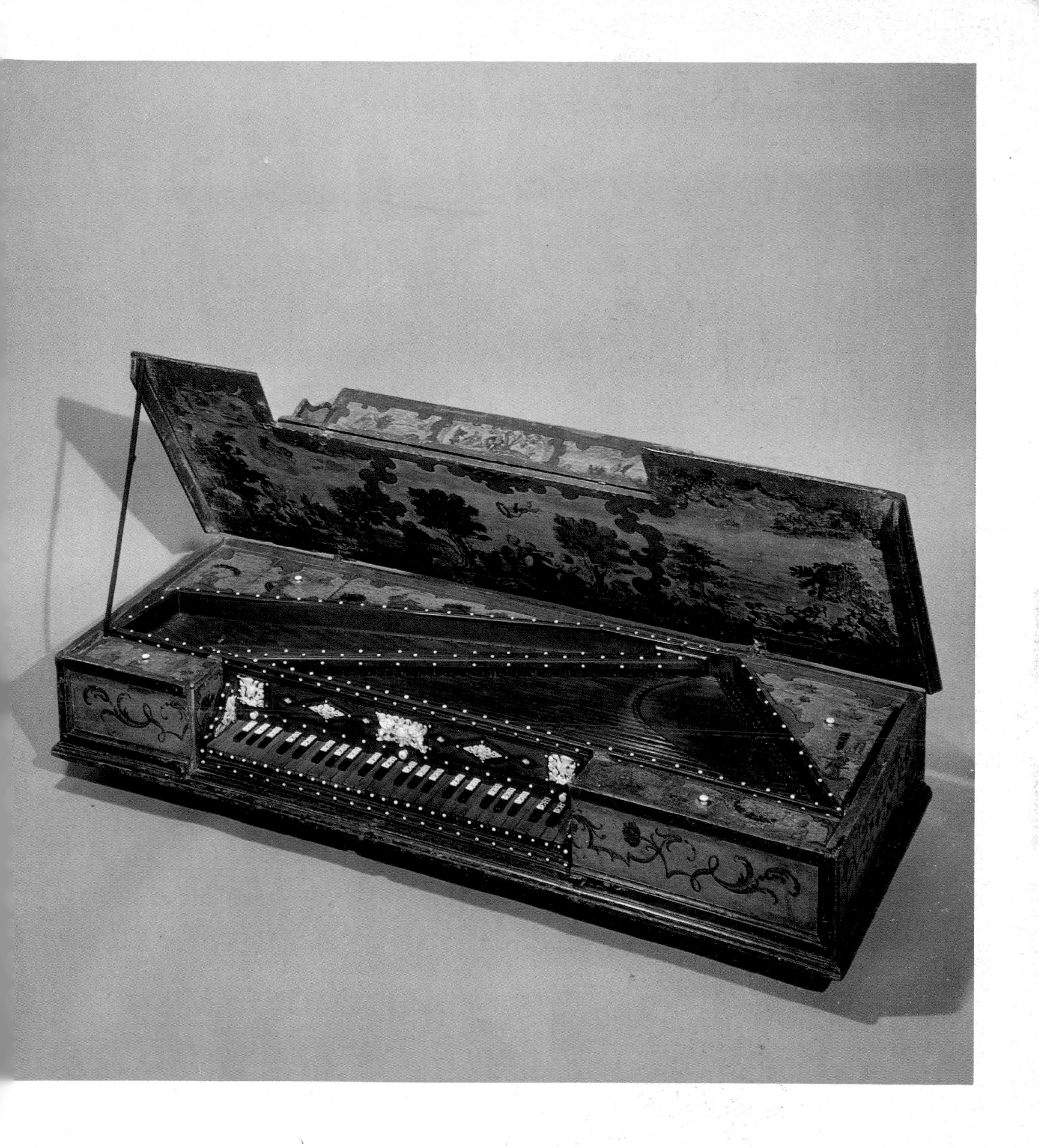

◄ III. — 19. **Italian harpsichord** (1619)

III. — 20. **Italian spinet** (1550)

III. — 21. **Flemish virginal** (*c.* 1580)

III. — 22. **English virginal** (1641)

III. — 23. **German fretted clavichord** (17th century)

III. — 24. **German regal organ from Switzerland** (16th century) ▶

III. — 25. **German Bible regal** (16th century)

III. — 22.

This is the oldest English virginal at present known. It was built by Gabriel Townsend who was born in about 1604 and whose death probably occurred in 1662. This maker was apprenticed to Thomas White I. He was admitted as a master of the guild in 1657-58. This instrument bears the inscription: "Gabriel Townsend *fecit,* 1641" and is the only instrument of his that we have. The picture painted on the inside of the lid is a fairly naïve representation of Orpheus enchanting animals with the sound of his lyre. The Victoria and Albert Museum in London has a virginal by Thomas White II on which the painting, executed at the same place, bears a strong resemblance to that of Townsend's virginal; from this it seems reasonably certain that these two pictures were the work of a single artist. The numerous initials E.R. (Elizabeth Regina) surrounding an escutcheon bearing the arms of England can hardly be related to Queen Elizabeth, who had died some time previously, and recall rather Elizabeth Stuart (1596-1662), daughter of James I and the Queen of Bohemia. The range of the keyboard is four octaves plus a third. Length: *c.* 69½ ins.

M.I., Brussels.
No. 1591.

III. — 23.

German fretted clavichord having four full octaves: the low *C♯* is missing. This instrument, by an unknown maker, has 23 double strings of which nos. 12-16 and nos. 19-22 each serve three notes. The 17th pair of strings serves four notes. The other pairs only serve one note each. The paper used for the decoration is similar to that used by Flemish makers in the 17th century. Length: *c.* 44 ins.

M.I., Brussels.
No. 1621.

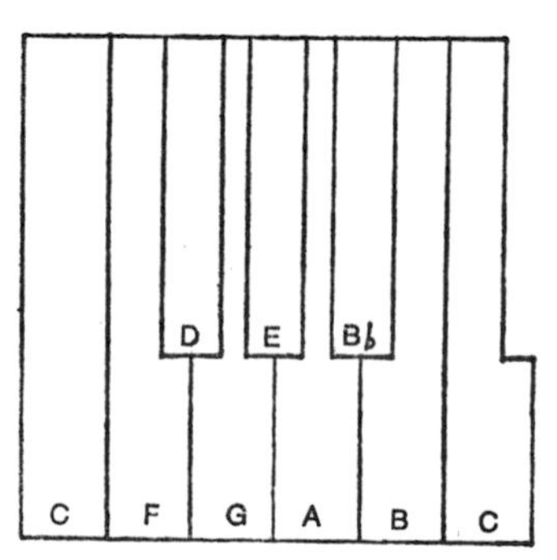

late in arriving and, at least in the case of the harpsichord, proved to have little success.

In the sixteenth century, the harpsichord, like the organ, did not have a very extensive keyboard. For this reason its lower octave had been reduced, the diatonic notes being retained so that the instrument could reach as low a note as possible. Only by changing the normal key-to-string correspondence was this possible, so either the *D* and the *E* or the *C* and the *D* would be sounded when the keys normally corresponding to the *F* and the *G* were depressed. In the "short" octave, as this type of arrangement was called, the only chromatic note that remained was the *B♭*, as may be seen from the example in the margin.

Like the harpsichord, the spinet and the virginal were keyboard instruments with plucked strings. They differed from the harpsichord in the shape of their sound-board and in the direction of their strings. Moreover, they never had more than one set of jacks, so that it was never necessary to give them a movable slide, for, there only being one stop, it never had to be rendered silent.

The harpsichord was characterised by a wing-shaped sound-board, somewhat like a horizontally placed harp, and its strings ran at right-angles to the length of the keyboard, as in our grand piano. The spinet also had a wing-shaped sound-board, but a much smaller one placed sideways on facing the performer, instead of reaching away from him as in the harpsichord. Consequently, the strings, again on a level with the keyboard, were placed across the board parallel to the length of the keyboard.

As for the virginal, it differed from the spinet in that it was contained in a rectangular case, and its strings were placed in a slanting position in relation to the keyboard, which itself occupied a different position. The difference in position of the keyboard on the two instruments may be thought of in conjunction with the fact that in neither case was the keyboard long enough to take up the whole breadth of the instrument; in the spinet it was nearly always centrally placed, whereas in the virginal it was sometimes in the centre, but more often to the left or to the right of centre. In the latter case, when the keyboard was situated on the right hand side, the name *muselaar* was used in Flemish countries rather than virginal.

In England, the first collection of music specifically for the virginal, the *Parthenia*, published in about 1612, depicts the instrument on its title-page. However, the name virginal seems in the sixteenth century to have been used for any keyboard instrument with plucked strings, as is shown in particular by the inventory of Henry VIII's musical collection (1547), which reads: "newe longe virginalles made harpe fashion", a description which befits the harpsichord. The same was probably true on the Continent where the virginal was sometimes known as the Flemish spinet.

An upright version of the harpsichord, the *clavicytherium*, mentioned and described in 1511 by Virdung, was mainly used in sixteenth-century Germany. It fell into disuse before being taken up again in a larger size and under different names by instrument-makers of the eighteenth century.

The only important keyboard instrument with struck strings

was the clavichord, the oldest known example of which, made by Domenico of Pesaro and dating from 1543, is now in the Instrumental Museum of Leipzig. At this time, and until the beginning of the eighteenth century, the clavichord had more keys than strings, so that one string might be struck by different keys at different places; according to where the string was struck it would produce a differently pitched sound. The adjective which describes this type of instrument is "fretted". This mechanism had one severe drawback: it was not possible to play at the same time two sounds belonging to the same string. It was not until the early years of the eighteenth century that it was decided to take the step of providing the instrument with as many strings as it had keys.

One of the most striking characteristics of the clavichord was its ability to produce a vibrato tone. As the tangent was a strip of metal fixed to the end of the key whose role it was to strike the string, this strip (in contrast to the action of a piano's hammer) did not fall back of its own accord after striking the string, but remained in contact with it for as long as the player's finger did not leave the key and allow it to return to its normal position. Thus it was possible, simply by applying a gentle and rapidy repeated pressure to the key immediately after depressing it, to apply the same sort of pressure by means of the tangent to the string, producing in this way a kind of quivering sound, which the Germans called *Bebung*; this sounded very much like a vibrato, but, unlike the vibrato that can be produced on bowed string instruments, it was only of short duration.

In the harpsichord as well as in the spinet and the virginal, the overall shape of the instrument, the manner of constructing the bridge, the placing of the tuning-pins, the material used for the keys and their shape tell us whether an instrument is of Italian, Flemish or English origin. French makers generally followed the lead of the Flemings.

During the Renaissance period, the organ, whose development had been relatively slow in the Middle Ages, was improved by some very important modifications and additions. We have said that the pedal-board was invented by Lodewijk van Valbeke in 1306. Its purpose was to operate, by means of a system of canes, the lower notes of the manual keyboard; it thus allowed the player's hands to be free to play in the middle and upper registers, and could at the same time provide a bass for the upper harmonies. Naturally, these lower notes could still, as before, be played manually.

In the second half of the century, a second manual keyboard appeared, and such a one is to be found at Rouen, dating from as early as 1386. Its pipes were enclosed behind a wooden screen in the organ-loft itself, behind the organist's back.

Later, the mixture stops, much esteemed during the Middle Ages, began to lose importance in comparison with individual stops which went to make them up, or were added to them as solo stops; these included the oboe, the flute, the crumhorn and the trumpet stops. In fact the role previously reserved for these solo stops had been to contrast with the full organ or with a mixture stop, but as polyphonic music had gradually evolved towards the equality of voices which found its ultimate expression in *a cappella* music, the organ had imitated this development by seeking

III. — 24.

German regal organ from the Abbey of Freuenfeld in Switzerland. The instrument dates from the end of the 16th century. This organ, of walnut, is richly sculptured. The reeds and pipes are enclosed in a box. A detachable lid enables the volume of sound to be varied. The two bellows are operated alternately by an assistant.
Length: *c.* 49⅜ ins.

M.I., Brussels.
No. 454.

III. — 25.

Regal organ of the "Bible regal" type. This rare instrument does not bear the name of a maker. It dates from the end of the 16th century. At first sight, it has the appearance of a large "Bible". The interior of this "Bible" is hollow and holds a keyboard (split into two halves) to which are fitted small reed pipes like those of the regal organ; hence the name bible regal organ given to this type of instrument. Once the "Bible" is opened, the keyboard may be taken out and fitted, along its whole length, to the lower sides of the "bible", whose two covers serve as bellows. The manner of tuning the notes of the lower octave remains a controversial point. The higher octave reproduces the preceding one; at the same time its pipes are not as long and thus produce a brighter timbre.
Size (when shut): *c.* 17 ins. × 13 ins. × 6⅞ ins.

M.I., Brussels.
No. 2703.

to individualise its different "voices" and could thenceforth scarcely be content with the old mixture stops and their attendant thirds, fifths and octaves. Hence the importance already apparently accorded to the independent stops at the end of the fifteenth century, when they were housed in the main chest of the organ.

To meet these increasing demands, the organ — as may easily be understood — became a more and more impressive instrument as a result of the continually increasing number of its pipes. The organ of the château at Blois, dating from 1451, already had 1,400 pipes, the largest of which were said to be wide enough for a man to pass through. The full organ at Amiens had more than 2,000 pipes in 1429.

Towards the end of the fifteenth century, German and Flemish organ-makers had introduced stopped pipes, pipes of inverted conical bore and reed pipes. The tremolo, obtained by juxtaposing two ranks of pipes slightly out of tune with each other, is met with for the first time at Hagenau in 1491.

French organs were characterised by their use of higher, more penetrating stops, such as the *cymbale*. Whereas elsewhere the pedal-board contained a variable number of pedals which was never less than ten, in Spain it had no more than seven or eight.

England and Italy lagged behind somewhat, for they continued to use an organ whose chief constituent was the mixture stops; at most they would have one independent and contrasting stop, and this would generally be a flute stop.

After 1450, compositions began to appear which were primarily intended to be played on the organ. One may mention here works by Conrad Paumann, Heinrich Isaac, Arnold Schlick and Paul Hofhaimer.

Though apparently in existence previously, a small organ of a special type, comprising a single rank of beating reed-pipes, began to be more frequently used after the beginning of the sixteenth century. This instrument, the *regal*, appeared for the first time on an engraving of Conrad Weidlitz dated 1519, in which the composer Paul Hofhaimer is portrayed at the keyboard. In the first place, the reeds were not provided with tubes to amplify the sound, but this development ensued almost immediately. With its beating reed, the regal may be related to our clarinet. The air was blown through a pair of bellows which an assistant operated alternately in a position facing the performer.

The regal organ was used wherever a full church organ could not be afforded, and also as a substitute for the harpsichord. Because of its particular timbre, the result of its beating reeds, Monteverdi chose this instrument to accompany the recitative of Charon in *Orfeo* at the point when Orpheus is about to descend into the infernal regions.

In about 1550, a native of Nuremberg, Georg Voll, invented a regal organ of a small size whose keyboard and rank of reed-pipes could be taken apart and fitted into a large hollowed-out imitation "Bible"; this was called a *Bible regal*. When anyone wished to play this instrument, they simply had to open the "Bible" and set up the keyboard and the rank of reeds. The hard boards which had looked like book-backs were metamorphosed into bellows, from each of which an air-duct led to the main part of the instrument.

The *mechanical organ*, numerous varieties of which are known to us today, seems to have been in existence as far back as the second half of the fifteenth century if we are to judge from the account-books of Philip the Good, Duke of Burgundy, since there mention is made of a pension paid from 1458 till 1467 to Jan van Steenken "*Meester van orgelen spelende by hen selven*" on condition of his showing to the Duke every instrument he made with a view to a possible purchase.

A few final remarks should be made before closing this chapter.

Following the lead of fiddlers, trumpeters and drummers, instrument-makers too had formed corporations in order to better the protection of their interests. The viol-makers of Antwerp in this way formed the guild *De Violieren* in 1480; its members included such renowned craftsmen as Borlon, Artus (d. 1579) and Willems. Under the patronage of Saint-Eloi, a guild of bell-founders including the Waghevens and Van der Gheyn families was formed in Malines. In France, in 1599, King Henri IV founded the *gilde des luthiers*.

Though the existence of these guilds promoted excellent craftsmanship in the making of instruments, since only qualified craftsmen were entitled to join them, they also fostered a certain amount of conservatism and consequently sometimes hindered new developments which might otherwise have borne fruit.

In England the word consort was used to describe a group of instruments of the same family and also works written for such a group, like the consort of viols. These instruments of differing sizes, were kept together in chests, or cupboards. At the beginning of the fifteenth century, three instruments were enough to make up a consort, since composers of the time did not write for more than three "voices". Later the number increased, so that Praetorius could write of a *Stimmwerk* of eight recorders.

The broken consort, on the other hand, consisted of an ensemble of instruments of various families, such as the lute, the pandora, the cittern, the viol and the recorder. Thereafter, instead of simply using the word consort to describe a homogeneous group, the term whole consort was used to distinguish it from the broken consort, the noun consort taking on a more general meaning.

IV - From Monteverdi to J. S. Bach

IV. — 1. **"A Young Student and His Sister"**

Historical Background

The period covering the years between the end of the sixteenth century and 1750 has been given various names by musical historians according to the point of view they have adopted. For some, the period might be called the Baroque era, for others the era of the *basso continuo*, and for yet others the era of the concerted style.

Those who favour the term Baroque era are mostly musicologists trained in German seminaries, and they justify their use of this term by the fact that the evolution of music ran parallel to that of the other arts, it thus being equally reasonable to speak of Baroque music as it is to speak of Baroque art. This terminology is fairly recent, and has not been unanimously condoned by musical historians of the Latin countries, who still generally prefer to refer to the period between the time of Monteverdi and that of Bach by a designation taken from the history of music itself.

As the present volume is an organological history of musical instruments, and therefore has no need to take aesthetic considerations into account, we need not go into the question of which terminological variant we prefer, for to justify such a choice would necessitate explanations requiring more space than is here at our disposal.

From the ninth century onward, music had developed continually towards a more and more complicated polyphony whose most complex manifestations appeared during the last years of the fifteenth century. In the sixteenth century, influenced by Renaissance tendencies, this polyphony became more clearly constructed, and its component voices took on equal importance. Composers began to "think in chords", and to try to establish once more an ideal balance between words and music. Finally, the use of chromaticism restored to music some of the passionate expression it had lost since the days of the troubadours and the trouvères.

However, although by means of the artifices that later came to be called madrigalisms this music had become rather more vibrant and warm, it had not yet provided an expression of individual passions. In order to make music that was both simple and personal, melody had to become the supreme element, freeing itself from its former bondage to the other voices; in other words, it was necessary to return to monody such as it had been known to the ancient Greeks. With the help of monody, the singer could identify himself completely with the individual he was supposed to represent; he could imitate natural diction, retard or accelerate his delivery, increase or diminish the tone of his voice without fear that the other voices would annul the effect of such means of expression; in short, his song could give vent to a thousand nuances of passion, exteriorising them without hindrance of any sort. What had, in the madrigal, been little more than an interplay of sound gently tinged with expressiveness thus became the potential expression itself of all human feelings. From that time on, the listener would not simply be charmed; he would feel the direct impact of expressed emotions.

Yet after so many centuries of polyphony there could be

no question of simply returning to a self-sufficient unaccompanied monody. This is why composers called on an instrumental bass having a purely supporting role as an accompaniment. Originally this bass was given to a lute with one or more *chitarroni,* or to a harpsichord and bass viol, whose job was to accompany the melody throughout with chords; for this reason it was given the name *basso continuo.* At a later date, when the orchestra was introduced, this bass was used in the same way, and indeed continued to be thus used until about 1750.

Accompanied monody immediately met with great success, and soon gave birth to vocal and instrumental forms which have survived to this day: opera, oratorio, cantata, sonata and concerto. Since, in such works, prominence was given to the soloist or to a small concerted group of instruments, their style came to be known as the concerted *(concertante)* style.

Before long, the same demands that had been made of voices began to be made of instruments too. Instruments of expressive potential were favoured, and for this reason the more neutral-sounding instruments were abandoned. Soon, accordingly, a number of reed instruments, such as the shawm, the crumhorn, the schryari, the bagpipe and the racket were dropped from common usage. By reason of their timbre and expressive potential stringed instruments were preferred to wind instruments.

Stringed Instruments

The lute continued to be extremely popular during the seventeenth century. In fact there were amateurs who devoted an immoderate amount of time and attention to it. The English lutenist Thomas Mace wrote in his *Musick's Monument* (1676): "... a Lute (should be kept) in a Bed, that is constantly used, between the Rug and the Blanket... only to be excepted that no Person be so inconsiderate as to Tumble down upon the Bed whilst the Lute is There, for I have known several Good Lutes spoil'd by such a Trick..." Mace was widely famed as a lutenist in his time, especially for his technique of the "shake" *(vibrato)*, which many players attempted to emulate with little success.

We drew attention in the previous chapter to the important role this instrument played in the sixteenth century. As its function was often to accompany a singer, and it would take the part of the lower voices — arranged in the form of chords — in transcriptions of polyphonic music, while the singer took the upper voice, and as it continued to be used in this way during the first decades of the seventeenth century, it became necessary to enlarge the instrument so as to give it a more consistent bass. By the end of the sixteenth century, lutes with prolonged necks (called *archlutes*) were already being made in Italy. The pegbox was no longer of a curved shape, but had been divided in two parts, one for the pegs of the melody strings, and the other, placed at the end of the neck, which held the pegs of the lower strings which were held away from the neck itself. Consequently, these strings could not be stopped, and each could only produce one note; they were used for the chords which accompanied the melodic line. This large type of lute included a type called the chitarrone, which was often

V. — 2. **German lute-guitar**
(17th century)

IV. — 3. **Italian penorcon**
(17th century)

IV. — 4. **German harp**
(17th century) ▶

◄ IV. — 5. **German bass viol** (1701)

IV. — 6. **German viola d'amore** (1742)

IV. — 7. **Italian viola di bordon** (18th century)

IV. — 8. **Violin by Andrea Guar** (1670) ▶

V. — 9. **Italian cello** (1690)

— 10. **German viola pomposa** (*c.* 1720)

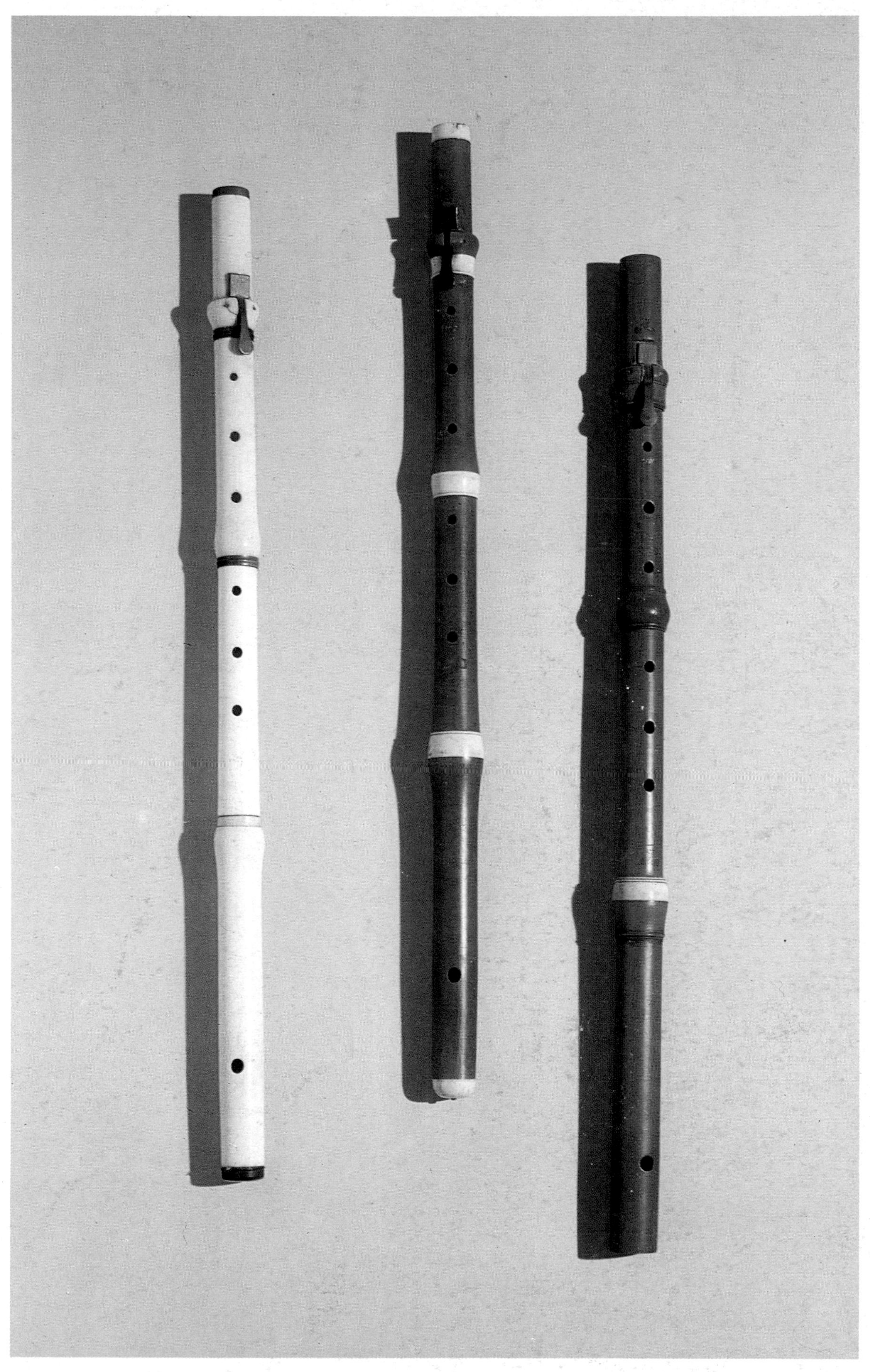

◀ IV. — 11. **French pardessus de viole and quinton**

IV. — 12. **Three transverse flutes** (18th century)

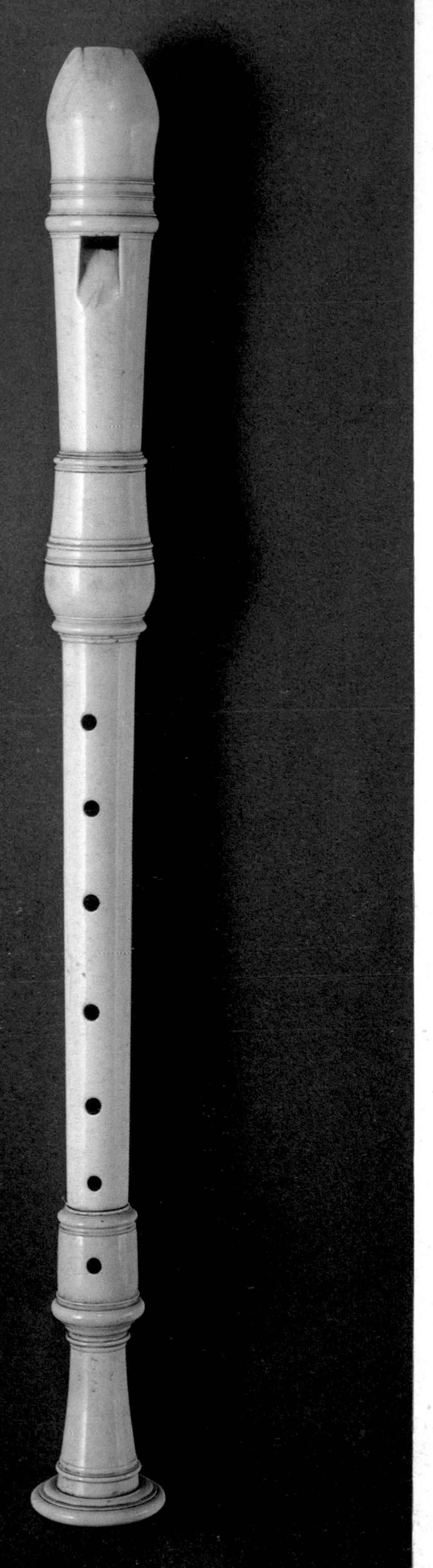

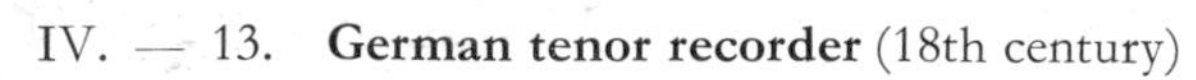

IV. — 13. **German tenor recorder** (18th century)

IV. — 14. **Three oboes** (18th century) ►

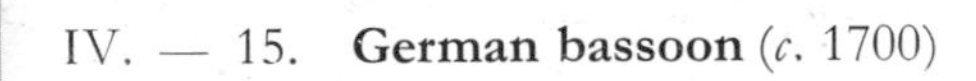

IV. — 15. **German bassoon** (*c.* 1700)

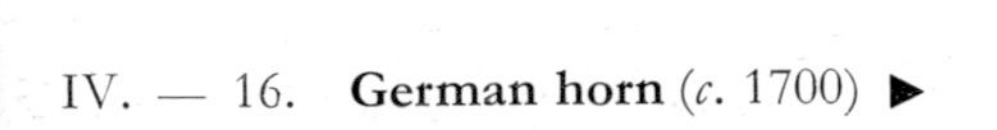

IV. — 16. **German horn** (*c.* 1700) ▶

IV. — 17. **Three German trumpets** (late 17th century

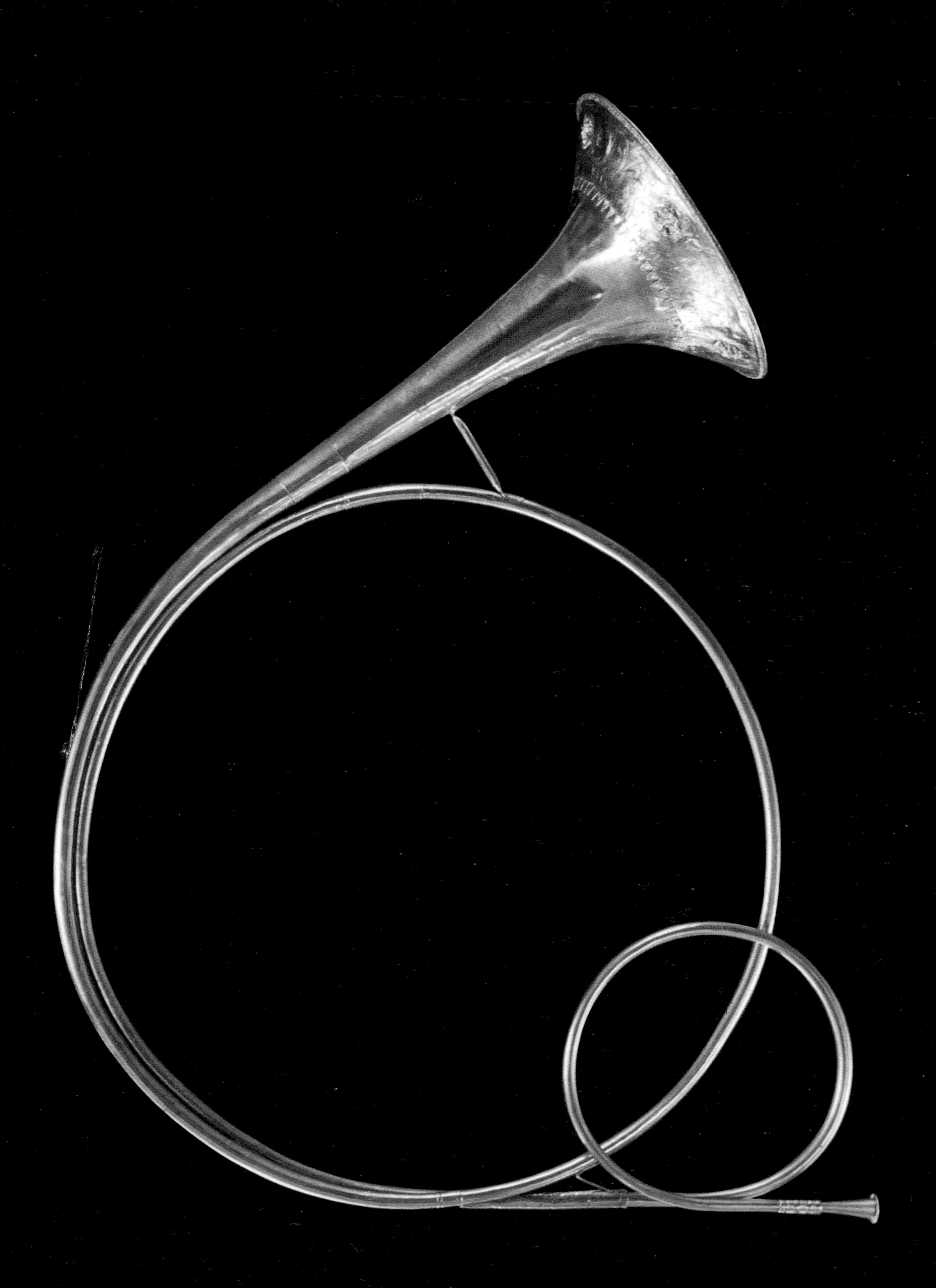

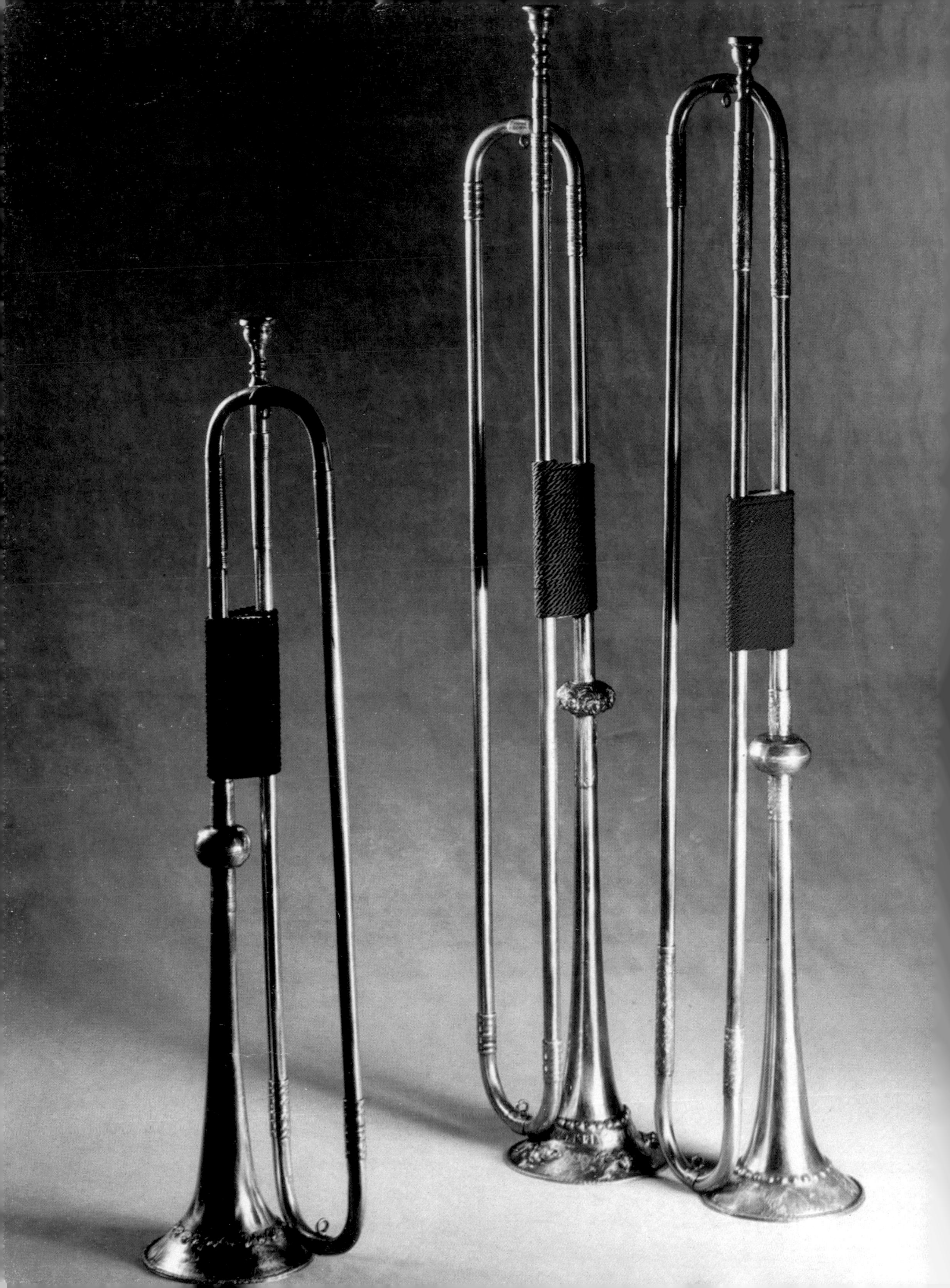

IV. — 6.
Viola d'amore built by Johannes Rauch at Commathau in 1742. Rauch was born at Hohenschwangau in about 1690; the date of his death is not known. The neck and scroll are not original. This instrument has 7 gut strings and 7 metal sympathetic strings. There are in existence several instruments attributed to this maker which are in fact only copies from workshops in Mittenwald. Length: *c.* $2\frac{1}{2}$ ft.
M.I., Brussels.
No. 1391.

IV. — 7.
Italian viola di bordone from the 18th century, by an unknown maker. The instrument has 6 gut strings and 16 metal sympathetic strings. The sound-holes are those of the viola d'amore, but are inverted and doubled. Length: *c.* $51\frac{1}{2}$ ins.
M.I., Brussels.
No. 231.

IV. — 8.
Violin, dated 1670, by Andrea Guarneri; this famous maker was born in 1626 and died in Cremona in 1698. Before 1670, his instruments show the influence of Amati; after this date he became influenced by his co-pupil Stradivari. This instrument is minimally rounded and the scroll is deeply carved. The varnish is of a yellowish colour. Length: *c.* $22\frac{3}{4}$ ins.
M.I., Brussels.
Unnumbered.

IV. — 9.
Violoncello by the maker Paolo Grancine bearing the label *"Milano* 1690". Only a few of this maker's products are preserved; he was probably a pupil of Nicola Amati. He worked in Milan between 1655 and 1692 and in building his instruments took his inspiration from the models of Amati. The sound-box is relatively flat. Length: *c.* 4 ft.
M.I., Brussels.
No. 3513.

IV. — 10.
Viola pomposa, bearing the label of Johann Christian Hoffman (1683-1750), a famous Leipzig maker who worked for the court of Saxony and that of Poland. The instrument was probably built in about the 1720s. The viola pomposa has 5 strings, the fifth of which is tuned in unison with the violin's *E* string.
Length: *c.* $31\frac{1}{4}$ ins.
M.I., Brussels.
No. 1445.

France and Italy the violin soon had as many adherents as the viol. However, France still boasted a number of first-rate viol players in the first half of the eighteenth century, the most notable of whom were Marin Marais and Antoine Forqueroy.

Before they disappeared, and as though to make a final stand against the onslaught of the new instruments, the viols extended their potentialities by introducing new members to their family. We shall briefly look at these additions before passing on.

Firstly, the *viola d'amore,* which was about the same size as the modern viola, and which, besides its six or seven ordinary strings, had seven sympathetic strings of copper; these were placed under the normal strings, and so could not be played with the bow, and would only sound in sympathetic vibration with the others.

Again, there was the *viola bastarda,* different from the bass viol in that its body was more elongated and its tuning-pegs were in a higher position. It was the English who thought of giving this viola bastarda (of Italian origin) sympathetic strings tuned in unison with the others; the resultant sound was sweet and full and had a sort of melancholy charm.

The viol had been introduced into England in about 1520, and had aroused the interest of Henry VIII to such an extent that he invited Flemish and Venetian viol-players to his court; it was in England too that a new instrument, the *lyra viol,* appeared in about 1600. This instrument also had sympathetic strings and was sometimes fairly tortuous in shape. It was used to perform divisions on a ground, or variations on a ground, or ostinato, bass. It passed from common usage in about 1680.

On the Continent, and particularly in Italy, the lira da gamba, an instrument which could have up to sixteen strings, two of them being drones, was used. Its function was mainly to provide chordal support for a sung melody.

The *viola di bordone,* also called the *baryton,* had a series of six to seven gut strings and a very large number of sympathetic strings which could be anything between seven and fourty-four, all of which were mounted on a sound-box no larger than that of the small bass viol. This sound-box too had rather tortuous contours. The gut strings were stretched over a narrow neck, itself placed on a wider neck behind which the metallic strings passed. In this way these could either be allowed to vibrate in sympathy, or could be plucked by hand behind the neck, with the thumb of the left hand. The origin of this instrument is unknown; it was also called the *viola di paredon,* and was said to have been constructed in prison by a prisoner awaiting execution, who received a pardon as a result of his invention. It was scarcely used outside Germany and was fairly short-lived as a result of the difficulties presented by the tuning of so many strings. The baryton certainly existed prior to the eighteenth century, for we have a work that was written for this instrument and dedicated to Prince Christian of Wurtemburg, who died in 1704. It was played in aristocratic circles up till the time of Haydn (1732-1809), for the latter wrote several compositions for the instrument to be played by his employer, Prince Nicolas Esterhazy, who was extremely fond of playing the instrument.

Finally, the bass viol itself was given a seventh string at the end of the seventeenth century; the first Frenchman to make use of this innovation was Marin Marais. Bach wrote his viola da gamba sonatas and Rameau his *Pièces en concert* for this seven-stringed bass viol. But with few exceptions it was for the six-stringed viol that the music of this period was written.

The invention of the violin is still attributed to Gasparo da Salo (born near Salo in 1540, died in Brescia, where he worked, in 1609), but there is no solid foundation for such an assertion; at the most, one can say that this maker was one of the first to make the new instrument, and the small number of his instruments that we have today are of a fairly primitive type. It was his pupil Paolo Maggini (1580-1630), the most renowned maker of the school of Brescia, who was the first to give the violin an elegant appearance similar to that which we know today. In fact, there was, at the time, no design which might serve the makers as a model for the instrument. Up to the time of Antonio Stradivari (Cremona, 1644/8-1737), the makers conducted their individual search for a suitable shape, and only later did a standard model exist which could be copied in all violin-makers' workshops. Maggini made rather flat instruments whose sonority was round and full; the Amati family settled in Cremona, and their most famous member, Nicola (1596-1684), later taught both Andrea Guarneri (1626-1698) and Antonio Stradivari; Amati violins were rather full-bellied and their sound was less strong. The same features are also characteristic of the Tyrolean school of Jacob Stainer (1621-1683), as well as of a great many Netherlands and Flemish violin-makers who worked in Rome. Jacob Stainer, in his day considered by the Germans to be the best living violin-maker, made violins whose neck often terminated in a magnificent lion's head; they were even more arched than Amati instruments, and had more rounded sound-holes.

The violin of Antonio Stradivari was nothing more than a combination of the models made at Cremona and at Brescia, but shaped with the hand of a master craftsman. Throughout all of his long life, Stradivarius strove towards perfection and brought to his violins modifications too numerous to list here; but no matter to what period they belong, his instruments always display a unity of conception, masterly craftsmanship, and exceptional sonority, so that today he has come to be considered the violin-maker *par excellence*. Hence, the hundreds of thousands of violins bearing the famous legend "*Antonius Stradivarius faciebat Cremonae* 17..." which reach us in great profusion, the majority of which are merely more or less servile mass-produced copies made by unscrupulous manufacturers, who have not hesitated to stick on their mediocre products copies of the famous, equally mass-produced, label.

Cremona instruments may be clearly recognised by their shape and, naturally, by their intrinsic value. They may also be recognised by their varnish, which gives them a warm colouration varying between yellow and a reddish brown; unfortunately, the formula for this varnish has been lost. However, it should not be thought that the varnish had any sort of effect on the instrument's

IV. — 11.

Pardessus de viole and quinton. The pardessus de viole is the work of the Parisian maker Pierre Saint-Paul whose instruments are characterised by their fine sonority; their outward appearance is not always as attractive as is the instrument shown here. The quinton bears the label of Jacob Stainer of Innsbruck, however this is clearly false as the instrument betrays French origins. The neck ends in a carving of a man's head.
Length: *c.* $24\frac{1}{4}$ ins., and 24 ins.
M.I., Brussels.
Nos. 219 & 139.

IV. — 12.

Three transverse flutes. *Left,* a French orchestral flute by the maker L. Lot (Paris, about 1740-1785). This ivory instrument has a key and a replaceable body part. *Centre,* a boxwood flute with ivory collars and a silver key, by the maker Nicolas Marcel Raingo of Mons (Belgium) who lived from 1746 to 1823. *Right,* a German flute in boxwood with one key, the work of the maker I. Denner (Nuremberg, died in 1735). These three instruments are tuned at least a tone below modern concert pitch.
Length: *c.* $24\frac{3}{8}$ ins., 24 ins., and 25 ins.
M.I., Brussels.
Nos. 2379, 2669 & 1056.

IV. — 13.

German tenor recorder, without a maker's name but bearing the inscription "Leipzig". The instrument is of ivory. Length: *c.* $19\frac{2}{3}$ ins.
M.I., Brussels.
No. 436.

IV. — 14.

Three oboes. *Left,* an oboe da caccia with three brass keys. The instrument is in three pieces, two of which bear the mark of I.H. Rottenburgh (Brussels, 1672-1765) and the third that of G.A. Rottenburgh (Brussels, 1709-1790). *Centre,* an ordinary oboe of German origin, having two keys. The maker was Grundmann Grenser, of whom no biographical details are known. *Right,* an oboe d'amore, also with two keys, the work of I.H. Eichentopf, who lived in Leipzig and of whom we have instruments probably made between 1724 and 1738.
Length: *c.* $28\frac{3}{4}$ ins., $23\frac{5}{8}$ ins., and 28 ins.
M.I., Brussels
Nos. 180, 962 & 971

IV. — 15.

Bassoon, with three brass keys, dating from the beginning of the 18th century. It is the work of Johann Christian Denner, born in Nuremberg in 1655 and died in the same town in 1707. The Denner family played an important role in the development of the conception of the clarinet.
Length: *c.* 48⅓ ins.

M.I., Brussels.
No. 427.

IV. — 16.

German horn (beginning of the 18th century) by Johann Leonhard Ehe (Junior) of Nuremberg. The name of this maker is engraved on the silver rim of the bell. In addition it bears a decorative Turk's head (the mark of the Ehe family) and angels' heads. This horn was to be played with crooks, one of which is shown here.
Length: *c.* 9½ ft.;
diameter: *c.* 34¼ ins.

M.I., Brussels.
No. 3152.

sonority; all that can be said is that if the varnish did not improve the sonority, it cannot have detracted from it either.

The violin of the seventeenth century was slightly different from our own: its bridge was shorter, and the neck was correspondingly shorter also. This meant that the strings were not so long, and consequently the angle formed between them and the shorter bridge was the same as that we know today with our longer strings and taller bridge. Since the string tension was greater than that in the viol, the bridge had a heavier burden to support. In order that the belly (which in the violin is a thin one) might be able to withstand the extra pressure exerted by the bridge, a small cylinder of spruce, the sound-post, was placed in the sound-box to the rear of the right foot of the bridge, inserted between the belly and the back. Under the other foot, running lengthwise under the belly, a strip of wood, the bass bar, was glued, to reinforce the resistance of the belly and also to transmit the vibrations of the left foot of the bridge. The neck of the violin, unlike most viols, has no frets.

All the elements which go to make up the violin have their necessary function, even if at first sight they may appear to be present only for aesthetic reasons. Thus, though some believe that the purfling (inlaid threads of wood) which set off the contours the body of the instrument is merely decorative, its real function is to protect the fragile wood of the instrument from possible cracks. The narrow waist facilitates the movement of the bow. The scroll is useful for hanging the instrument up. The fact that the violin's neck is rounded instead of being flat, like that of the viol, may be explained by the different manner of holding the instrument. If the shape of the sound-holes has changed over the years, this has been as much for practical as for aesthetic reasons, for their shape and position play a considerable part in balancing, amplifying and projecting the instrument's sound. The shape of the sound-holes and their position on the belly differ from one maker to another; the same is true of the shape of other elements. This is why it is relatively easy for a well-informed connoisseur to identify the school, if not the maker, to which a violin may be attributed.

From its inception, the violin was regarded above all as a solo instrument; therefore, its possibilities were quickly explored and exploited as they were gradually discovered. In 1542, Ganassi explained in his *Regola Rubertina* how the bow should be held in the execution of pizzicati. When Monteverdi used the violin, even though only in orchestral scores, he demanded of the player a technique which extended to playing in the fifth position. In 1627, the technique of playing the instrument had advanced so far that Carlo Farina, in some of his compositions, required it to imitate the guitar, the sound of hens, etc., which can only be achieved by means of a well-developed technique. The Italian, Farina, who was one of the first violinist-composers to write sonatas for his instrument, established a school in Germany, where he was attached to the court of Dresden, and his pupils and in their turn their pupils made efforts to surpass their master in the sphere of difficult feats. In this way, Westhoff — who in 1682 commanded the admiration of Louis XIV — and Walther went one better than Farina by requiring the violin to imitate, for instance, the hen, the cuckoo, the thundering of an organ, the bagpipe, etc., feats which demand an amazing virtuosity. But in this second half of the seventeenth century another aspect of violin technique was represented in Germany; for in this country where polyphonic music had never really lost its hold, the violin was often played on two strings simultaneously (double-stopping) and was given three- and four-note chords to play; this technique was to lead up to the sonatas for solo violin of Johann Sebastian Bach. A different sort of technique, practised above all by Heinrich Biber (1644-1704), was the use of *scordatura* (tuning the string to notes other than those normally used).

England remained untouched by this movement, and rather was influenced by the Italians. As for France, for a long time yet viols were held in higher esteem, the violins being considered suitable at best for the common people. In 1636, Mersenne wrote that nothing could be more delightful or powerful than the *vingt-quatre violons du Roy,* the orchestra Louis XIII had created in 1626; but an orchestra whose players could only attain the third position and limited themselves to playing suites of dances could not have aspired to a high level of virtuosity; nonetheless, the fact of only being able to reach this third position would in no way preclude the possibility of a certain perfection of playing. It was not until 1692 that sonatas were written which were to raise the violin to the level it had already attained in Italy and in Germany; and these violin sonatas were written, not by a violinist, but by a harpsichord player, François Couperin le Grand.

It was Marco Uccellini (1610-*c.*1679) who first reached the sixth position, and he was also responsible for the technique of the *tremolo* (very rapid short movements of the bow); it is said to have been Scarlatti who, in 1701, first played in the eighth position.

Though there were a few great violinists in the seventeenth century, it was really in the first half of the eighteenth century that the great masters of the rapidly spreading instrument made their appearance. From then on numerous "methods" were published, dealing with the technique of the instrument — the mode of playing, the way to hold the bow, the way to hold the violin itself, etc. These treatises were written by pedagogues of frequently differing persuasions, and whilst not actually contradicting each other, they show fairly curious differences of technique. For instance, according to which method is followed, the instrument might be placed on the front of the chest, or on the shoulder; it mattered little whether the chin was to the right or to the left of the tail-piece. We need not dwell on these divergences, which simply go to show that some sort of technique was in the process of being formed. A collection of sonatas published in about 1738, the *Sons harmoniques* by the Frenchman Mondonville, contains a series of works designed to bring into play both natural and artificial, both single and double harmonics. Here we have an incontestible enrichment of violin technique. In about 1750, staccato playing was introduced, and Tartini insisted on certain improvements to the bow. It was not long before this celebrated violinist-composer wrote his well-known treatise *Arte del Arco,* which comprised fifty variations on a theme by Corelli.

IV. — 17.

Three trumpets. *Left,* an alto trumpet in *G.* An inscription engraved on the edge of the bell gives the maker's name and the town in which he worked: *"Iohann Wilhelm Haas in Nurnberg"*. This inscription is completed by the depiction of a running hare, which was the trade mark of J. W. Haas. Like Kodisch (see below), he was fond of decorating the edges of his bells with angels' heads. In the *centre,* a trumpet in *D♭*, made by Johann Leonhard Ehe I who lived at Nuremberg (1638-1707). At the time there were in the same town three men of the same name all practising the same trade. Five instruments by Johann Leonhard Ehe I have survived and may be seen in the collections of Leipzig, Eisenach and Brussels. *Right,* an alto trumpet in *D.* This instrument has the following on the edge of its bell: *"Macht Iohann Carl Kodisch Nurnb.* 1693". Of this famous maker, who was born and died in Nuremberg (1654-1721), we have twelve instruments which may be found in the catalogues of several collections such as those at Michigan, Nuremberg, London, Basle, Berne, Munich, Berthout, Salzburg and Brussels. The decoration of the bell is characterised by a border of angels' heads chiselled in brass and standing out in relief. Length: *c.* $24\frac{3}{8}$ ins., 30 ins., and $30\frac{3}{4}$ ins.

M.I., Brussels.
Nos. 1176, 1177 & 1180.

Kit, or "pocket-violin".

If we study contemporary engravings, we find that generally the violin was held in a position slanting downwards and the bow was held at a point rather further from the end than is usual nowadays. It is easy to explain why this was so: in fact the bows of the time were straight, and sometimes even slightly convex, rather than being concave like our own; their tips were pointed, and this feature was known technically as the *tête de brochet* (pike-head); finally, the bow itself was shorter and lighter and facilitated a particular way of playing with an articulated or even *martelé* phrasing. The hair of the bow was free, and did not yet have to pass through a wedge; its tension was regulated by means of slanting teeth, or *crémaillère*, which could not be adjusted by such fine degrees as are possible today. In Italy at the end of the seventeenth century, bows could be found whose tension was regulated by a screw, as is the case today, but it is a Parisian, François Tourte, who must be given the credit for having, in about 1780, originated the modern bow — concave, longer than before, with the hair passing through a wedge and the tension regulated by a screw. By an odd coincidence, John Dodd arrived at the same result at the same time in England.

The second member of the violin family, the *viola*, is larger than the violin and consequently deeper in pitch, being tuned a fifth lower. Its body is between 16 and 17 ins long. However, at the period with which we are dealing, it was scarcely regarded as an instrument to be used widely. It was usually played by violinists who demanded, to enable greater facility, that the instrument should be as small as possible; this is why many old violas have bodies no more than 15 ins long. Thus, they could not be tuned in the normal way. On the other hand, violas existed whose bodies might be up to nearly 19 ins long; but these were a version of another instrument, called the *tenore*, of seventeenth-century Italian origin. This tenore has today disappeared, and was, in effect, an intermediary between the viola and the *violoncello*.

Precisely when the first violoncello (now more commonly called the cello) appeared is not known. We know only that Andrea Amati made one in 1572, and that this was given by Pius V to Charles IX. It is also known that the cello was for a long time the rival of the viola da gamba, which was sometimes even given precedence over it in ensembles to which violins had gained admittance; the reason given for this was that the sonority of the cello was too strong for it to be a useful accompanimental instrument. On the other hand, not only because of this powerful sonority, but also because its tuning in fifths permitted a more advanced technique of playing, it was fairly quickly taken up as a solo instrument. The first cellos were probably played after the manner of the bass viol, the bow being held with the palm of the hand facing upwards. It is difficult to say when the position of the hand was changed; Quantz (1697-1773) was the first to describe the new position, in a treatise he published in 1752.

In the works of Bach, we sometimes find the indication: *violoncello piccolo*. This was an instrument measuring about 40 ins in height and being something like a five-stringed viola, the last string being tuned to an *E* as on the violin.

In France, another instrument, the *quinton*, was played; this was not, as is often thought, a five-stringed *pardessus de viole*. In fact, the quinton had a rounded neck, whereas the viols, as we have seen, had flat necks. It was meant to be played like the violin, in other words, on the shoulder. Admittedly, some of its features such as the flat back, the sound-holes and the shoulders were derived from the viol, and these are partly responsible for the confusion between the two instruments. The quinton, a hybrid instrument, had very little success.

Finally, the *viola pomposa,* said to have been the invention, in about 1720, of J.S. Bach, was not, as some believe, a member of the viol family, but of the violin family, since it was constructed like the viola, but had five strings; its history was fairly brief.

Wind Instruments

Whereas in the Renaissance period, the recorder was made in a single piece, it now had three detachable parts. The joints between the parts were generally embellished with bone or ivory collars. It was no longer necessary to have two corresponding holes at the bottom, the one for a right-handed and the other for a left-handed player, for now that the two lower sections were detachable, players in either manner simply had to twist the lower section one way or the other to suit their own requirements. The bore became narrower and more conical; the instrument's bevel-edge was closer to the mouthpiece and wider. These alterations gave the instrument a sharper tone, which corresponded to the ideal of the time; the sweet and rounded sonority of the Renaissance disappeared. Although the recorder had to maintain its position against the more and more popular transverse flute, there were composers who used both instruments in the course of a single composition; this was the case with Lully, Purcell, Handel and the great virtuoso Quantz, who was the teacher of Frederick the Great, himself an excellent flautist.

It should be noted that flute-makers were not numerous enough to be able to form their own guild, and had to join other guilds which often had only a tenuous connection with their own craft. In France, the makers of transverse flutes and recorders belonged to the guild of chair-leg manufacturers!

The transverse flute itself had undergone certain changes. It too was made in three sections, and even, after 1750, in four; the cylindrical bore of the sixteenth century became a conical bore; its widest diameter would be at the head end, and this might be up to about 2 inches wider than the diameter at the foot.

One of the most famous of all makers of the transverse flute and the recorder, Jacques Hotteterre, known as le Romain, published in 1707 a treatise called *Principes de la flûte traversière*. He was without doubt one of the greatest contributors to the development of the instrument. There appears in his treatise an illustration of a transverse flute having a key, the same instrument that was used by all the virtuosos of the seventeenth century, and was even played by some who lived at the beginning of the nineteenth century. This flute was in *D*, and its key was used to obtain *D*♯. When he was staying in Paris in about 1726, Quantz

Cor anglais.

Oboe d'amore.

(who later wrote an important treatise: *Versuch einer Anweisung die Flöte Traversière zu spielen,* 1752) attempted to refine his instrument by adding a second key which gave *E♭*, but this project was a failure.

The *musette,* an instrument extremely fashionable with the seventeenth- and eighteenth-century aristocracy, had also been brought to perfection by Jacques Hotteterre, who was one of a family of players and makers of wind instruments, and who was born in about 1684 and died in Paris in about 1760; the musette was decorated with pompons, fringes and ribbons. Besides his pieces for the transverse flute (1708 and 1715) and his chordal compositions for the musette (1722), Jacques Hotteterre also published his treatises *Principes de la flûte traversière, de la flûte à bec et du Hautbois* (1707) and *Méthode pour la musette* (1737), which are of exceptional interest for the instruction they give, and which were reprinted a number of times.

Either of two men may have been the inventor of the oboe: Michel Philidor, a crumhorn player living in around 1659, or Jean Hotteterre (died 1691), the grandfather of Jacques Hotteterre. Whoever actually invented it, it was at this time that the oboe came into existence, as a consequence of the great improvements which had been made to the shawm. There are a number of things which enable us to distinguish between the two instruments: the shawm was made in a single piece, did not have a key, its bore was wide and its bell relatively large, whereas the oboe was made in three pieces, had three keys, a narrow bore and smaller bell. The holes in the oboe were not so wide as those of the shawm; the double reed was longer and narrower and not protected by a pirouette, but rather held directly in the player's mouth, allowing, by means of lip pressure, firmer control of the sound.

The oboe was first played in public by Jean Hotteterre in 1657. Shortly afterwards, and certainly before 1660, it was admitted to the court of Louis XIV, and was accorded the honour of being introduced into the *Grande Ecurie du Roy,* an ancient institution dating from the time of François I and consisting mostly of wind instruments and drums, occasionally joined by violins and tromba marina, whose function was to participate in processions and ceremonies of the musketeers. One year later, Lully, the director of court music, wrote a march for oboes. According to Michel de la Barre, a member of the *Grande Ecurie* from 1702 till 1705, Lully's promotion to the directorate brought about a total decline in the use of all the old instruments with the exception of the oboe. It was claimed, in particular, that the musette should be left to the shepherds. In actual fact, the musette was excluded from the orchestra, but as we have already seen was still just as widely played in aristocratic and bourgeois circles. It was natural that the oboe, a recent instrument that had only just been included in the orchestra, should retain its place there. Of the older wind instruments, only the recorder survived this purge, since we find that it was still used in chamber music.

For ease of fingering, and above all to avoid crossed fingers, wind instruments were made with more and more keys. Some variants of the oboe began to be made, the most important of which were the *oboe d'amore* and the *oboe da caccia.* The oboe d'amore

IV. — 18.

Carillon of Antwerp Cathedral. In all, it has 47 bells from different periods. The deep bell is the oldest, having been cast by J. and W. Hoerken in 1459. Of the others, 36 date from between 1655 and 1658 and were cast by the brothers Fr. and P. Hemon, 3 by J. Dumery (1767) and the 7 smallest by Fr. Van Aerschot (1904). Each bell may be struck either by a hammer or by a clapper. The hammer striking the bell is activated by a cylinder itself attached to the clock. On the other hand, the clapper is attached to a keyboard and pedal-board by means of wires.

Antwerp Cathedral.

IV. — 19.

Double-manual harpsichord by Hans Ruckers the Elder, the Antwerp maker. This instrument, dating from 1612, underwent *ravalement* in 1774 at the hands of another maker of harpsichords, Pascal Taskin (1723-1793), a native of Theux (near Liège) who lived in Paris and was the most renowned maker of his day. Hans Ruckers had founded the Ruckers dynasty at Antwerp. He was born in about 1550 and died after 1620. The case and sound-board are decorated by paintings of the Brussels artist A. Fr. Van der Meulen who was attached to the court of Louis XIV. The King himself and some members of his court appear on the lid, and, around the case, a panorama of a number of towns is to be found, amongst which Audenarde has been identified. This harpsichord is unusual in its two manuals which do not, as was normally the case, operate different stops; on the contrary, so as to facilitate transposition, the two are tuned a fourth apart from each other. Length: *c.* 7½ ft.

M.I., Brussels.
No. 3848.

did not come into being until around 1720. It was larger and sounded a minor third lower than the normal oboe. Its shape differed from the oboe's in that it had a pear-shaped bell; however, such a shape was already known in the seventeenth century, since it could be met with in the tenor oboe.

As far as we know, the oboe d'amore was played for the first time in an opera by Georg Philipp Telemann: *Der Sieg der Schönheit* (1722). Although some composers, such as Bach, Georg Schürmann and others, appreciated its sonority and used it in their works, it fell into disuse a few years later.

The oboe da caccia was in reality simply an oboe d'amore which sounded a major third lower. Some early examples had a flared bell, but before long it was made only with a globular bell. In about 1760, the tube was bent so as to facilitate manipulation, and from then on it was called, not oboe da caccia, but cor anglais. This innovation is attributed to Jean Perlendès of Strasbourg. Opinions differ as to the origin of this curious name. Since sometimes the instrument is found to have had a sharp angle instead of a curve in the tube, some believe that the instrument was originally referred to as the *cor anglé,* of which cor anglais would be a later corruption. Others are not satisfied with this explanation on the grounds that it does not account for the use of the word *cor* (horn); for this reason they maintain that the oboe da caccia was called cor anglais when its tube became curved because it then came to resemble (in shape) a *hunting-horn* in use in England at the time. The first use of the cor anglais in music for the theatre was in Gluck's *Alceste* (1769).

We shall say no more here about the bassoon, the bass of the oboe family, for it remained pretty well what it had been during the Renaissance period, and only after 1751 did instrument-makers really begin to be interested in it.

Apparently, the double bassoon, made in wood or metal and sounding an octave lower than the bassoon, was invented in Germany at about the end of the sixteenth or the beginning of the seventeenth century. According to Burney, its shape was that of an enormous bassoon and it was over six and a half feet high. Although already known for some years in Germany, it did not yet exist in England when Handel wished to use it in his *Fireworks Music* (1748), and he considered having one specially made by Stanesby.

In the previous chapters we have always spoken of the shawm as being a double-reed instrument. However, we also said of the mediaeval shawm that it was also possible that the term might refer to a primitive type of *clarinet*, hence an instrument with a single reed mounted on a sort of mouthpiece enclosed in a cap. The French used the word *chalumeau* (shawm) for such an instrument in the sixteenth and seventeenth centuries, in the same way as the German *Schalmey* — a double-reed instrument — was used. Fairly soon, attempts were made to refine the French chalumeau in Germany, and it was in this way that at the end of the seventeenth century Johann Christoph Denner (1655-1707), taking this instrument as his starting point, modified it to the extent of creating an instrument which was quick to establish itself and which we know today as the clarinet. He gave the instrument

IV. — 20.

Flemish virginal bearing the following inscription: "*Johannes et Andreas Ruckers fecerunt*". This instrument, which also has the rose-hole of Hans Ruckers the Elder, is interesting in that in the lower part of the instrument, over the range of two octaves and a fourth, it has a special stop called, in Flemish, *Rommelbas* and imitating the sound of the bagpipes. This is obtained by sliding a batten holding metal hooks under the strings without touching them. As soon as the strings are set in vibration they come into contact with these hooks and thus yield this distinctive sonority. In his *De Organographia,* Praetorius describes an identical stop, calling it *Harfenzug*. The instrument's range is four octaves, the first of which is short.
Length: *c.* 56 ins. *M.I.,* Brussels. No. 2927.

IV. — 21.

Clavecin de voyage (travelling harpsichord) invented by the Parisian maker Jean Marius, who was also one of the inventors of the piano. As from 1700 Marius had obtained a licence to build *clavecins brisés,* as they were also called. The one shown here can be closed by folding it on itself so as to form a rectangular box. Since this harpsichord was intended to be taken on journeys the maker has substituted lead jacks for wooden ones, which would have been over-sensitive to climactic changes. Cristofori, who was in charge of the de Medici collection, has left us a description of a similar instrument in that collection.
Length: *c.* 51¼ ins.
M.I., Brussels. No. 555.

IV. — 22.

Geigenwerk built in 1625 by the Spanish priest Raymundo Truchado of whom no biographical details are known. This instrument has four wheels operated by a crank, and above are stretched 45 gut strings of decreasing length and thickness. With the help of metal hooks operated by the keys of a manual, these strings are brought into contact with the wheels, which thus act as bows. The instrument might be termed a "one-man hurdy-gurdy string quartet". Its range is four octaves, the first of them short.
Length: *c.* 5 ft. *M.I.,* Brussels. No. 2485

◄◄ IV. — 18. **Flemish carillon** (1459-1904)

◄ IV. — 19. **Flemish harpsichord** (1612)

IV. — 20. **Flemish virginal** (early 17th century)

IV. — 21. **"Clavecin de voyage"** (*c*. 1700

IV. — 22. **Spanish "Geigenwerk"** (1625

FRAY RAYMVNDO TRVCHADO:INVENTOR:1625:

IV. — 23. **German clavichord** (1744)

IV. — 24. **French harpsichord** (1679) ►

IV. — 25. **French positive organ** *(Louis XIII Period)* ►►

IV. — 23.

Clavichord (1744) by the Hamburg maker Hieronymus Albrecht Hass. This unfretted clavichord has two strings to each key. A third set of strings, playing an octave higher, has been added for the 22 lowest strings. The etchings which adorn the lid show a view of the town of Altona. H.A. Hass was born in 1689 and died after 1744. The instrument's range is five octaves.
Length: *c.* 5⅝ ft.

M.I., Brussels.
No. 2518.

IV. — 24.

This double-manual harpsichord bears the inscription: "*Fait par moy Vincent Tibaut à Tolose* 1679". We know nothing about the life of this maker. The entire instrument is richly decorated with marquetry showing birds and phyllomorphous motifs which surround a coat-of-arms, itself of marquetry. The keyboard, with a range of four octaves plus a fourth, has a broken octave in the bass. The stops are of 8 ft., and 4 ft. Length: *c.* 81½ ins.

M.I., Brussels.
No. 553.

IV. — 25.

French positive organ (Louis XIII) by an unknown maker. This instrument has show-pipes of gilded tin, a piccolo stop, also having tin pipes, and a bourdon stop having stopped wooden pipes. The piccolo is unusual in that though it has a sixth and three octaves, the highest octave is pitched in the same register as that immediately below it. The bellows are operated with the aid of a leather thong at the right of the instrument.
Width: *c.* 30¾ ins.

M.I., Brussels.
No. 453.

this name because in its higher register the new instrument recalled the sonority of the trumpet (*clarino* in Italian).

Denner's innovations may be briefly described: he dispensed with the cap so that the reed was in direct contact with one of the player's lips, the other one resting on the beak-shaped mouthpiece; thus the lip pressure exerted on the reed allowed the production of harmonic sounds which would otherwise have been unavailable. Further, wishing to enable the instrument to play high harmonics, he reduced its size and the width of its bore. The bell was flared so as to give it the shape of a trumpet-bell. Finally, so as to obtain a fuller range and to avoid a four-note gap between the highest natural sound and the first of the harmonic sounds, he introduced further improvements; these we cannot examine in great detail here, but they served in particular to remedy the lack of homogeneity of timbre which had at first been noticeable in the different registers. Denner's son, like him a native of Nuremberg, and Berthold Fritz of Brunswick added in their turn further refinements to the clarinet.

In accordance with the usual practice of the time, Denner made his clarinets in three sections with collars at the joints, mostly in ivory.

In the first place, the clarinet was played by applying the upper lip to the reed, and not, as nowadays, the lower lip. It was the clarinettists of Mannheim who first played the instrument in the latter way, and it was they whom Mozart heard when he first encountered the instrument (in 1777). Even today, it is possible to find clarinettists who prefer to play with the reed against the upper lip.

Although Germany was the country of its origin, the clarinet was first played as an orchestral instrument in Belgium; this was when, in 1720, Jean Adam Faber, *maître de chapelle* at Antwerp cathedral, gave a performance with orchestra of a mass composed by himself. In France, the first to use this instrument was Rameau in his opera *Zoroastre* (1749), and not, as is commonly believed, in *Acanthe et Céphise*.

The French hunting-horn (*cor de chasse*), which had originally been straight like the posthorn, became longer, and for reasons of practicality, curled in on itself. It was also given a narrower bore, permitting a more exact reproduction of harmonics of the fundamental sound. It was French makers of the first half of the seventeenth century who added these refinements. The instrument's French origin was further emphasized when it was imported to England in 1661 and given the name *French horn*. Twenty years later, Count von Sporck introduced it into Bohemia.

This horn was bent in two and a half circles some time during the reign of Louis XV (1713-1774), and has remained in this form since. Although the Germans were fairly quick to take it up in ensemble playing — for it may be found in the orchestra of J. J. Fux (1660-1741) — the French did not hear it in this way until German horn players were engaged with the orchestra of La Pouplinière to play in Paris in 1750.

The cor de chasse was made of a single tube and could therefore produce only a limited number of notes — the fundamental and its own harmonics. If the length of the tube could be modified, the fundamental note would change, and bring with it the possible harmonics. This led to the invention of crooks, which were small tubes of various lengths which could be fitted on to the body of the horn between the detachable mouthpiece and the main tube, lowering the note by the corresponding amount. In this way, different fundamental notes could be sounded, as could their harmonics. Some consider this invention to date from 1715; others place the date rather later, but it was certainly before 1750. With these greatly increased possibilities, the French horn took on a separate existence, while the old cor de chasse survived and went its own way.

Rose-hole form by Ruckers.

In spite of such improvements, the French horn still presented certain drawbacks, for if a player wished to change the note, he had to replace one crook by another, an operation which was bound to take some time, however quickly it was carried out. It was then that an important discovery was made by a German horn player, Hampel. In 1760, attempting to produce a muffled sound on the normal French horn, this man pushed a cotton pad into the instrument's bell. He must have had quite a surprise to discover that, instead of muffling it, the pad had the effect of raising the note by a semitone. Thus, by introducing a foreign object into the bell, it was possible to slightly change the pitch of the note; furthermore, by varying the extent of insertion of the pad, the change in pitch could itself be varied. From that moment one can say that the chromatic horn was born. It was soon found that the hand could perform the same job as the pad, and much more easily. For this reason, the pad was abandoned, and from then on it was the player's hand which, inserted in the bell, would be used to modify the pitch of each note.

During the period from Monteverdi to Bach, the trumpet, the trombone and the cornett — in other words, those wind instruments which had both a separate mouthpiece and a cylindrical tube — underwent relatively few modifications. However, it is worth mentioning a somewhat curious fact: Bach often wrote for the trumpets in a very high register, and such parts are very difficult to perform; on the other hand, the French masters of the time wrote works which never contained such high parts for the instrument. It seems probable that the technique of high trumpet-playing was unknown in France.

The *tromba da tirarsi* (slide trumpet), having a mouthpiece fixed into a very long neck on which the body of the instrument could slide, was used by Bach in several of his cantatas; the only example which has come down to us dates from 1651, was made in Naumburg in Saxony, and is today part of the collection at the Instrumental Museum of Berlin.

There appeared in England in about 1690 the *flat trumpet*, so called because a slide inserted in the loop nearest the player enabled him to play certain semitones which would give him the minor scale. This instrument was used in the music for the funeral of Queen Mary in 1695.

The trombone, descendant of the sackbut, did not undergo any changes. In fact, it had from its inception satisfied all the demands that could be made of such an instrument. As far as we know, it was Monteverdi who first used it in an orchestral score when he had a group of five differently pitched instruments to play the prelude to the scenes in the underworld in *Orfeo* (1607). He was to use it again three years later in a *Sonata da chiesa*.

It should be recalled that from the beginning of the seventeenth century on, the horn and the trumpet were sometimes given mutes which were inserted into the bell so as to muffle their sonority.

Percussion Instruments

Writing of the kettledrum in the chapter on the drum in his *Harmonie Universelle*, Mersenne says: "*A quoy l'on peut adjouster le tambour d'airain que l'on frappe du baston pour joindre son bruit aux sons des cymbales. La peau de ce tambour se bande avec des chevilles*". (To which may be added the bronze drum, which is struck with a stick and whose sound is combined with that of the cymbals. The skin of this drum is attached with pegs.) It seems from this description that the kettledrum of the time was very similar to that which we know today. The way in which kettledrums were introduced to France during the reign of Louis XIV was rather unusual. Having, in the course of numerous victories, captured such drums from their enemies, the French troops developed a taste for them and started to play them; they became a regimental trophy, as sacred as each regiment's standard, and Alain Manesson, the mathematics tutor to the pages of Louis XIV, wrote in his book *Les Travaux de Mars ou l'Art de la guerre:* "The player of the kettledrums should be a man of valorous heart, and he should rather perish in combat than allow himself and his kettledrums to be delivered up to the enemy".

The carillon, which had started life in Belgium, soon spread to neighbouring countries. From the seventeenth century on, they could be found in Holland, north Germany, England and northern France, and their manufacture was often entrusted to founders who were natives of Flanders, Louvain or Brussels. There were also others, some of whom became famous, such as Franz (1609-1667) and Pieter (1619-1680) Hemon of Amsterdam whilst at Malines worked the Van der Gheyn and Waghevens families. It was the Hemons who were the first to file down the insides of the cast bells so as to tune them exactly.

The number of bells per carillon continued to increase. Any carillon which did not possess at least fifty bells was considered of little importance. Now, the cylinders were activated automatically by the clock; often they had over a thousand pins which in turn activated the mechanism which operated the hammers for the corresponding bells; these bells were fixed. As the cylinder was perforated all over its surface with holes arranged in symmetrical lines, all that needed to be done for a different tune to be played was for the position of the pins on the cylinder to be altered.

Generally, the English carillon system was not the same as that used on the Continent. Instead of being fixed and struck by a mobile hammer, the bells were suspended in the manner of ordinary church bells; the melody they played was not harmonised as it was in Continental carillons; there was no prefabricated drum which could play a given tune, but instead men activated the bells according to a system known as bell change-ringing, in which the order in which the bells were rung was constantly changed. Consequently, the succession of sounds produced did not result in a melody, artistically speaking, even though the bells were operated according to strictly established rules.

Soon the carillon began to be used in instrumental ensembles. At first, the orchestral carillon consisted of bronze hemispherical sections scaled to different sizes and struck by the player with two mallets. Later, these bells were replaced by bronze bars of varying length and thickness. Apparently, Handel was the first to use such chimes, in the well-known chorus of girls in his oratorio *Saul* (1738).

As for that other percussion instrument, the drum, it remained much as it was in the previous era, apart from secondary improvements. We shall merely mention that it was in 1706 that it first appeared in music for the theatre, namely in the opera *Alcyone* by the viol-player Marin Marais.

Keyboard Instruments

The main reasons behind the development of the harpsichord during the course of the seventeenth century were the fact that the lute provided less scope than it did for accompanying melody as a continuo instrument, and also perhaps because at Antwerp, which had become the great centre for the manufacture of harpsichords, a second keyboard had been devised for the instrument.

The existence of a double, or even sometimes a triple, keyboard was to result in two things: firstly, both keyboards could be used at the same time in playing so as to make a clearer distinction between the timbres; on the other hand, once such a practise was in operation, the player did not have to make a break in his performance in order to change the stops.

The latter result was due equally to the fact that the sliders that had in the Renaissance period been placed on the right of the keyboard were replaced by more readily accessible levers at the front of the instrument. The invention of this mechanism is often attributed to the Antwerp manufacturer Jean-Daniel Dulcken, called Le Hessois. In any case, Thomas Mace reports that in England John Hayward had, by 1664, attempted to facilitate the changing of stops by means of pedals; though interesting, this attempt met with little success. Arrangements operated by the knees were also used. Italian harpsichords differed from the others in that they only had a single keyboard and only one or two 8-foot stops and one 4-foot stop; its body terminated in a fairly tapered point and its outward appearance was sober.

Flemish and French harpsichords (we are here concerned with those made by the great manufacturers: Ruckers, Couchet, Dulcken and Tibaut) were characterised by their two keyboards, having the same set of stops as that in the Italian harpsichord, but divided over the two keyboards; this made it possible to obtain different degrees of volume according to whether one or the other of the keyboards was used on its own, the greatest volume of sound being obtained by coupling the two keyboards. The body was relatively deep and on the heavy side, and the wood used was certainly not so fine as that used by the Italians. The chromatic keys were generally in bone, whilst the diatonic ones were in black-tinted wood.

It is easy to distinguish German harpsichords from the others, for their body is most frequently shaped in a double curve, as follows: Z. some also have a 16-foot stop, which cannot be found in harpsichords of any other country in that period.

(The English harpsichord never possessed a nasard stop.)

Besides the characteristic shape of a case, experts can distinguish a harpsichord's country of origin by other characteristics, such as the size of the keys and the names given to the various stop — lack of standard names often giving rise to doubts as to which stop should be used.

In the previous chapter we commented that the harpsichord was — like the organ — of itself incapable of yielding nuances of crescendo and decrescendo, and it was only considerably later that a system of shutters (or swell-box), which we described, was used to obtain such effects. This was the invention of two makers working in partnership, Burkat Shudi and John Broadwood of London, who applied to the harpsichord the principle of the organ's swell-box which could already be found in 1712 in an organ made by Jordan for the church of St. Magnus the Martyr in London.

Although the range of the keyboard was greater in the seventeenth century than it had been in the sixteenth, it was not found sufficient for the eighteenth. Therefore, harpsichords with more extended keyboards were constructed. However, since it was found desirable to continue to play on instruments of the famous makers of the previous century, such instruments were enlarged by the addition of keys both in the high and the low register and, of course, by the corresponding addition of strings; this procedure was known as *ravalement*. Because of this, it is very seldom that one comes across a seventeenth-century harpsichord that has not undergone the treatment of *ravalement* during the eighteenth century. This modification was really only successful in the hands of certain reputable makers, who themselves manufactured harpsichords, such as the famous Pascal Taskin (1723-1793) of Theux, near Liège, who was the custodian of the instruments at the Royal Chapel in Paris as well as being custodian of the instruments of the King's chamber.

Makers even went so far as to construct *clavecins de voyage*, in other words, harpsichords which were not too hard to transport from one place to another. These were folding instruments which, once folded, had the appearance of a long box. In order to make them, harpsichords had to be constructed in three movable parts which however were required to adapt themselves perfectly to their musical purpose on being unfolded into the normal shape of a harpsichord. Further, the keyboard section of each of these three parts was movable and could be inserted under the soundboard to make the instrument less cumbersome to carry. Finally, since wooden jacks were too fragile to endure the rough treatment and changes in climate that were inseparable from travelling, the jacks were made of lead. It was in 1709 that Jean Marius — who was also a piano builder — took out a patent for the construction of this instrument, which he called the *clavecin brisé*, and which had been one of the fruits of his fertile imagination.

The advent of accompanied monody led to the use of the harpsichord as an accompaniment instrument for the voice or for a melodic instrument. Since chromaticism was beginning to make more and more demands, it became awkward still to have to use the "short octave" which had been used in the previous century, and which lacked the *F*♯ and the *G*♯. Yet it was not wished to extend the range of the keyboard by two supplementary keys at the bottom. For this reason, in order to save space and at the same time to fit these two new notes into the lower octave, the first two black keys were divided into two parts, each of which activated a different string, as may be seen from the accompanying diagram. This kind of octave was known as a "broken octave". "Short octaves" and "broken octaves" which use different systems of tuning, and can be found on spinets as well as on harpsichords, regals and clavichords.

At this time, too, instruments using fixed notes did not have a tempered scale such as was to be in use later, in fact from the time of J.S. Bach onward. An instrument which can avail itself freely of any note, such as the violin, is able to make a difference between an *E*♭ and a *D*♯, the latter being one "comma" higher than the former; on the other hand, when tuning an instrument whose notes were fixed, such as the harpsichord, one or the other of these two had to be chosen, and it was always the sharpened note that was used. This entailed a serious drawback: when a singer or a violinist was performing a work in a flat key, the accompanying harpsichord player could only offer sharp notes. The resulting discrepancy was most disagreable to the sensitive ear. For this reason there arose the idea of using the same procedure as that of the "broken octave" in order to get the flat notes needed; in other words, the black keys for *D*♯ and *G*♯ were divided into two so as to obtain in addition respectively *E*♭ and *A*♭, as may be seen in the diagram apposite.

The Instrumental Museum of Brussels is the only one to possess an instrument in which the "broken octave" is combined with enharmonically tuned black keys. This is an instrument that was made in 1619 by the Corsican, Giovanni Battista Boni. It is worth noting that ten years after Boni, a German organ-maker, Gottfried Fritzsche, arrived at the same solution with regard to the organ.

It need hardly be said that an instrument made in such a way, although providing a viable solution to a delicate problem, could not achieve widespread propagation, for it demanded of the instrumentalist a rethinking of his technique. And man is well known to be lazy by nature. It was for this reason that in the time of J.S. Bach it was felt desirable to give an equal value to all the semitones of fixed-note instruments. This was the "equal temperament" which had been a dream of the sixteenth century and, artificial though it is, we still abide by this "equal temperament" today; for even if our pianos do give us mathematically equal semitones, these are semitones that have been fabricated "against nature".

The clavichord underwent an important modification in the first half of the eighteenth century. We referred to this in the previous chapter. From being fretted it became unfretted

Organ pipes

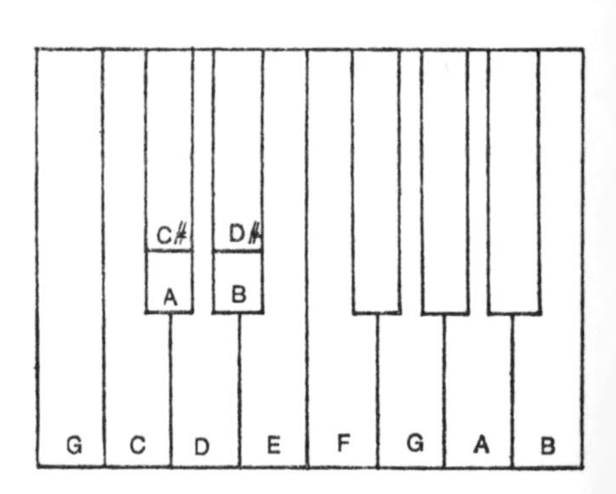

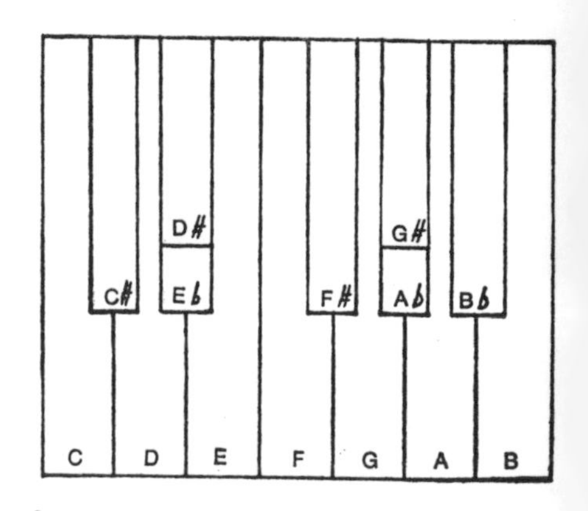

— in other words, each key corresponded to its own string. We have every reason to believe that this innovation was due to the German maker Daniel Tobias Faber of Crailsheim in Saxony, andis said to date from around 1726. As a result of it, the scope of the instrument was enlarged since now any chord of a number of different notes was possible on it. Moreover, in order to give more volume to the lower strings in the two octaves of the bass register they were doubled with thinner 4-foot strings. Finally, so as to prevent certain parts of the strings from vibrating, they were provided with cloth dampers.

The largest range attained by the keyboard of a clavichord was of five octaves, a development dating from roughly 1753, the year in which Carl Philipp Emmanuel Bach, an enthusiast of the instrument, published his treatise *Versuch über die wahre Art das Clavier zu spielen.*

After being held in such contempt by the higher classes during the Renaissance that in Germany it was called *lyra mendicorum* or *Bauerleyer* (beggar's or peasant's lyre), the hurdy-gurdy in the eighteenth century suddenly became fashionable, especially in France, to a degree never previously known. This was a result of the vogue for the pastoral — *bergeries* and *paysanneries.* It could be called the "François Boucher style" after that man's lintels, panels and fireplaces which were decorated in consciously pastoral and idyllic style, and which were a transposition into a refined and affected society of a more down-to-earth reality. The aristocracy and the *haute bourgeoisie* became affectedly captivated by the hurdy-gurdy just as they had already begun to be infatuated with the musette.

This infatuation was detrimental to a fair number of fine old lutes, for since the demand for hurdy-gurdies exceeded the rate at which they could be produced some makers adapted these lutes as hurdy-gurdies; theorbos and even guitars suffered the same fate. If such a maker as Charles Bâton was capable of making successful adaptations of this kind without too much harm to the instrument the same was not always true of makers less notable for their good taste. Bâton made a considerable contribution to the rebirth of the hurdy-gurdy for his decorations of the instrument included a fine sculpted head placed above the pegbox which gave his instruments a much sought-after artistic interest. Tuition books were soon written for the hurdy-gurdy, the most interesting of which is that by Jean-Baptiste Dupuits (1741). The numerous works written for the instrument could also be played on the musette since both instruments had in common the same register, nearly the same range, and the same pastoral character.

Since the appearance of the hurdy-gurdy and up to the present day, several inventors have been tempted to make other instruments based on the same principles (rubbed strings and keyboard). None of these inventions won the hoped-for success. However, we should pay some attention to the invention of a native of Nuremberg, Hans Haiden, who lived in the seventeenth century. This was an instrument called the *Geigenwerk* or the Geigen-instrument of which Praetorius gives an account. It was in the form of a harpsichord, but under the strings, instead of the jacks, was placed a series of wheels edged with rosin, each of which corresponded to a given number of strings. These wheels were set in rotation by a pedal. Then a key merely had to be pressed for it to push the corresponding string against the moving wheel by means of a mechanism which had a hook at the end; operating in the same way as a bow, this wheel sounded the string for as long as the contact was maintained. Since there were as many strings as there were keys, and since on the other hand all the wheels were constantly in motion, the geigenwerk could be made to play all the combinations of notes that were possible on any keyboard instrument.

Haiden's instrument is lost. However, the Instrumental Museum of Brussels has, from the same period, a unique instrument which bears a startling resemblance to it and which was made, in 1625, by the Spaniard, Fr. Raymundo Truchado, who claims to have been its "inventor". The basic difference between the two instruments is that in Truchado's model the wheels are operated by a crank placed at the rear and thus necessitating the participation of a second person, whilst in Haiden's it is the player himself who operates these wheels with the help of the pedal.

Whereas the organ of the Renaissance was characterised by stops whose timbre was often incisive, among which were those which imitated wind instruments, it was modified in the course of the seventeenth century by the addition of sweeter and softer stops which imitated the human voice or stringed instruments; these were used in preference to the earlier ones. The tremolo was also introduced, this being an artifice by means of which the air was only allowed to enter a pipe by fits and starts to produce a continuous and more or less pronounced tremolo which often degenerated into a quavering sound. Thus, in attempting to emulate the human voice, it was sometimes made to imitate its worst defect.

In previous organs, the various stops did not sound equally well; in other words, some were inimical to others by reason of a too great power of tone which, when two were used in combination, rendered the weaker virtually inaudible. Now they were all calibrated according to their volume, and from then on the player was able to choose any combination of stops he wanted without any fear of a less than satisfying result; in this way, the instrument graduated from being one for straight-forward musicians to one which attracted the attention of virtuosos.

Two great schools were formed at that time : that of Amsterdam with Sweelinck (1562-1621) and his pupils, who were mostly of north German origin and who were later to give their native localities the benefit of the instruction they had received, and that of Venice with the Gabrielis, the younger of whom, Giovanni, lived from 1557 to 1612.

Before going on to examine the structure of the organ itself and to discover in what respects it differed from one country to another, we should say a few words about the organ case.

By "case" is meant the carpentry working, either in single or double woodwork, which encloses all the working parts of the instrument: the pipes, the mechanisms and the bellows. In keeping with the various periods, this changed in appearance so as to conform with the architectural aesthetic of the time and not to jar with the style in which the reredos, the pulpit and the stalls were worked. This is why, in the Gothic era, it was provided with panels in which ogives and rosaces were sculpted, sometimes even panels painted by celebrated artists, and these panels acted as shutters which enclosed the pipes when the organ was not in use, in order to protect them from dust. During the Renaissance period, the decorations consisted of foliated scrolls, more or less grotesque curlicues and articulated statues, some of which might seem out of place in sacred precincts. Above the case, we find, for example, an eagle which is set in motion, often by a complex mechanism operated by a pedal, and which the organist can cause to beat its wings, or a figure of St. Peter whose eyes turn to bless the congregation, or again, a Moor's head whose "face trembles when the sweetest tones of the organ are heard" but whose "eyes roll in their sockets and teeth snap together when the volume of the sound increases". The paintings on the panels were not content simply to represent God the Father, Christ and the Saints, but depicted also the gods of antiquity, heroes, such as Hercules, and satyrs and fauns. The case of the seventeenth century was more sober, for these excesses disappeared, leaving on the turrets only a few pagan memories in the form of those caryatids and harpies which give the impression of supporting them. It may be added that until the beginning of the eighteenth century, the show-pipes, in other words those which were visible to the congregation, were gilded or chequered. However, it should be made clear that in general the French organ screen, apart from having undergone certain foreign influence in some regions of the extreme south and of the north-east, avoided the showiness and peculiarities mentioned above and had, rather, a more classical style. In the eighteenth century, there was a tendency for the case to be curved and for its decoration to consist of panels, in the wood of which were artfully sculpted musical instruments and heads of angels. As for the turrets, which served to throw into better relief the different sizes of pipes, these had already appeared in France by about 1550. At first, they were placed at each side in the shape of a semicircle or a mitre, but they were often replaced in the eighteenth century by a single central turret, although to speak too precisely on such matters would be to tread dangerous ground since even if general tendencies may be seen in the construction of cases, each maker nonetheless retained a certain freedom in his conception of them.

With regard to the instrument itself, we have here to deal with two great schools, the French, and the Dutch and German. One of the main elements by which they may be distinguished is the pedal-board. From the fifteenth century on, this was made up of pull-downs, which were a type of wooden strip connected to some of the manual keys so that they could be operated by the feet. These small pieces of wood, projecting from the floor in two slightly sloping ranks, at first served merely to sound a few of the deeper pipes; having between 8 and 10 keys, this pedal-board was gradually developed to the point of having as many as 32 and even 35 by using *ravalement*. This was the French style pedal-board, the form of which survived up to the beginning of the nineteenth century, and it was not well adapted to smooth playing or the performance of rapid passages. By contrast, the Germans fairly quickly adopted a pedal-board with longer keys and closer spacing, whose keys could be played equally well with the heel as with the toes; thus the German style pedal-board, rather than being restricted to the playing of a succession of long-held notes, allowed the addition of a supplementary voice which could be joined with the higher-pitched voices that were being developed on the manual keyboards. In short, the use of such a pedal-board in Teutonic countries corresponded well with the temperament of the Netherlanders and Germans which inclined them towards a type of music whose architecture was articulated on several levels of sound, whereas in the Latin countries complex polyphonies were not held in such high esteem. This may also be seen in the sort of stops of which the various pedal-boards were composed. Whereas in the seventeenth and eighteenth centuries the French style pedal-board abandoned the deep and fairly restricted stops it had featured since the Middle Ages and simply used 8- and 4-foot stops in the tenor register, only returning to 16-foot stops at the end of the eighteenth century, the German style pedal-board of the seventeenth and eighteenth centuries was lavishly supplied with 32-, 16-, 8- and 4-foot flue- and reed-stops.

The French organ, which flourished particularly between 1650 and 1750, as a rule had its manual stops modelled on a specific type: there was a principal manual, called the *grand orgue* and using the 16-foot stops, a secondary manual, the *positif*, using the 8-foot stops, and two smaller manual keyboards, the *récit* and the *écho*, and also, in some organs, a keyboard called the *bombarde*.

The Dutch and German organ offered a greater diversity. Many stops were added after 1500 to the organ of the Netherlands, above all in the north; the southern Low Countries were notable for their use of the transverse flute stop.

Germany reigned supreme in the realm of the organ, since there more than in other countries the instrument was obligatory in church services. This is because, Germany being under the sway of the Protestant religion, the congregation always participated in the services by its singing, and was accompanied in this by the organ. This was the main reason for which stopped pipes, of which there were some very small ones on the pedal-stops, were particularly preferred to reed-pipes, whose tone was too bright for accompanying voices, whilst in France, where the organ was more frequently heard as a solo instrument, these reed-pipes, due to the variety of timbres and loudness they featured, prevented any occurrence of monotony in the succession of the numerous pieces which were played in the course of a service. According to the testimony of Andreas Werckmeister in his *Orgelprobe* (1681), reed-pipes were considered in Germany to be stops "fit for a madman". It is worth noting, too, the distinctive and typical stops used in the south of Germany: 16-foot violone, 8-foot viola da gamba, and 8-, 4-, and 2-foot salicional. Finally it should be mentioned that the organ-builder Gottfried Fritzsche, whom we have already cited in the section on the harpsichord, built the first five-manual organ (sometime after 1629).

As for other countries, they remained traditional. The Spanish organ generally divided its full stops into high registers and low registers, and tended to place its clarion, trumpet and bombarde pipes *en chamade*, that is, projecting horizontally towards the inside of the church; Spain also produced some organs with two pedal-boards, placed one above the other.

In Italy, the double-manual organ was unknown, and pedal-boards developed so little that at first they did not have any stops of their own.

In England, where the baroque style remained unknown, there was no thought of building, as elsewhere, an organ of great scope. We have come a long way from the time of the legendary great organ of Winchester (tenth century). Until 1536, the English organ made do with one keyboard and 6 stops. After that date, examples may be found which have two manuals and about 15 stops. It is perhaps permissible to see in this poor state of the instrument a consequence of the prohibitions introduced by certain ruling powers. For example, it is known that Cromwell thought the organ "too Catholic" an instrument. It was not until 1720 that Christopher Shrider adapted a pedal-board to an English organ for the first time, and this pedal-board consisted of no more than a few notes.

V - The Classical Period

V. — 1. **"Flute Concert" (Frederick the Great at Sans Souci),** by A. Menzel

Chanot violin

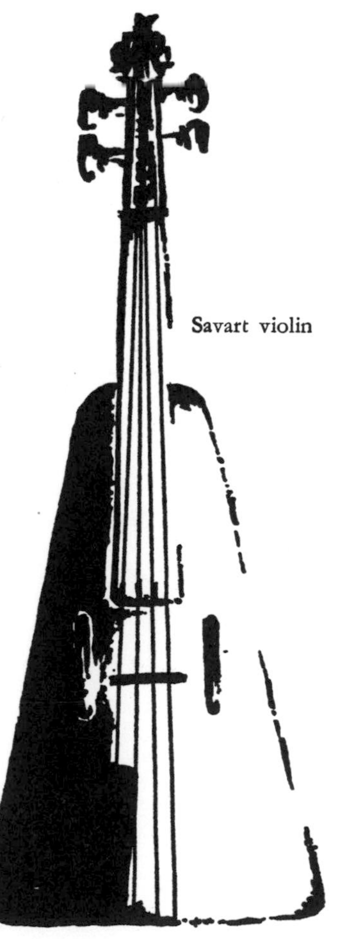
Savart violin

the small movable devices by which the strings were gripped and shortened resembled crutches (*béquilles*). This system was patently better than the previous one using hooks, but it entailed certain drawbacks; the use of fourteen pedals was somewhat awkward for these were placed in two ranks, an upper and a lower, it being impossible to arrange them all on the same level; and the weight of the instrument had been considerably increased, making it less manageable. For this reason, in 1812 Sébastien Erard made a harp having seven pedals, but each capable of a double movement; that is, according to whether it was lowered one or two degrees, the pedal brought into play one or two of the forks thad had replaced the crutches and did their job. It was advantageous that the fork should have replaced the crutch; it consisted of a brass disc on which were two polished studs between which the string passed; when the disc turned, the two studs gripped the string without breaking or fraying it (a fairly common defect with the crutch system); moreover, this system shortened the string without displacing its axis.

Of the other innovations, one was the addition of a sort of soft pedal to certain harps, this being a pedal which operated — either opened or closed — a shutter built into the body of the instrument so as to strengthen or to mute the volume of sound. This was the same principle as that of the swell-box which the English maker Jordan had already applied to the organ in 1712, and which was used in conjunction with some harpsichords in the second half of the eighteenth century.

The violin was decisively victorious over the viol; it was far better adapted to virtuoso playing than the older instrument, and its tone was more brilliant. However, it was quickly noticed that on occasions when it was called upon to take the role of soloist with one of the new, larger orchestras, and when it had to make itself heard in bigger halls, the power of its sonority was still not sufficient. It could only be made so by increasing the tension of its strings, and to do this the instrument itself had to be strengthened and its parts modified to a certain extent. In addition, its neck was lengthened, so that longer strings could be used. So that it could more easily withstand their tension, the neck was modified. From being a simple extension of the sound-box, it developed a slight backwards tilt in relation to the sound-box and, furthermore, it was made thinner in order to facilitate the passage of the player's hand which supported it at the same time as playing on it. So as to obtain more notes at the top of each string, the fingerboard also was extended. The top of the bridge took on a more pronounced curve so as to accentuate the different planes on which the strings were situated. Again, as the strings, more tightly strung than before, exerted through the bridge a stronger pressure on the sound-board, the latter's resistance had to be increased by making the bass bar longer and thus giving it extra support.

From what we have just said, it may be deduced that the violins of the previous age no longer satisfied the new demands, and if it was still felt desirable to use them, they had to be subjected to certain structural alterations. This happened to a good many of them. Not even violins of the great masters were immune from this sort of transformation. This is why it is now rare to find, for example, a Stradivarius which still has its original neck. It was precisely the Stradivarius model of violin which lent itself most readily to these alterations, because it was broad and not very arched, whereas the more pronounced arches at the front and back of those instruments made by the Amatis and by Jacob Stainer made such operations more difficult to conduct.

For every new, or even merely altered instrument, there was a new technique of playing. However, here we are touching on a field we have no need to go into for our present purposes. It will be sufficient to point out that a new way of holding the instrument came into being and was advocated by Leopold Mozart, the father of Wolfgang Amadeus, in his treatise on the art of the violin, *Versuch einer gründlichen Violinschule* (1756), which had a great influence on the music of that time: the violin was to be placed against the chin. However, the earliest position was still used by some, for when Spohr came to introduce the use of the chin rest in 1820 he placed it, not at the left as we would today, but over the tail-piece itself.

Despite the degree of perfection that had been attained in the manufacture of the violin, there were still makers and acousticians who sought to modify its structure in order to give it a greater or better balanced sonority, or again in order to perfect its timbre, etc. It is worth mentioning the violin of François Chanot, which had no sharp angles and had C-shaped sound-holes, and that of the acoustician Félix Savart (1791-1842), the shape of which was trapezoidal and which had rectilinear sound-holes. The lack of general success these models met with may be attributed to various causes, chief of which was that interesting though such innovations were they did not compensate for certain snags they entailed, notably a lack of manageability.

Taking his idea from the violin of Chanot, Georg Staufer, a Viennese maker, made, in 1823, a cello having the same form, giving it frets on the neck and six strings, as if it were a guitar: he called the instrument the *arpeggione*. Franz Schubert (1797-1828) wrote a sonata for this instrument which was not published until after his death.

As we have seen, the modern bow was thought up in about 1780 by Tourte, and almost simultaneously by Dodd in England. It subsequently benefited from notable improvements which were the work of makers who made bows as well as violins, such as Nicolas Lupot (1758-1828), and, in later years, the Vuillaumes, to whom we must add Tubbs, Voirin and the Peccate brothers.

Since the strings of the violin and of the instruments of the same family were more tautly strung, the bow had to be made heavier. The number of horsehairs used in the bow was increased and might total as many as 150. Tourte gave the bow a concave incurvature so as to make it more pliable, and as a result of this modification, was obliged to build up its head. In order to prevent the bow from slipping in the fingers, Tartini (1692-1770) had carved grooves in the stick, for as we have pointed out, in those days the bow was held by the fingers on the stick itself, thus further away from the nut than is usual today. These grooves continued to exist as a result of sheer force of habit, having since lost their justification, as violinists had begun to hold bow near the end to

V. — 2.

Spanish guitar bearing the mark "*Cassas Baña*" and dating from the beginning of the 19th century (Cassas worked at Baña, in the district of Leon). The back, of broad strips separated by white threads, is flat. The sides, the belly, the fingerboard and the pegbox are encrusted with mother-of-pearl, while the pegs are of ivory. The rose-hole is in vellum. The instrument has 5 double strings. Length: *c.* 38½ ins.

M.I., Brussels.
No. 3184.

V. — 3.

Rose-hole of a cittern built by the maker Gérard Deleplanque, who worked at Lille from 1755 to 1790. The instrument has 14 frets and 11 metal strings; it is dated 1774. Length: *c.* 30¼ ins.

M.I., Brussels.
No. 2509.

V. — 4.

Harp by the Parisian maker Holtzmann who lived at the end of the 18th century. This instrument has 7 pedals which enable each of the strings to be raised a semitone by means of hooks which shorten their vibrating length.
Height: *c.* 64¾ ins.

M.I., Brussels
No. 3916

V. — 5.

Violin (1750) by the Belgian make[r] Benoît-Joseph Boussu, who worke[d] at Etterbeek from 1750 to 178[0] This finely wrought instrument is [a] copy of an Amati. The bow, whic[h] is French, is by an unknown make[r]. It has a nut of open-worked ivory. The adjusting screw has a knob [o]f the same material. The horseha[ir] is loose and the ring is missing. Length of violin: *c.* 28⅞ ins.

M.I., Brussel[s]
Nos. 2781 & 23[illegible]

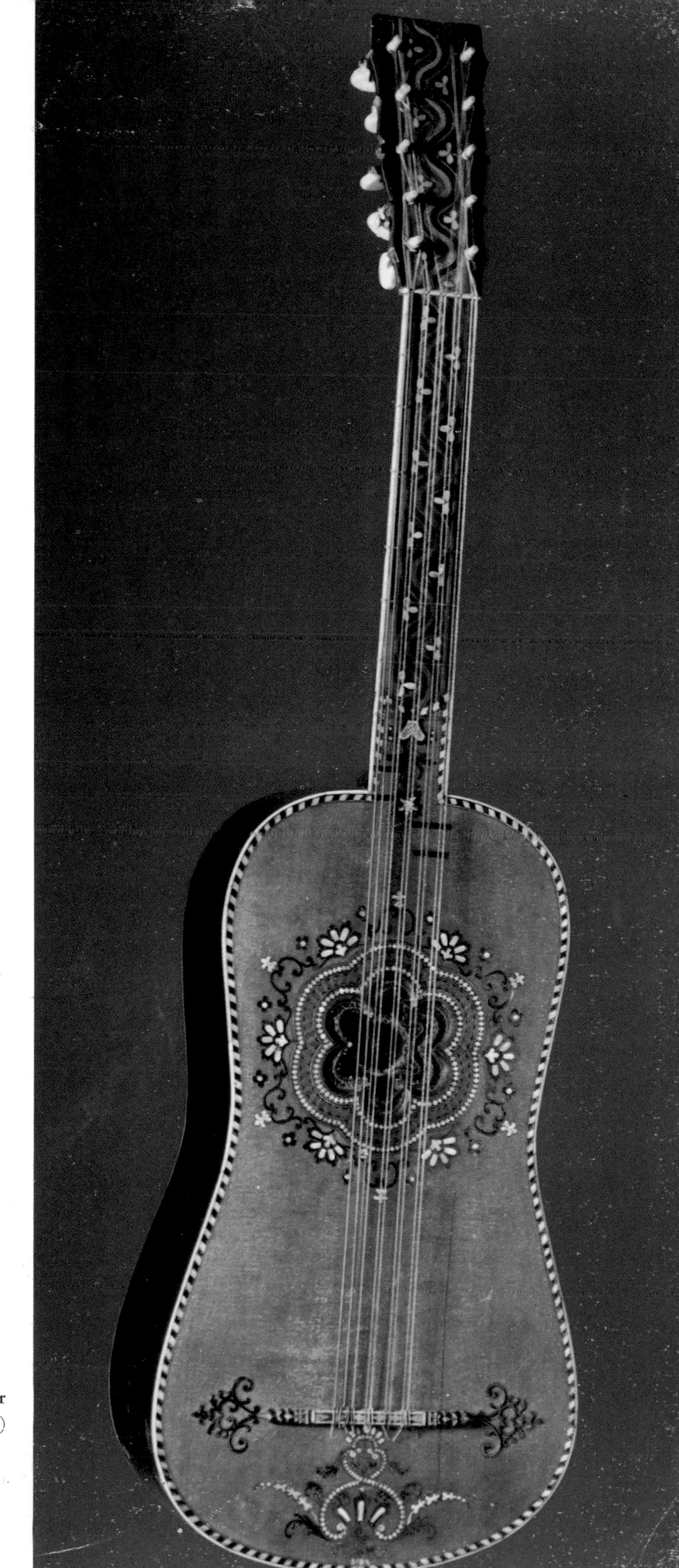

V. — 2. **Spanish guitar**
(early 19th century)

V. — 3. **Sound-hole of a French cittern** (1774)

V. — 4. **French harp** (18th century) ▶

V. — 5. **Belgian viol**
(1750)

V. — 6. **French lu**
(1750) ►

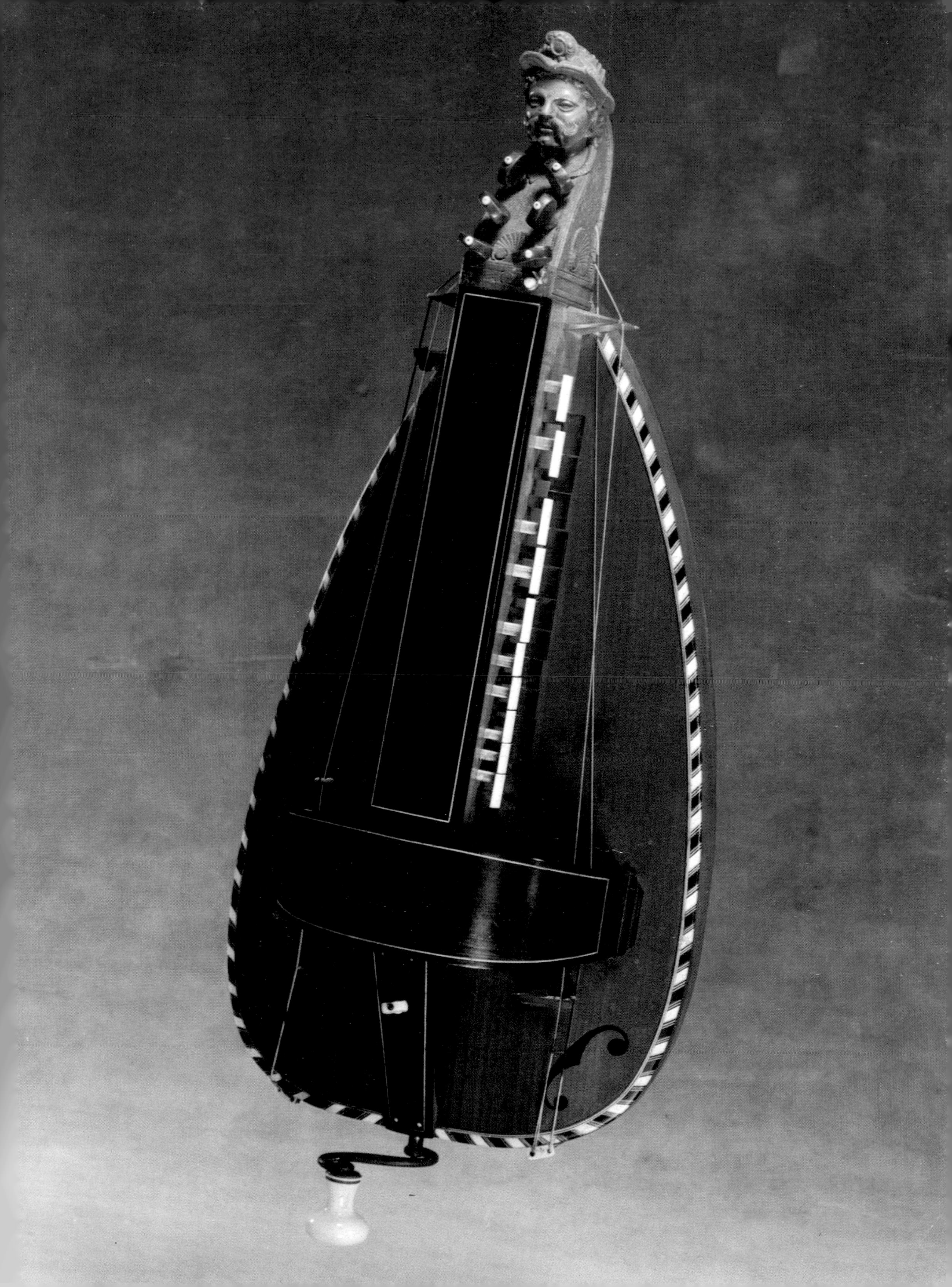

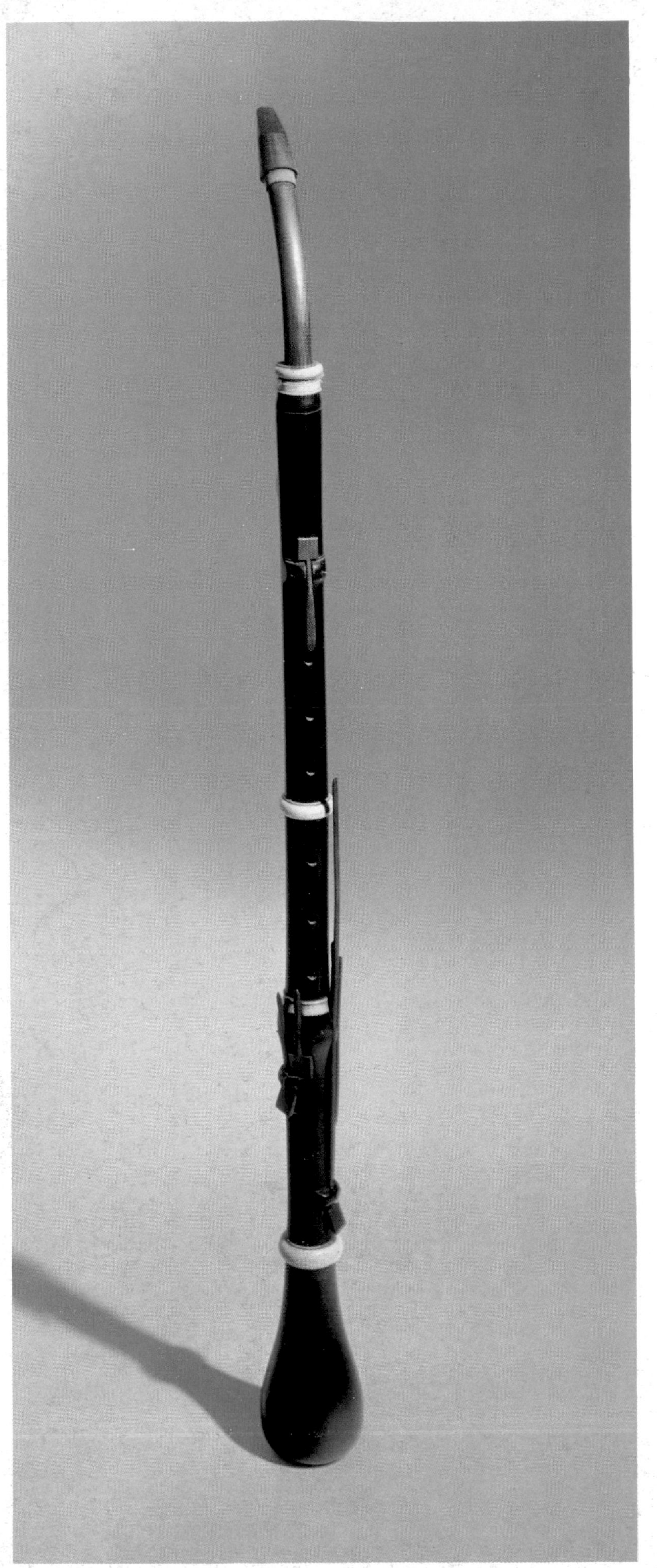

V. — 7. **Belgian clarinette d'amour**
(18th century)

V. — 8. **Belgian key bugle**
(early 19th century) ▶

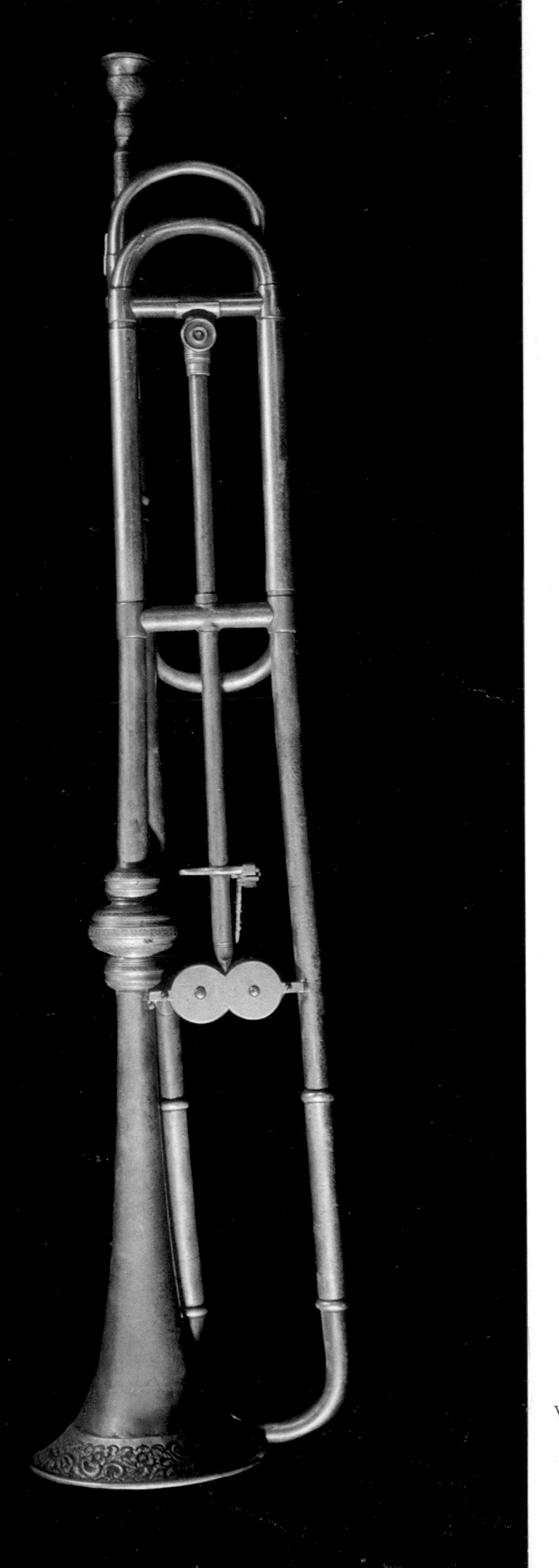

V. — 9. **English trumpet**
(19th century)

V. — 6.

Lute-vielle by Jean Louvet, the third of a succession of makers in the Louvet family. He worked in Paris in the middle of the 18th century. The instrument dates from 1750. The adjustable "trumpet" string is placed underneath the "fly" string. It rests on a mobile bridge like that of the tromba marina. Besides citterns and hurdy-gurdies, Louvet the Younger made violins and even harps. He edited music and organized concerts in France for Johann Stamitz.
Length: *c.* 26⅜ ins.

M.I., Brussels.
No. 521.

V. — 7.

Clarinette d'amour by Godefroid Adrien Rottenburgh. This "woodworker" was active in Brussels where he was born in 1709 and died in 1790. This fine instrument is tuned in *G*, and is of boxwood. The mouthpiece tube is of copper and is slightly curved; there are 6 keys.
Length: *c.* 35¼ ins.

M.I., Brussels.
No. 2595.

V. — 8.

Key bugle made by C. Devaster in Brussels at the beginning of the 19th century. This instrument has 6 silver keys with engraved silver plating. The body is of an alloy of copper and zinc (pinchbeck). By releasing the first key, which opens by means of a spring, the instrument can be raised a semitone.
Length of tube: *c.* 53⅛ ins.

M.I., Brussels.
No. 2738.

V. — 9.

English slide trumpet by J. Goddison (London, 1838-1898). Besides the slide mechanism, the instrument is provided with 7 crooks which fit into each other. The slide trumpet was still played in England when it had been abandoned on the Continent in favour of valve trumpets.
Height (without crooks): *c.* 26 ins.

M.I., Brussels.
No. 3157.

allow it more freedom of movement and greater control over playing.

The reason we have given the names of a number of renowned bow-makers above is that bow-making is a delicate art and it takes a man of considerable skill to succeed in it. For this reason, bows of quality are rare. Sometimes the nut was decorated with inlays of tortoiseshell, silver or gold, although these had no bearing whatsoever on the quality of the bow itself.

Wind Instruments

The recorder now passed from favour, and its place was decisively won over by the transverse flute, whose sound, though not always so soft, was more powerful. It became so fashionable that even monarchs and the most powerful of the bourgeois did not disdain to play it, whether well or badly. Besides Frederick II, King of Prussia, who composed several works for the instrument, we find Stanislas, King of Poland, the Prince of Carignan, the farmer general La Pouplinière, who also had his own orchestra, and many others played the instrument. They even went so far as to have their portraits painted, transverse flute in hand; it was all in the accepted style of the period.

On account of such an infatuation, and also because the instrument seemed to hold such high hopes of a brilliant future, the makers did their utmost to endow it with new refinements. The same was true of other wind instruments.

At first, it was allowed that the keys served for the production of the chromatic notes, but before long this rule came to be less strictly observed. The flute (for from now on we shall so refer to the transverse flute) as it was known in 1774, had four keys. We do not know who added the last three which yielded, respectively, *F*, *G*♯ and *B*♭ (we cannot, in fact, count as a second key that which Quantz added in about 1726 so as to obtain *E*♭, since this innovation was abandoned immediately). After 1774, Florio, an Italian flautist who lived in Paris and in London, added two supplementary open keys, *C* and *C*♯. In 1786, the German flautist Tromlitz added the long *F* key. In France, Tulou's (1786-1865) eight-keyed flute was played.

Not every flautist necessarily adopted these innovations, some of them, taking as their point of departure the five-keyed flute, preferring to add to their instruments those of the new keys that best served their requirements.

Till the time of Boehm, of whom we shall speak in the next chapter, no further improvement of importance was to be brought to any aspect of the key mechanism.

The first metal flutes, for which Miller was responsible, appeared in about 1810. The use of this material allowed the English flautist Charles Nicholson (1795-1837) to make the holes considerably larger, thus giving his instrument a stronger and more brilliant tone.

The clarinet in turn was given supplementary keys: firstly, shortly before 1764, the third and fourth keys, and then, two years later, the fifth key which was the work of Fritz of Brunswick, whilst in 1791 Xavier Lefèvre of Paris added the sixth.

Here we give the successive additions in so far as we can determine them from the numerous clarinets of the time that have been preserved. However, the Parisian maker Amlingue is on record as having, as early as 1782, made six- and seven-keyed clarinets. In 1791, at the same time as or shortly after Lefevre's addition of a sixth key in Paris, the Berlin maker Floth produced an eight-keyed clarinet.

As may be seen, this was a period during which one innovation followed rapidly on another and it is not always easy to establish their chronology. As with the flute, the clarinet was often made to the specifications of the virtuosos who played it, and we find Anton Stadler (1753-1812), for example, obliged to extend his instrument in order to be able to reach the low notes of Mozart's *Clarinet Concerto* (1791). In his opus 26, Spohr explains what the clarinettist has to do to obtain such an extension.

It is the Russian, Ivan Müller (1786-1854) who must be accredited with the invention of the modern clarinet, with its thirteen keys. Now the instrument acquired a purer tone and could be used to modulate into keys that had till then been beyond its reach. When Müller presented his invention at the Paris Conservatoire, a committee, which included the composers Méhul, Gossec and Cherubini, found fault with it and declared the instrument worthless. However, far from being discouraged, Müller set about eliminating the imperfections of his clarinet, notably the system of padding the keys, and the instrument was greatly improved in 1817 by the Parisian maker Gentelet, working under the inventor's directives; now it commanded unanimous support, and entrenched itself so firmly that even after the introduction of the Boehm system (of which we speak later on) the thirteen-keyed model continued to be used all over Europe, and even in America.

The alto clarinet is mentioned for the first time in 1792. However, in Germany an alto clarinet of quite a different type had existed since 1770, when the maker A. Mayrhofer and his brother created a seven-keyed alto clarinet whose bore was narrow and whose upper part was bent back; in about 1800, rather than being made with a curve, it was made with a right-angled bend: this alto clarinet, in *F*, called the basset horn, was later given the straight shape which is known to us today.

The bass clarinet was made for the first time in 1792 by the maker Louis Lot, in Paris. He called it a *basso tuba*. Independently of him, Grenser of Dresden also made a bass clarinet in 1793. In 1807, this instrument was to be perfected by Desfontenelles, who constructed a model with seven holes and twelve keys.

In the same year, Dumas invented a different kind of clarinet, called the *basse guerrière*, and in 1810-11 a similar, but larger, clarinet called the *contrebasse guerrière*. In 1812, Sautermeister, in Lyons, made a *basse-orgue*, and in 1835 Catterini of Bologna made a *glicibarifono*. But it is to Adolphe Sax of Dinant, at the time still living in Brussels, that must go the credit for having in 1836 given the bass clarinet its present form, that of twenty keys attached to a body in boxwood. It may be noted in passing that an Italian maker called Papalini attempted to reduce the length of the bass clarinet and thus to make it easier to handle by making it and its bore in a zigzag shape, but this invention did not meet with the hoped-for success.

The *clarinette d'amour*, which was used for the first time in the opera *Themistocle* (1772) by Johann Christian Bach and which a pear-shaped bell like that of the oboe d'amore, from which it had also taken its crook, was very quickly forgotten. Nevertheless, it was still used in chamber music in about 1800 in the Low Countries, above all in Brabant and Flanders.

It should be noted that of all the wind instruments the clarinet possess the widest range, since it is divided into three registers, the low, the middle and the high, and these taken together extend to four octaves plus a fourth. It has a great and varied scope in performance: it is capable of rapid or difficult passage-work, made easy by the precision and adaptability of the key mechanism, of smooth *legatos*, made possible by the addition, in 1823 by C. Janssen in Paris, of sliding rollers which enabled the player to pass smoothly from one key to another, of trills, repeated notes, etc.; depending on which register is used or on the loudness of tone, the timbre might be suave, biting, piercing, or even neutral. In short, the clarinet is to the wind instruments what the violin is to the bowed string instruments. Mozart was the first to exploit all its resources and Beethoven did not omit to use it in the majority of his orchestral works.

Finally, it should be noted that there is a difference of timbre and of manufacture between French and German clarinets: generally the bore of the latter is narrower and their single reed shorter, thereby producing a more acidulous and penetrating sonority.

Military serpent

The Count of Adhémar claimed to possess an oboe made by Hotteterre and having two silver keys; furthermore, the model given as an example of the oboe in the *Encyclopédie* of Diderot and d'Alembert — begun in 1751 and completed with its supplements in 1777 — also shows two keys. However, in Germany at this time, the oboe would have three keys, two of which were added in 1727 by the maker Gerhard Hoffmann; this means that the Germans previously had a one-keyed oboe. Clearly, the subject is open to much controversy. However that may be, we can be certain that as from the end of the eighteenth century or the beginning of the nineteenth, the French oboe had four keys, the last two of which were added by Sallantin, a teacher at the Paris Conservatoire; this we are told by his successor Gustave Vogt (1781-1870) in an unpublished *Méthode pour le hautbois*. Vogt states that at the time the German oboe had up to nine keys, but that this increase in the number of keys was considered to have more disadvantages than uses. In Paris, preference was still shown for the four-keyed oboe.

As with the clarinet, the oboe was made differently in France and in Germany. The French workshops continued the tradition of the Hotteterres: the tube was very narrow, and on the outside did not have the rings on which the keys had been fixed in the previous period; these were attached directly to the tube with screws; the tone was thinner and more brilliant. On the other hand, in Germany and in Austria oboes were thicker and consequently more solid; they might have up to ten keys and these were fixed on with rings.

The bassoon, which had not seen any notable improvements during the period, was given two keys in addition to the two already existing in about 1750; the fifth arrtved in 1760, and afer that date the numder continued to grow until, in 1827, Adler was able to introduce a bassoon he had made with fifteen keys.

In 1782, Dominique Porthaux had considered replacing the metal crook with a wooden one, but this innovation was a total failure. In 1816, Asté (also called Halary) made bassoons of copper, wishing to use the same material for this instrument as that (which he planned to use for the *ophicleide* or keyed serpent which we shall be coming to presently) for which he had already built prototypes at this time.

Apart from the fact that it was made with six keys at the beginning of the nineteenth century by Schuster of Vienna, the double bassoon scarcely changed during the classical period. It reached France in 1800, when Haydn's *The Creation* was performed in Paris. Like the bassoon, and following the example of German military music, it was taken up by certain French infantry bands.

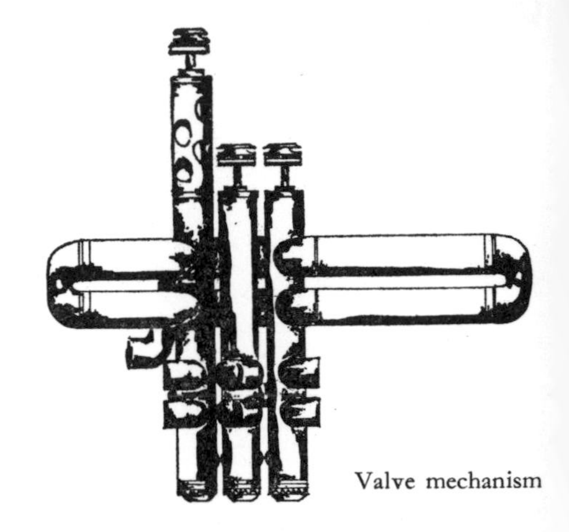
Valve mechanism

With regard to brass, there was nothing really new before the start of the nineteenth century. In 1810, Joseph Halliday of London built an instrument with conical bore that was provided with keys, and gave it the name of *Kent-horn*, because the Duke of Kent immediately made use of it in his military band. When Napoleon fell, the British staged a triumphal entry into Paris (1815), and the French heard this instrument for the first time. The maker Asté made use of the opportunity to acquire one and immediately started work on plans to build a keyed horn of a larger model. In fact, the Kent-horn was known on the continent as the *keyed horn* (*cor à clefs*), or *keyed trumpet* or even *keyed bugle*. It was in 1817 that Asté presented three instrumental prototypes to the *Académie royale des Beaux-arts de l'Institut de France* in order to apply for a patent; one of these was a keyed horn which sounded lower than the Kent-horn and to which he gave the name of ophicleide. It was not until 1821 that he obtained a patent for an eight-keyed ophicleide, though soon he increased the number of keys to twelve. However, even before it had been patented, this new instrument had already been used to enrich the orchestral palette, since it was used for the first time in 1819 in Spontini's opera *Olympie*. In spite of a tone that was vulgar to such a point that Mendelssohn used it in *A Midsummer Night's Dream* (1826) to imitate the roaring of a lion, the ophicleide filled a role as the bass member of the keyed bugle family and, until about 1850, remained the principal bass instrument in military bands; at that time it was replaced in Germany and Belgium by the *tuba*, a valve instrument.

At the Paris Conservatoire, the ophicleide replaced the *serpent*, a wind instrument with mouthpiece which owed its name to the fact that it had a long, broad tube that was curved in the shape of an "S", and sometimes even a double "S". In short, the serpent was none other than the bass of the old cornett. Tradition has it that it was invented by Canon Edme Guillaume who lived at Auxerre at the end of the sixteenth century. However, it would seem that the instrument could be found several decades earlier in Italy and even in France in about 1450, notably in the church at Sens. In fact, the serpent was much used in French

Crescent

churches to support the voices of the singers in unison. At the time when it gave way to the ophicleide, the latter took over this role from it, as well as its part in military bands. As with the other wind instruments, the serpent was provided with keys over the course of the years. In about 1780, a certain Régibo of Lille thought of giving it the form of a bassoon. This innovation was taken up again in about 1800 by Frichot, a French maker domiciled in London, who, instead of wood, used brass as his material, calling his instrument the *bass horn*. Before long, this instrument was embellished with a dragon's head at its extremity. It spread rapidly through England and Germany, and only returned to France in this new form in 1815, at the time of the invasion of the allied forces. For this reason, this *military serpent* was known there either as the *English serpent* or as the *Russian bassoon*.

It may be noted in passing that in 1799 the Belgian composer Gossec, one of the founders of the Paris Conservatoire, wrote a *Méthode de Serpent*.

The bass horn, furnished with supplementary keys, became chromatic. It was in this form that it served as a basis for another instrument, the *bass tuba*, invented in 1835 by Wieprecht and Moritz in Berlin.

The keyed bugle, the ophicleide, the bass horn, and virtually all the brass instruments having keys, were to gradually disappear and give way to instruments using valves.

The invention of valves in 1815 by Heinrich Stölzel, of Saxony, (although this mechanism seems to have been discovered, though not applied, earlier in the century by the Silesian, Friedrich Blühmel) made it possible for those metal wind instruments with a mouthpiece to take very important steps forward.

Apart from the trombone and the tromba da tirarsi, which had slide mechanisms, no other instrument with a metal tube, such as the horn and trumpet, could yield any different fundamental notes or their harmonics without recourse to crooks of different sizes which had to be fitted manually into the body of the instrument. The snag was that this operation took quite some time. The best thing would have been for it to be carried out mechanically, or in other words automatically.

This is what Stölzel achieved by linking secondary tubes of differing length to the instrument's body. If these tubes remained closed, only the principal tube, that is, the only one that had existed previously, emitted the appropriate fundamental note and its harmonics. If, on the other hand, thanks to the system called the valve system, a secondary tube was opened so as to come into play together with the principal tube, it extended this by its own length minus the length of the principal tube between its inserted ends, and consequently modified the fundamental and its harmonics. Thus if, for example, instead of one secondary tube, three were used, each having a different length, three extensions of the principal tube could be obtained by opening each of the secondary tubes in turn in the manner described above. Thus, a total of four different fundamentals could be yielded. Furthermore, if, instead of a single secondary tube, two of these tubes were brought into play at the same time, or the three together, still more corresponding extensions of the principal tube could be obtained, hence a greater number of fundamentals and their harmonics. So in this way, thanks to the valve system, the instrument could without difficulty give a chromatic succession of fundamentals and their harmonics. At first, Stölzel's valves were rectangular in cross-section, but after 1818 they became cylindrical.

The horn was the first brass instrument to benefit from the valve system. Shortly afterwards, the trumpet was fitted with it; however, for some time it continued to be played using the older systems — the slide trumpet (especially played in England), that with crooks and the keyed model. The valve horn and valve trumpet were introduced to France in about 1825.

Next came the *cornet*, which had once been a hunting instrument, and to which Asté added valves in 1828. Its tone was rather vulgar; however, Rossini used it in his *William Tell* in 1829.

At the end of the eighteenth century and the beginning of the nineteenth there was a greatly increased contact with the East; it was in this way that certain Asian instruments appeared in Europe. One such, in particular, was the *sheng*, a free-reed instrument originating in the region which today forms Laos and Cambodia. This instrument prompted the Austrian, Anton Haeckl, to invent the *physharmonica*, which consisted of free reeds which were set in vibration by the air contained in bellows. As these were too clumsy, Buschmann of Berlin took up the elements of the physharmonica in 1822 and made two more manageable instruments: the *mouth harmonica* and the *accordion*. For his part, the Englishman Charles Wheatstone in 1829 invented the *symphonium*, characterised by reeds which could only vibrate if released by buttons which served as keys. The reason we mention this instrument, whose existence was short-lived, is that it gave rise to the *concertina*, invented in England in 1844, which enjoyed a great vogue, and which is still frequently played by clowns of the present day.

Percussion Instruments

Those which had been played in the previous period continued to be used. There were practically no new instruments apart from the *triangle*, made from a cylindrical rod bent, as its name implies, in the shape of an open triangle. It existed well before this date, since, in 1585, J. Cellier introduced one that was mounted with six rings whose tinkling was added to that of the rod when it was set in vibration by being struck either with the hand or with a straight rod, itself of steel. J. Cellier called this sort of triangle a *cimballe*.

The triangle itself became part of the orchestra at the beginning of the nineteenth century. It belonged to what, in orchestral parlance, was known as the "Turkish band", a term which designated the noisier group of percussion instruments. The name was used because the Turks had these instruments, as well as others like the *crescent*, in their military bands, and made abundant use of then; Westerners in the course of their campaigns against the Ottomans in the seventeenth and eighteenth centuries, became familiar with them and adopted them for their own military bands. The first to use this "Turkish music" were the Prussians, the Poles and the Russians; then, in the eighteenth century, it spread over

. — 10.

arpsichord made in London in 73 by Burkat Shudi and John roadwood. The archives of the roadwood house seem to indicate at this harpsichord was offered by ederick the Great of Prussia to the npress Maria Theresa of Austria. has two manuals, two pedals and e stops. The left pedal operates e characteristically English "ma-ine stop". The right pedal opens series of boards which Shudi called e "Venetian swell". These boards, an arrangement like a Venetian ind, enable the player to vary e intensity.
ength: *c.* 107¼ ins.

M.I., Brussels.
No. 1604.

— 11.

uare piano by Meyncke Meyer d Pieter Meyer of Amsterdam 782). This instrument does not ve escapement. It possesses a stop erated by two levers. This orte", releasing the dampers, is vided in two sections, each cover-g half of the keyboard. This ano's hammers are covered in ather; its range is 5 octaves.
ength: *c.* 58 ins.

M.I., Brussels.
No. 2953.

all Europe. Soon it was seized upon for theatre music, which would make use of one or other of its elements, if not all of them at once, and particularly when the opera in question dealt with "turqueries"; examples are the bass drum in Gluck's *Les Pèlerins de la Mecque* (1764) and in Mozart's *Die Entführung aus dem Serail* (1782), the cymbals in Gluck's *Iphigénie en Tauride* (1782), the triangle, bass drum and cymbals in Grétry's *Caravane du Caire* (1783), etc.

The crescent consisted of a stand surmounted by metallic crescents and circles on which were suspended jingles and small bells which were sounded by shaking the stand. It was used only in military bands. One of the first mentions of it dates from 1783, and concerns the crescent which was a part of the Duke of York's band. It was barely used at all after 1840, except in Germany, but at the end of the nineteenth century it made its appearance in the symphony orchestra of the Impressionists.

It is worth mentioning that one of Haydn's "London Symphonies" (1791-1794), the *Military Symphony*, was sometimes known as the *Turkish Symphony* because, besides the usual percussion section, it called on a triangle, cymbals and bass drum.

Keyboard Instruments

The harpsichord, which at the time of Ruckers had a keyboard of four octaves, extended its range by seven notes at the bottom and five at the top. By this means, the harpsichord now had a range of five octaves, and as we have already said in the last chapter, many harpsichords belonging to the previous period were transformed in such a way as to offer an equally extensive keyboard themselves. This operation of *ravalement* was carried out especially in France, and two great artists in this field were François-Etienne Blanchet II (1729-1766) and his Walloon apprentice, Pascal Taskin (1723-1793) who, a few months after the death of his master, succeeded him, at the same time marrying his widow. We may point out that his nephew Pascal-Joseph Taskin (1750-1829), who had also made the journey from Theux to Paris at a very early age, set out to rival his uncle, whom he was later to succeed, by marrying Blanchet's daughter, and thus became his uncle's son-in-law.

In 1768, Pascal Taskin introduced his "buff" harpsichord, so called because the quills placed at the end of the jacks had been replaced by small pieces of buff-leather, hardened in oil. It is thought by some that a similar practice was current in the sixteenth and seventeenth centuries. Whatever the case may be, it must be allowed that Pascal Taskin had made several attempts, notably with darts and even fragments of horseshoes, before succeeding with the pieces of buff-leather in obtaining a softer plucking of the strings. This search for a softer stop for the harpsichord, which had had to do without one hitherto, was motivated by a desire to bestow on it a quality which its younger rival, the pianoforte, already possessed, and so to enable it to put up a fight on equal terms with it.

In addition, the same Taskin, having replaced the sliding stops first with knee-pieces and then with pedals so that the stops could be changed more easily, created a stop whose express purpose was to produce every possible variation of loudness from *piano* to *forte*, though in this he did not succeed completely, since such treatment was contrary to the nature of the plucked string.

Finally, as we have already pointed out in the previous chapter, Burkat Shudi, John Broadwood's associate in London, used a series of planks in the form of a shutter in order to obtain *crescendi* and *decrescendi* on the harpsichord; he patented this device under the name of the Venetian Swell. This shutter, taking the place of a lid above the sound-board, could be opened to different degrees so as to release the sound, and was operated by a pedal.

All these attempts to enable the harpsichord to carry off a victory over the new invader that was the piano — which was still at a growing-up stage — were in vain. The piano was about to establish itself permanently. However, Rossini (1792-1868) still claimed to prefer the use of the harpsichord in the teaching of singers.

The *clavicytherium*, or upright harpsichord, which had fallen into disuse for two centuries, reappeared, but in a larger format, and was made by makers such as Delin (1751), Despinois (1763) and Obert (1763).

We may now pass on to the instruments with struck strings. First of all, we find the clavichord again, its keyboard having reached a range of five octaves in the first half of the eighteenth century, and the instrument now being unfretted rather than, as before, fretted. This instrument was to undergo no further modifications. It was at the end of its evolution, and would shortly give way to the piano. Certain composers continued to show a fair amount of appreciation for it. Of these, Carl Philipp Emmanuel Bach (1714-1788) considered that to play the clavichord was the most difficult of all things and that one could not judge a harpsichord player until one had heard him play the clavichord, for — as Bach's pupil, the Alsatian Nicolas-Joseph Hüllmandel also declared in his *Encyclopédie méthodique*, published by Framery and Ginguené — "practising the clavichord is excellent for perfecting one's touch. The slightest difference in the pressure of the fingers can be heard on it, and the least irregularity can create a bad effect".

Aside from its expressive qualities, the clavichord had one or two defects, not the least of which was an extremely weak, seemingly secretive sonority. The mechanism by which the string was struck allowed it to produce a variety of dynamic levels, either in contrast or in a constant build-up, but in view of the instrument's tonal weakness, its notes could not be sounded with a strong enough contrast or with a sufficiently pronounced build-up to satisfy the demands the Romantics were soon to make to the end of expressing their egos. This was why the clavichord's life drew to a peaceful close at the end of the eighteenth century, though not before it received the tribute of C.P.E. Bach's attachment to it, an attachment that is apparent in several of his works, and particularly in that moving piece *Adieu à mon clavicorde* which the composer addressed to his favourite instrument at a time when he and it were forced to part, and in the second of his *Sonaten für Kenner und Liebhaber* (1779) where, already, hints of Beethoven's music crop up.

It was the piano that was to set its seal on the classical period. It was invented in three different places by three makers of different

V. — 12.

Triangular piano in the form of a spinet by the maker Johannes Schmahl and dating from the middle of the 18th century. The strings are on a level absolutely parallel with the keyboard. The leather hammers are arranged as in the Viennese piano mechanism. They are threaded on a string that is held by a peg. There is only one string to each key; on the other hand, the instrument has five stops: a mute — a silk ribbon — a felt damper, a harp stop, a forte and a transposing stop. Length: *c.* 46¼ ins.

M.I., Brussels. No. 1630.

V. — 13.

Grand piano, bearing on the left-hand side of its sound-board the original label: "*Jean André Stein faiseur d'orgues, de clavecins et organiste à l'Eglise des Minoristes à Augsburg* 1786". A pupil of the famous Strasbourg organ-builder Jean André Silbermann (1712-1783), Jean André Stein (Hildesheim 1728 - Augsburg 1792) concerned himself mainly with making numerous pianos, the balance of whose sound and whose solidity were praised by Mozart himself. In this piano the row of dampers is still operated by means of a knee-piece which could be operated by either the left or the right knee. It was not until 1789 that Stein replaced the knee-piece by a pedal. The range of the keyboard is five octaves. Length: *c.* 84¾ ins.

M.I., Brussels. No. 163[illegible]

V. — 10. **English harpsichord** (1773)

◀ V. — 11. **Dutch square piano** (1782)

V. — 12. **German triangular piano** (*c*. 1770)

V. — 13. **German grand piano** (1786)

V. — 14. **German square piano** (1783) ▶

◀ V. — 15. **Glass harmonica** (18th century)

V. — 16. **French flute-playing organ mechanism** (1838)

V. — 17. **Dutch componium** (1821)

nationalities and within a relatively short space of time. It did not establish itself immediately, for at first it suffered from a number of imperfections which made it impossible for the instrument to compete with the harpsichord. But since it had from the first displayed resources which corresponded to a mode of expression which was beginning to make itself felt, the makers of this new instrument, far from balking at the difficulties, sought to eliminate its defects, and gradually succeeded in doing so.

The idea of making an instrument with struck strings and keyboard is a very ancient one, for it had already been realized in the Middle Ages with the dulcimer, the clavichord, and possibly with the mysterious échiquier.

Since the invention of the piano came at a time when the harpsichord reigned supreme it is hardly surprising to find that it was soon known as the "harpsichord with hammers"; in fact, its case was the same shape as the harpsichord's, its strings were disposed in the same direction as the harpsichord's with respect to its keyboard, and thus it could not be related to the clavichord; and besides, the latter was hardly used outside Germany at the time, and it used a fixed tangent to strike the strings, rather than the hammer which had, in the piano, been free-moving from the first.

At any rate, it was as a *gravicembalo col piano e forte* that Bartolommeo Cristofori (1653/5-1731) introduced his invention in 1709 or in 1711. He built about twenty similar instruments. Two of these have come down to us; one of them dates from 1720, and already has two strings for each note, and it may be found in the Metropolitan Museum of New York, and the other, of 1725, is in the Instrumental Museum of Leipzig. The latter possesses the very important escapement mechanism which establishes a connection between the key and the hammer, obliging the latter to fall back into place without a jolt after it has struck the string. Moreover, the same model that has been preserved at Leipzig has the means of playing *una corda*, in other words, it is possible to move the hammers so that they strike only one of the two strings tuned in unison that go to make a course; in this way, the hammer only striking one of the two strings, a less powerful sonority could be obtained. This possibility of moving the hammer was subsequently to be abandoned, and was only taken up again later, when the wooden frame was replaced by a metallic frame. In 1716, the Parisian maker Jean Marius, who had in 1700 invented the *clavecin de voyage*, introduced a piano which he called *clavecin à maillets* (harpsichord with hammers). Finally, the German Schröter introduced the court at Dresden to a similar instrument in 1722.

Neither Cristofori nor Marius nor Schröter knew each other and it was probably because such an idea was "in the air" (for such things have frequently been known to happen) that they all independently arrived at the same result. Of these three makers only Schröter admitted having been inspired by the pantaleon of Hebenstreit, which was not surprising, since they knew each other, living in the same town, and the pantaleon was played all over Germany and particularly in Dresden, where Hebenstreit had been attached to the Polish Royal Chamber since 1708 in order to play his instrument there.

In Germany it was, above all, Gottfried Silbermann (1683-

1753), one of a family of instrument makers, who, taking his lead from Cristofori's mechanism, tried to improve on it. In 1736, he presented a *Hammerclavier* he had made to J.S. Bach, but the latter was critical of its high notes, finding them too weak-toned. Silbermann once more set about his labours and, in 1747, Bach registered his complete satisfaction with the results of them.

Soon, in Germany, the wing-shape that had been taken over from the harpsichord was abandoned in favour of rectangular shape and the lay-out of the strings of the clavichord was adopted; by these means, the piano became smaller and less expensive.

Just as the clavicytherium, the upright harpsichord, was now again in production, upright pianos began to be made, and these appeared in two forms: firstly there was the pyramidal shape, exemplified in the piano built in 1745 by the German maker Friderici of Gera, then later, more closely derived from the clavicytherium, came the *Giraffe piano*, whose shape may be thought of as that of a piano identical to a harpsichord whose sound-board was placed vertically instead of horizontally.

The *pyramidal piano* met with hardly any success. On the other hand, another piano, whose case, instead of being rectangular, was in the shape of a spinet, such as those built by Schmahl of Ulm, was favourably received.

The first pianos still had many points in common with harpsichords. Although all were naturally instruments whose strings were struck with hammers, they also borrowed from the harpsichord certain stops, which were later gradually to disappear, and sometimes the swell-box too. Thus, at first English pianos had a lute stop and a Venetian swell. Johannes Schmahl's piano, whose construction is a small miracle, offered the following stops: damper, sourdine I, sourdine II, lute, and also a mechanism by which the keyboard and hammers could be displaced so that the latter came opposite the next string upwards and the music could be transposed up a semitone. As for the maker Johann Gottlob Wagner of Dresden, he constructed in 1783 a small piano which had four stops giving sourdine, forte, fortissimo and lute. All this proves that if by now most preferences went for the pianoforte, there was nonetheless a certain regret concerning the different capabilities possessed by the harpsichord.

In 1783, John Broadwood introduced the use of the pedal on the piano; until then, knee-pieces or buttons had been used to operate the registers. The first pianist to make consistent use of this pedal pianoforte was the composer John Field (1782-1837).

Soon — it is not known why — the rectangular piano was known as the *square piano*. The first English square piano was made in 1765 by Johannes Zumpe. This maker, like some others, the chief of whom being Jacob Kirckmann, was of German origin and had been compelled to leave his homeland because of unemployment after the Seven Years War. These makers had settled in England which derived the benefit of their experience in the making of pianos. They were joined by Burkat Shudi, who came from German Switzerland.

The first *upright piano* was built in 1807 by William Southwell of Dublin. As the tension of the strings over the sound-board had become extremely strong (in a modern piano it can be as much as twenty tons) and also since the makers had to make an opening in this board through which the hammers could pass to strike the strings, makers found themselves faced with a delicate problem which was not solved until, in 1777, the Londoner, William Stodart reinforced the sound-board with tubular bars. This system was improved in 1808 by Isaac Hawkins in Philadelphia. A still stronger reinforcement was provided by placing parallel metal bars over the strings; it is still disputed as to whether this improvement was the work of John Broadwood in 1821, or of Sébastien Erard (1752-1831), an Alsatian who had settled in Paris and founded the famous firm which is still in existence today, and who specialised in making pianos and harps. Finally, in 1825, the American, Alpheus Babcock of Boston moulded in a single piece the first frame entirely in cast iron. All these improvements led to the possibility of using longer and thicker strings which had a more powerful sonority.

Let us now go back to the beginning so as to trace the evolution of piano mechanism, whose role is of the first importance.

The first mechanism, known as single action, was used in Cristofori's first pianos, in those of Silbermann and those of his pupil Zumpe, who introduced it to England. Its chief characteristic was that the hammer was fixed onto the frame rather than to a key. When the key was depressed, it came into contact with the hammer which in turn struck the string. This mechanism, clearly a very simple one, did not give much control over tone-production; besides, if the key was struck too hard, there was a risk that the hammer might rebound and in this way strike the string for a second time.

For this reason, Cristofori introduced the double action mechanism on his 1726 piano. This action, taken up by Silbermann and improved by Zumpe, was dubbed the pilot mechanism. In fact, the mechanism had a hopper or pilot, fixed on the end of the key; when the key was depressed, the hopper operated a lever which passed the impulse on to the hammer. After striking the string, the latter fell back into its initial position.

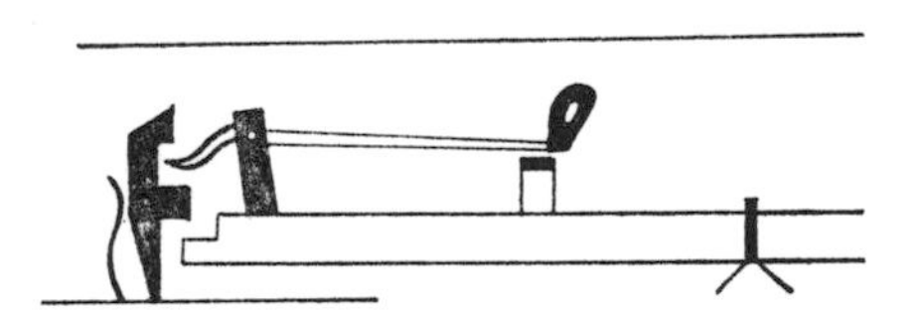

Already the result was better, but still it was not adequate. It was then that Erard, who had already invented a sort of double-pilot hammer action perfected, in 1794, the escapement mechanism which allowed the hammer to free itself of its activating lever at a distance of two millimetres from the string. This mechanism had the advantage over the pilot mechanism of making the hammer's contact with the string more precise, but did not yet allow a rapid repetition of the hammer's striking of the string since the key had to return to its normal position and the hammer to its original position before the mechanism could again be activated.

It was not for another thirty years that this rapid repetition was possible, despite the many efforts of makers of different countries who were bent on resolving this problem, and it was once again Sébastien Erard who, in 1822, created the double escapement mechanism, which he introduced to the public at the time of the 1823 Paris Exhibition. This was an invention of genius that has since never been paralleled in this field.

As for the German mechanisms, their chief characteristic was that the head of the hammer was placed towards the player, the rest of the mechanism being further away. Thus this was a head-to-tail arrangement. It is possible to distinguish between the *Stossmechanik* and the *Prellmechanik* by ascertaining whether the hammers were attached to the frame or to the keys.

In about 1770, the Augsburg maker Johann Stein provided the *Prellmechanik* with an escapement. His pianos are characterised by the short course of their hammers and their extremely light touch, imitating that of the clavichord. Since Stein's daughter Nanette, left an orphan, married in 1793 the pianist Andreas Streicher, himself a piano-maker who transferred Stein's piano-making business to Vienna, the mechanism with which these pianos were provided came to be known as the "Viennese action". It was after having for the first time played on a Stein piano in 1777 that Mozart adopted it as his favourite instrument, as we can see from many letters he wrote to his father.

The introduction in 1826 of felt-covered hammers is attributed to the French-naturalized German maker Johann Heinrich Pape (1789-1875), the possessor of a fertile imagination, for he is known to have been the father of at least 137 inventions. Also, conforming to a general tendancy of makers who, since Southwell, sought to reduce the size and the height of the upright piano, and taking his lead from Robert Wornam's cottage piano (1811) — the principle of which had been taken up in France by Ignace Pleyel (1757-1831) — Pape succeeded in building an upright piano so small that it was no larger than a small chest of drawers; this he called a console. However, this invention of Pape's would not have had any particularly striking significance if, in order to preserve the power of an ordinary upright piano, he had not thought of crossing strings, or overstringing. In fact, thanks to such overstringing, he was able to use strings — in an oblique position — that were just as long as those on a normal upright piano; furthermore, since all the strings passed over the centre of the sound-board, their tonal power was increased and conditions were more favourable to the production of harmonics. In short, Pape's *piano-console* soon became the equivalent of what the *pianino* has become today, for the invention was exploited, sometimes with minor variations, by foreign makers who even applied it to their ordinary upright pianos and their square pianos.

Finally, the damper, as its name implies, served to damp the sound of the string after it had been struck; this too underwent some developments. At first, this piece of wood which had at its end a bit of felt, was in the form of a jack, in imitation of the models used on the harpsichord. This type persisted until about 1830, though already, in 1800, the damper could be found directly fixed by means of supports to the case of a square piano. We can say no more about it here without going into details that are too technical. It should suffice us to add that, as from the second decade of the nineteenth century, two ways of making the damper act on the string can be distinguished in upright pianos: the one, known in France as the blade mechanism, is applied to the string below the point at which it is struck by the hammer, whilst the other, which the French call the bayonet mechanism (because the damper is activated by a metal rod bent in the shape of a bayonet) damps the string at a point above the point of impact. Each of these methods of damping had its partisans, but it was certainly

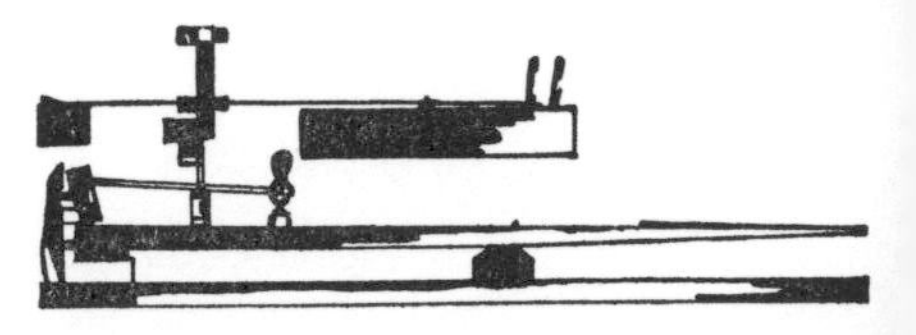

V. — 14.

This small square piano in Louis XVI style bears, on the inside of the instrument, the following manuscript inscription: "*Johann Gottlob Wagner / Orgel und Instrumente-Macher / Dresden* 24 *Decbr* 1783". This maker was born in Medingen (near Dresden) and died in Dresden itself in 1789. He was a pupil of Gottfried Silbermann. Johann Gottlob and his brother built about 800 keyboard instruments. We know of five still in existence in different museums: Berlin, Leipzig, Eisenach, Nuremberg and Brussels. The piano shown here shows certain characteristics of construction which recall those of the clavichord. It has four stops: mute, forte, grand forte and harp. Finally it should be pointed out that this piano already has the adjustable blade type of escapement mechanism. The keyboard has a range of four octaves and a fifth.
Length: *c.* 43¾ ins.

M.I., Brussels.
No. 1628.

V. — 15.

Glass harmonica, invented by the American physicist Benjamin Franklin (1706-1790), later to become Ambassador to France. The instrument shown here dates from the end of the 18th century and is by an unknown German maker. Franklin's invention consisted of fitting into a horizontal axis rows of glass bowls ranged in a semitonal series and overlapping each other without touching. The axis was rotated by means of a pedal, and since the bowls turned with it, it was necessary only to rub them with a moist finger for them to begin to vibrate and to sound. This instrument has 46 glasses, giving it a range of three octaves plus a sixth. The glasses yielding chromatic notes are edged with a gilt band.
Length: *c.* 50⅜ ins.

M.I., Brussels
No. 411

V. — 16.

Flute-playing organ mechanism by the Parisian maker Davrainville, dating from 1838. It was presented by Louis-Philippe to the officers of the French corvette *La Recherche* which had sailed around the world. The cylinder bristles with studs and staples which, once the cylinder is in rotation, lift copper keys; these open the valves of the wooden pipes. This mechanical organ has 32 pipes. Height: *c.* 30¾ ins.

M.I., Brussels. No. 459.

V. — 17.

Componium, bearing the mark: "*Diederich Nicolaus Winkel invenit et fecit, Amsterdam an.* 1821". Winkel, who died in 1826, also invented the metronome and a machine for weaving. The componium includes two distinct parts: on the one hand, the orchestrion and on the other, the componium which composes variations on an 80-bar theme. The orchestrion part has nine stops, a triangle and a drum. Height: *c.* 107¼ ins.

M.I., Brussels. No. 456.

the first, which acted on the string at a more central point, — thus where the vibrations were more pronounced — that was the more effective in fulfilling its appointed role.

The first composition which we are certain to have been specifically written for the piano dates from 1731 and was the work of Lodovico de Pistoia who, in the same year, wrote a set of twelve sonatas. Later, a number of works were inscribed "for the harpsichord or the pianoforte", for an individually pianistic style was far from having been established. It is still disputed as to whether such and such of Mozart's sonatas was written for the piano rather than for the harpsichord, and such doubts are greatly increased by the knowledge that by reason of its structure the Viennese action, with its shorter gap between hammer and string and its lighter touch, yielded a sonority which came quite close to that of the harpsichord, whereas the English and French mechanisms, giving a more powerful tone, had revolutionary effects on both composers and performers.

Though, in 1770, Clementi, an Italian who had settled in England and who was at the time barely 18 years old, wrote his *Sonatas for harpsichord or pianoforte*, he emerged three years later as an incomparable virtuoso of the piano and in 1817 published his famous *Gradus ad Parnassus*, a collection of studies for this instrument, and himself became a piano-maker. Moreover, the keyboard works written in Paris after 1770 clearly tended towards a pianistic style. It needed only the invention of the double escapement mechanism, which was taken up by makers the world over, for the harpsichord to be finally consigned to oblivion and for the race of virtuosos whose activities were a feature of the Romantic era to be born.

The organ hardly developed at all during this period. Organ-makers in the Low Countries were especially conservative, continuing to build the instrument on the basis of the principles of the first half of the eighteenth century.

French organ-making was halted by the Revolution; it was to flourish anew after 1840 with the romantic organ, conceived on different lines. In Italy a second manual and an independent pedal-board made their appearance. In England, only two cathedrals possessed organs that had pedal-boards with their own stops.

Finally, in Germany, stops imitating stringed instruments, such as had already appeared the South, became more widespread after 1750.

Mechanical Instruments

It will be recalled that we mentioned one Jan van Steenken, who seems to have built for Philip the Good, Duke of Burgundy, one, if not more, mechanical organs. We have no other evidence of this beyond a surviving document. It should also be mentioned that there exists in the Paris Instrumental Museum a mechanical spinet, of the seventeenth century, that is described and depicted by Buchner (*Mechanical Musical Instruments*, London).

In reality, it was not until the nineteenth century that there was any dissemination of automatic musical instruments. This is not the place to consider automatic toys, even those which played music, whose main purpose was to provoke amazement and curiosity rather than any musical interest. If this had been the case, we should have had to go back to Alexandrian times in order to trace the history of such devices, for in those days artificial birds were already made to sing, and then to speak of the mechanisms in use during the Renaissance, passing on to the already complex mechanisms of the eighteenth century; it was such mechanisms as these that enabled makers like Vaucanson (1709-1782), who was a highly skilled engineer, to construct decidedly rare musical toys, such as a tabor-player, a player of the transverse flute, and (nothing whatever to do with music) a duck which ate and digested food. Besides all these there were innumerable musical clocks, made above all in the Tyrol, which, at the striking of the hour, set in motion a cylinder like that of the carillon except that it was of wood and had studs and strips instead of nails, and these operated a series of pipes fed by air from a blower.

It was on the same lines (cylinder, pipes and blower) that small mechanical organs were built in the first half of the nineteenth century; these had only one set of pipes (which might correspond to the trumpet or the flute stop, for example) but their cylinder would move from left to right whilst rotating, so that they would not play the same tune again; the cylinders thus contained several fairly short pieces which followed one after the other, or else a single, longer work, such as an opera overture. When the cylinder had run its course it could be replaced by another, just as today we can replace one gramophone record by another. Of the most famous makers of this kind of instrument was the Frenchman Davrainville.

We now come to a unique and extraordinary instrument, one whose ingenious mechanism still provokes astonishment and admiration: this is the *Componium*, which its inventor, Diederich Nicolaus Winkel, so called because it was capable, once it had been set in motion and without any further attention, of playing a theme and so many variations of it that, with each variation lasting five minutes, it would take 138,000,000,000,000 years to exhaust them all. Obviously, we cannot here explain all the details of the technique behind such an achievement, atthough we may point out that the mechanism was based, not on one, but on two cylinders, each moving on its axis at the same time. However, neither of these had a continuous set of studs and strips. After a fixed stretch on which there were studs and strips there followed a further stretch of the same length which had none. Thus, if only one of the cylinders was set in motion, two bars of music would be heard, followed by two more bars, this time of silence. Moreover, since the second cylinder was made in the same way as the first, but with its bars of silence corresponding with the first cylinder's bars of music, all that was needed was for the two cylinders to turn at the same time in order produce a continuous stream of music The two could, in combination and in the course of one revolution, play the theme and seven variations. But, since each of the cylinders could be displaced to a greater or lesser extent by a longitudinal shifting operated by a mechanism which, once set in action, worked automatically, it was impossible to foresee the extent of shift it would impart to each of the cylinders or even to a single one, leaving the other to continue on its course without being shifted either to the right or to the left. As a result of these successive shifting movements of which neither the frequency nor the extent either to left or to right could be foreseen, since these were decided automatically by the mechanism alone, it was not always the same set of studs and strips on the second cylinder that followed those of the first, and vice versa. From this may be seen the multiplicity of the possible combinations engendered by such a system. We should add that the instrument had five different "stops" for its upper wind-chest, and for its lower wind-chest, four that were distinct from the others; the mechanism could bring these nine "stops" into play — still in an unpredictable way — either singly or by combining two, three or more of them, and in addition to the stops there was a triangle and a drum; consequently, here too, in this department of the componium's sound-production, there was a multiplicity of possible combinations.

Winkel, who was also the real inventor of the metronome, ruined himself in the research and execution of this prodigious instrument which he completed in 1821.

The mechanical organ with only one cylinder having metal studs and strips could be met with in a smaller form; this was the *barrel-organ*, in which the cylinder and blower were operated by a cranking device. It was possibly invented by the Modena maker Barberi (hence its French name of *orgue de Barbarie*), and he certainly played an important part in its dissemination. This cylinder, like those of musical clocks, contained several tunes which could be changed either by manually shifting the cylinder or by using a hand-lever. The latter method is still used today on barrel-organs.

Again, we should mention the *musical boxes* which made their appearance at about the end of the eighteenth century. They operated on the principle of a disc with studs which set in vibration a series of chromatically tuned blades (see Plate VI. - 17).

VI Romanticism and Impressionism

VI. — 1. **"The Orchestra of the Opéra" (Chabrier can be identified in the box),** by Edgar Degas

Historical Background

The great steps forward made in the production of wind instruments at the beginning of the nineteenth century were followed up throughout the whole period of Romanticism, thanks to the interest shown by composers in the varied and richly contrasting colours that could be drawn from these instruments.

The strings did not form the core of the orchestra any longer, but were rather balanced against the wind instruments, and in certain passages of orchestral works this balance might be swayed, sometimes even favouring the predominance of the wind instruments. The percussion also began to exercise a particular attraction for composers.

Now, the orchestra was enlarged both at the top and at the bottom: piccolos, trombones, double basses, double bassoons, bass tubas, etc. made their appearance. Sometimes it would happen that a composer — as is especially the case with Wagner — would include in his orchestra an instrument which would be specially made for him.

It follows that, in order for them to make themselves heard in the middle of a more and more sizeable orchestral ensemble, instruments which had a softer sound and a smaller voice, such as the clarinet and the transverse flute, had to be reconstructed with a larger bore so as to give them a greater sounding power.

In fact, Hector Berlioz (1803-1869) dreamed of a monster orchestra which would comprise no less than 467 instruments to which might be added massed choruses of 360 singers. To give an idea of this orchestra, details of which are given in Berlioz, *Traité d'instrumentation* (1844), we can say that it was made up of all the types of instruments to be found in the Beethovenian orchestra, but that there were many more instruments of each type and in addition a large number of others, either new or not previously used in an orchestra: on the one hand, 120 violins, 40 violas, 45 cellos... 12 bassoons ... 16 horns, etc., and on the other hand, among the newcomers, 4 *octo-basses* (invented shortly before by Vuillaume and abandoned almost immediately), 5 *saxophones*, 2 bass tubas... 12 pairs of antique cymbals on different notes, etc.; finally, believe it or not, this gargantuan orchestra required 30 harps and 30 pianos, instruments which till then had only been thought of as soloists.

This dream of Berlioz, was not realised by him but rather, sixty years later, by Gustav Mahler (1860-1911), in 1910 at Munich, when he produced his Eighth Symphony, called the "Symphony of a Thousand" because its first performance was given by a thousand musicians (more than half of whom were choral singers). Many composers of the Romantic era, starting with Meyerbeer and Wagner, together with many composers of later periods turned to this famous *Traité d'instrumentation* for ideas about the sorts of orchestra to use and how to use them.

A book such as the present one is not the place to include a study of the Romantic orchestra. It should suffice to give some idea, as is done above, that this orchestra — by virtue of both its size and its diversity — cannot be compared with the classical orchestra, and its aims were altogether different.

The classical orchestra had replaced the previous period's

concept of intensity with a concept of colour. The emancipation of timbre was emphasized, and that considerably, in the Romantic orchestra since, now that music had to express the ego with all its passions and to depict colourful and even fantastic scenes in forms that now were much freer, it had also to enrich its orchestral palette with new colours which could be given different shades and could be used for strong contrasts.

In other respects, the "king" of instruments was to be the piano; the improvements which had been made on it, and, above all, the system of double escapement, dating from the early years of the nineteenth century, transformed it into an instrument which could respond to the most difficult demands of the great Romantic virtuosos, as well as of the composers such as Moscheles, Chopin, Thalberg and Liszt, to name only the chief amongst them. The improvements which it was to undergo subsequently were only of a secondary nature.

Debussy, with whom in certain aspects one may link composers like Ravel and Roussel, heralded the advent of musical Impressionism at the end of the nineteenth century, when composers continued to make use of the large orchestra of the Romantics, though to different ends. Here, far from being concerned with dramatic expression and the outward aspect of things, music was composed of refined nuances which served to express subjective states and rare and delicate feelings. It can be seen from this that the orchestral resources were deployed in a quite different way. Timbres became atomised, dispersed over the music, combined in totally new combinations of sound, which were sometimes rendered more transparent and limpid by the use of harps and divided strings which very often served as an accompaniment to the wind instruments, which in turn were treated with the greatest delicacy imaginable. The use of the *glissando* — on the strings and the harp as well as on the trombone — was widely exploited. Finally, instruments of exotic origin, such as the xylophone, the castanets, the crescent, and the *tam-tam* (all percussion instruments) were now frequently used in symphony orchestras.

Stringed Instruments

Towards the middle of the nineteenth century, the guitar had acquired an even greater popularity than previously. In Vienna, some of the Romantic composers played it. In Paris, more or less well-written Romances were composed with guitar or harp accompaniment; those of Loïsa Puget were particularly highly thought of. In Spain, the guitar remained the popular instrument *par excellence*, but already Fernando Sors, or Sor (1778-1839) — who settled in Paris in 1813 — had opened up new horizons for it by treating it as a virtuoso instrument. Such composers as Weber and Berlioz were interested in the guitar, as was Paganini, who, it seems, was a virtuoso performer on this instrument as well as on the violin.

In 1854, the Spaniard Antonio Torres built a guitar whose sound-box was larger than usual and whose belly was strengthened on the inside by cross-pieces disposed in a wheel-spoke formation, which enabled the vibrations to be transferred to the greatest possible area of the belly. This system can still be found in guitars

VI. — 2.

Double-action harp by the French maker Erard. The harp shown here, however, was made in the firm's London branch. The pedals, 7 in number, can be placed in three positions, thus giving three different notes for each string. The pedal operates a disc by means of rods and levers passing inside the column and cross-piece; by turning through a quarter or a half of a revolution the disc shortens the string and raises the note either a semitone or a tone.
Height: *c.* 70⅞ ins.

M.I., Brussels.
No. 2487.

VI. — 3.

Chromatic harp invented by Gustave Lyon, director of the firm of Pleyel. The diatonic strings are placed diagonally in relation to the chromatic strings. This arrangement on two planes makes it possible to dispense with pedals. Since the string tension is liable to vary under different atmospheric conditions it is regulated automatically by a mechanism in the cross-piece.
Height: *c.* 74 ins.

M.I., Brussels.
No. 3867

VI. — 4.

Lyre-guitar by the maker Roudhlo[illegible] Nauchand of Paris. The belly of this instrument has two rose-holes and is adorned with incrustations of mother-of-pearl. The tail-piece is glued to the belly. The body assumes the shape of an ancient lyre, very fashionable at the end of the nineteenth century. The 6 gut strings are tuned as in the modern guitar.
Length: *c.* 31⅛ ins.

M.I., Brussels
No. 26[illegible]

VI. — 2.
French double-action harp
(19th century)

VI. — 3. **French chromatic harp**
(20th century)

VI. — 4. **French lyre**
(late 19th ce

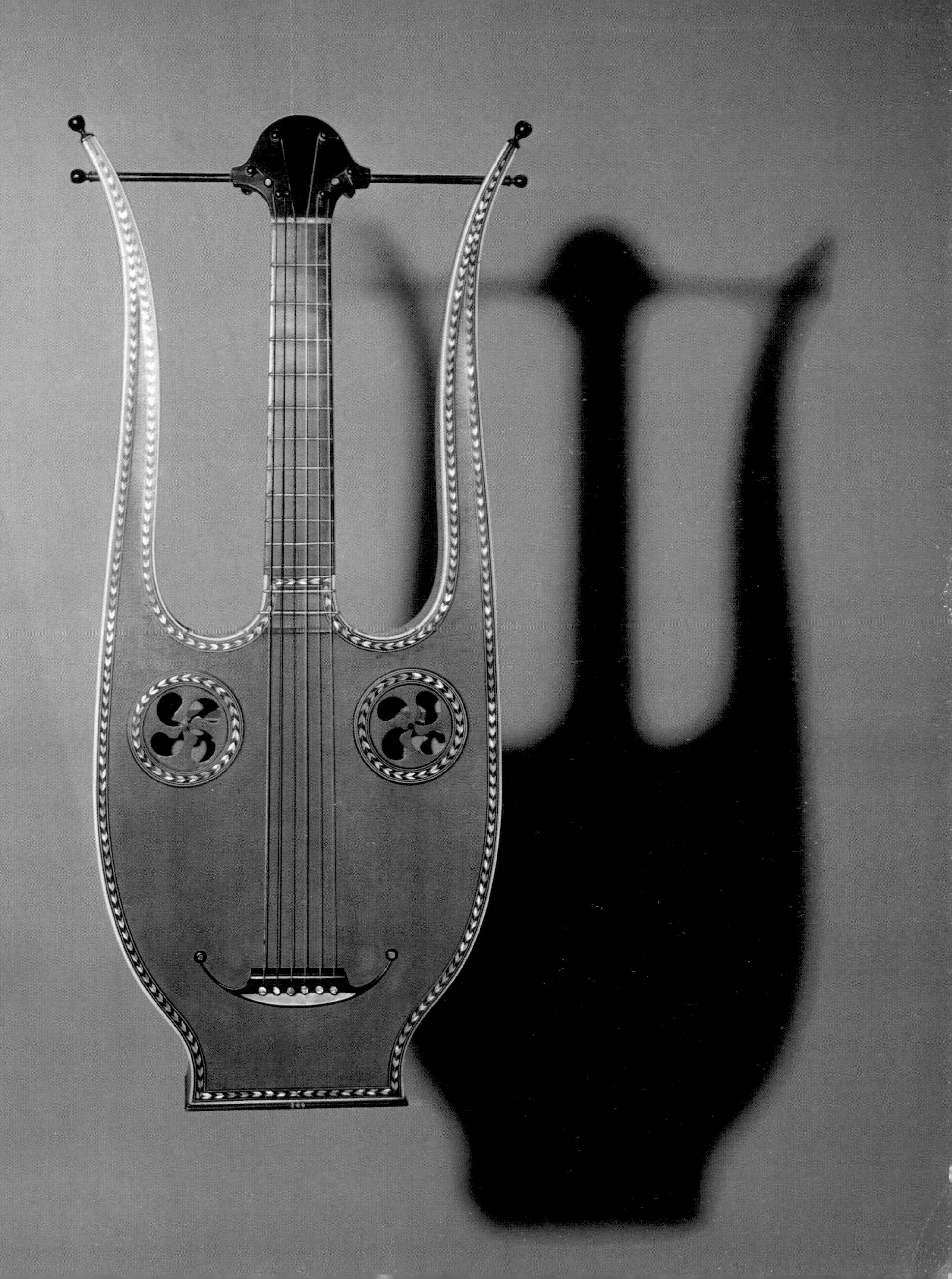

'I. — 5. **Three violin bows**
(19th century)

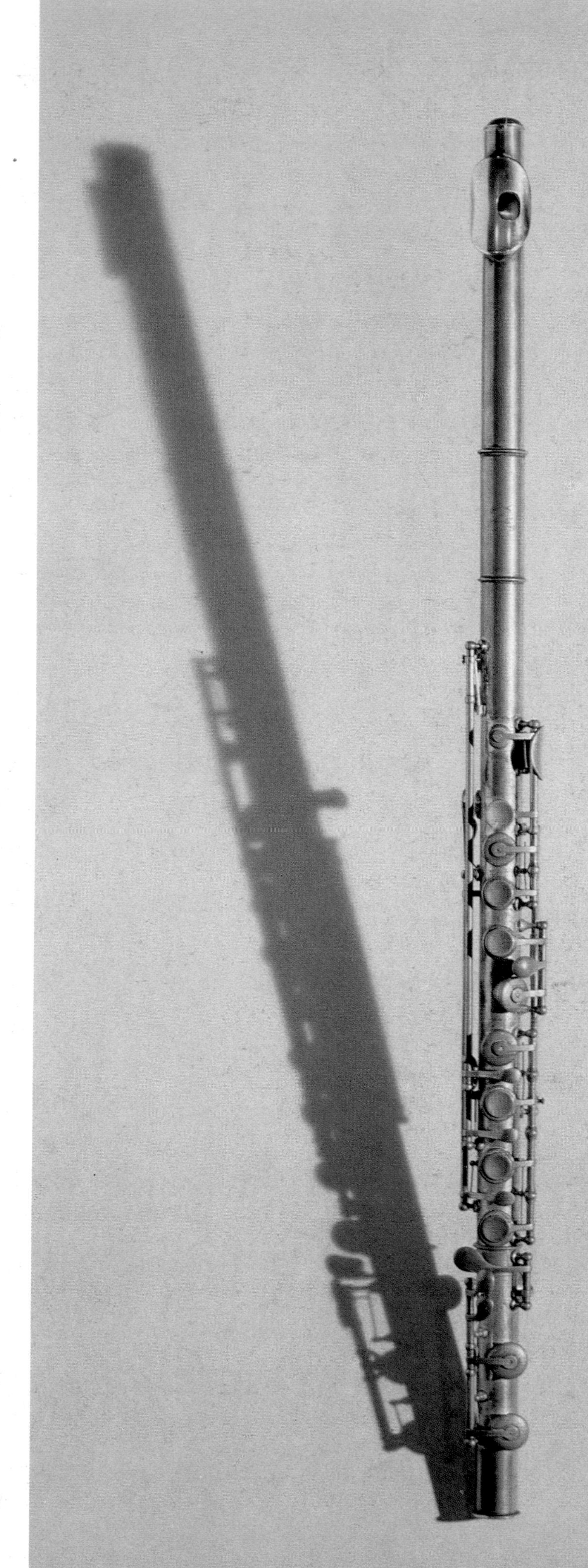

VI. — 6. **German transverse flute** (1847)

VI. — 7. **French contrabass clari**
(*c.* 1890)

8. **French tenor saxophone**
(19th century)

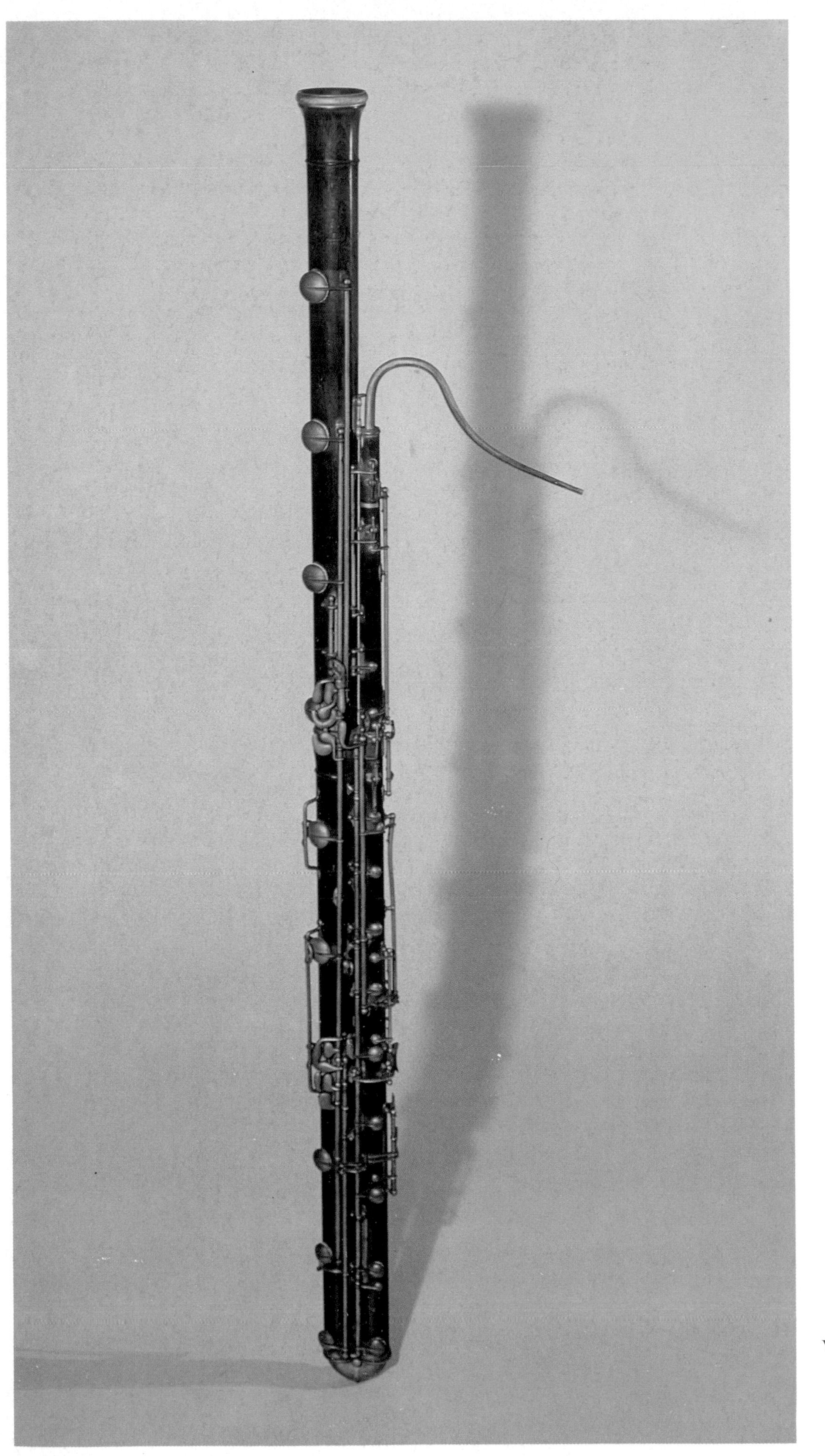

VI. — 9. **French bassoon** (1862)

VI. — 5.

Three violin bows; from left to right: violin bow, bearing no signature, attributed to Dominique Peccate (1810-1874) of Mirecourt. The nut is of tortoiseshell decorated with gold and bears the Latin adage "*iuvat pietas*". In the centre a violin bow by the London firm of Hill and Sons. The head, the mother-of-pearl knob and the nut, in mother-of-pearl and tortoiseshell, are decorated with gold. Finally, a violin bow with nut and knob of ivory embellished with gold and mother-of-pearl, signed by F.N. Voirin of Paris on the occasion of the 1878 Exhibition. Voirin was born at Mirecourt in 1833 and died in Paris in 1885. Length: *c.* 29 ins., $29\frac{1}{4}$ ins., and $29\frac{1}{3}$ ins.

M.I., Brussels.
Nos. 3482, 3437 & 3481.

VI. — 6.

Silver transverse flute, with mouthpiece plate and springs in gold, by the maker Theobald Boehm (Munich, 1794-1881). This instrument bears the manufacturing number 41 which enables us to date it 1847. To facilitate its maintenance, Boehm provided this flute with an ebony stick. In his system of needle springing he had recourse to an invention of A. Buffet the Younger of Paris. It will be noticed that this flute does not yet have the $B\flat$ key which was added only later by the Italian Briccialdi. Length: *c.* $24\frac{3}{8}$ ins.

M.I., Brussels.
No. 1084.

VI. — 7.

Contrabass clarinet by the Parisian maker G.A. Besson (last decade of the 19th century). On the metal bell of the instrument is inscribed: "*Système prototype, Paris, 96 rue d'Angoulême*". This is apparently one of the instruments made by Besson before he settled in London to found the Besson firm there. The instrument consists of a metal bell having 2 open keys and 3 wooden tubes of slightly conical bore joined by metal sleeves. Besides the keys already mentioned this contrabass clarinet has 12 closed and 8 open keys. Apparent height: *c.* $53\frac{3}{4}$ ins.

M.I., Brussels.
Unnumbered.

of high quality, except in those made in Germany. It was Torres, too, who built a guitar in cardboard, except for its belly, which was in fir wood, in order to be able to test his theories on the guitar's resonance.

The technique of playing changed, too. Previously, the guitar was plucked either with the fingers or with a plectrum. From then on, the strings might be struck and, when it came to plucking them, this might be done with the nails rather than with the finger-tips (a mode of playing already used by the Welsh harpists in their *eisteddfodau*). Still further effects made their appearance, like the *campacias* (open-string effects added to the playing of unrelated chords, and the *rasgueado* (more often reserved for folk music and rarely introduced into classical playing), obtained by turning the right hand from the wrist so that it rises high enough for the little finger to touch the lower (drone) strings whilst the other fingers slide over the whole or a part of the strings, thus producing an arpeggiated chord whose intensity and duration can be varied.

Among the virtuoso guitar players of the Romantic period who did most to propagate the instrument were the Frenchman Napoléon Coste, who invented the seven-stringed guitar, and the Spaniard Francesco Tarrega.

The pedal harp of Sébastien Erard was further improved, between 1835 and 1838, by his nephew Pierre Erard, who placed part of the pedal mechanism in a sort of bowl which served as the instrument's base, and since it was a part of the instrument, reduced the heigh of the instrument.

Despite the high degree of perfection it had attained, the pedal harp still had certain limitations, notably that of being unable to yield rapid chromatic passages, for the same string had to play three successive notes, and again in long passages of constant modulation the player had to make different and repeated movements of the pedals. This is why Gustave Lyon, affiliated with the firm of Pleyel and, later, its director, set about making a chromatic harp without pedals. In this field he had had a precursor in the figure of Johann Heinrich Pape, who had had the same idea in 1843, but whose methods of construction were quite different, and in any case had not been put into practice.

Thus in 1894, Gustave Lyon built a chromatic harp without pedals, in which each note of the chromatic scale had its own string. Without realising it, and in a different way, he put into practice an idea that was already old, that of placing the diatonic and chromatic strings on different planes and distinguishing them, as on the piano, by their colours, black and white. Whereas the pedal harp had 47 strings, the chromatic harp had to use 78. This raised a problem of string tension, for now that this was considerably greater as a result of the increased number of strings, it was liable to distort the instrument's shape. For this reason, after several unsuccessful attempts, Lyon decided to build a harp entirely in metal: the fore-pillar, the neck and the body — making it fairly heavy, for such a harp weighed about a hundredweight. In 1896, Lyon provided it with dampers; later, so as to counteract the variability of string tension that resulted from changes in humidity, he went on to use metallic springs attached to the string ends which controlled their tension automatically.

Obviously the chromatic harp without pedals quickly won its detractors and defenders. It, too, was not perfect (for example, it was incapable of yielding *glissandos*); quite simply its qualities and defects were different from those of the pedal harp. Each of the two firms, Erard and Pleyel, who had given these harps their respective names, sought to demonstrate their instruments' qualities by commissioning works, which would make them known, from two of the masters of the time. It was in this way that, in 1904, Claude Debussy wrote his *Danses sacrée et profane* for chromatic harp without pedals and orchestra, whilst immediately afterwards (1905-6) Maurice Ravel in his turn provided (but this time for the firm of Erard) a work called *Introduction and Allegro* for pedal harp accompanied by flute, clarinet and string quartet.

In view of the increased size of the harp after the beginning of the nineteenth century, miniature, or at least smaller harps had been planned. The composer Louis Spohr (1783-1859) declared that his wife, who had learnt to play on a single-action harp of Nadermann, was unable to come to grips with the harp of Erard.

Thus small harps, designed to be played in salons started to come into fashion. In 1798 an English maker, Edward Light, invented a small harp of the same size as the mediaeval harp which, like the latter, could be placed on the knees; however, he provided it with seven keys which were operated by the player's fingers and shortened the gut strings, thus serving the same purpose as the pedals on a large harp; hence its name, the *dital harp*. Only after 1830, the year in which Pfeiffer started manufacturing it in Paris, did this instrument have any real success, and even then it was short-lived.

Another small harp, which its inventor Gustave Lyon called the *harp-lute*, was made in 1897 at the request of Richard Wagner, who had wanted, in *The Mastersingers*, to use the lute sonority that his text required. Unfortunately, the lute was not played in Wagner's time, and it was awkward, if not impossible, to find a player to do it (though the same would no longer be true today). This was why Lyon, seeking solely to recapture this lost sonority, and not concerned with creating an identical instrument, built this harp-lute, whose sound-box and the special way of mounting its strings enabled the required effect to be produced. The harp-lute, all of whose strings were of metal, was built on the same principle as the chromatic harp without pedals.

In the group of bowed string instruments, the family of viols had completely disappeared, and although we still find the viola d'amore making episodic appearances in Meyerbeer's opera *Les Huguenots*, this is a rather exceptional case, the composer using it deliberately to add local colour. The only trace left by this family was in that the shoulders of the double bass bore some resemblance to those possessed by the viol.

The viola, which Mozart had already used as a concertante instrument, as had Beethoven in his last quartets, was admitted to the rank of soloist, a privilege well merited by an instrument of such qualities. It was in this role that Berlioz used it in his symphony in four parts, *Harold in Italy* (1834).

The double bass was modified a little. The model having three strings tuned in fifths was superseded by a double bass with

VI. — 8.

Tenor saxophone in ***B♭*** by Adolphe Sax (Dinant 1814 - Paris 1894). The tenor also exists in *C*. The range is of two octaves and a fifth. The double spatula does not yet exist. The mouthpiece is of ebony and the bore is conical. The instrument consists of four pieces cut from a plate of brass and welded together. Length: *c*. 30¾ ins.

M.I., Brussels.
No. 3765.

VI. — 9.

Boehm system bassoon (1862), patented by Triébert of Paris. The geometrical division of the tube already established by Theobald Boehm is applied here. The mechanism is very precise but from the practical point of view extremely complicated, even though it was conceived in the first place in order to facilitate playing. There are in existence only three instruments built in accordance with this principle. This instrument was the work of Frédéric Triébert (1813-1878), third in the descendency of the Triébert family.
Height: *c*. 52⅛ ins.

M.I., Brussels.
No. 3119.

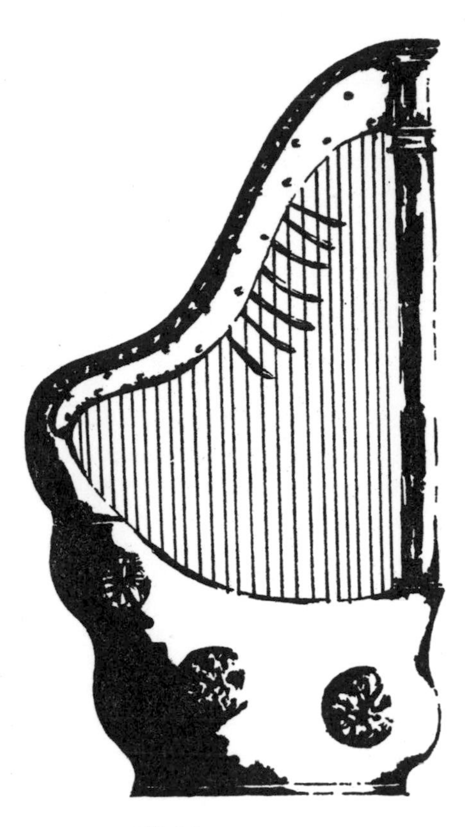

Dital harp

four strings tuned in fourths. Nowadays, double basses are some times made with five strings, the lowest of which is tuned a third below the string above; this innovation was the work of the Parisian makers Bernardel and Gand. If the (four-stringed) double bass was sometimes used as a soloist, this was due to the great virtuosity shown by some of its players.

Wishing to obtain a still deeper instrument, Jean-Baptiste Vuillaume in 1849 invented the *octo-bass*, more than four yards high and having three strings; he perfected it in 1851. It was impossible to use the fingers to shorten the strings of this gigantic instrument, which reached down four notes lower than the double bass. Steel "fingers", operated by levers, had to be used to do this. Although Berlioz, with his imaginative enthusiasm, had not hesitated to include this instrument in his equally fantastic orchestra, practical reality soon consigned it to the level of a curiosity; few examples of it have survived, one of these being preserved in the Paris Conservatoire Museum.

The bow of the double bass also underwent a certain development. The so-called Dragonetti bow was very arched and short; it was excellent for playing with a staccato touch, but not well adapted to legato playing. Rossini, at the time living in Paris, had commissioned it from Daniel Dragonetti himself, and was responsible for its introduction in France. It was not until some time later that a slightly longer bow with a slanting nut appeared; Bernardel and Gand were the first to think of this bow after 1883. It was subsequently improved by Vigneron, but was still too heavy and therefore too tiring to be used in playing modern works. It was a young maker, Thomassin, who, after about 1903, made a bow weighing 4 ounces whose efficiency was equal to that of Vigneron's bows, which never weighed less than 4½ ounces.

In Central Europe, the bow of the Viennese double bass virtuoso Simandl was used. This bow was held in the same way as that of the viol, in other words the hand was turned to face upwards and exerted a less forceful pressure on the strings so that certain nuances of pianissimo could be played, as could all the harmonics, whose presence helped to give the double bass a brilliant timbre.

Of the instruments with rubbed strings which originated in the Romantic and pre-Romantic periods, and whose existence was ephemeral, however interesting they may have been, four are worth mentioning here.

In 1890 an Austrian, Alexander Stelzner, built an instrument that was larger than the cello and was tuned a fourth lower. The new, elliptical instrument was called the *cellone*, and its inventor intended it to replace the double bass, which he considered to be too large for chamber music.

In order to combine the capabilities of the violin and the viola (which is tuned a fifth lower) Hermann Ritter (1849-1926) of Würzburg in 1876 added a fifth string to the upper register of the viola, tuning it in unison with the violin's *E*-string; hence the name of *viola alta* that it was given.

At the beginning of the twentieth century, the same maker built the *Tenor-Geige* (tenor violin), an intermediary instrument between the viola and the cello. In fact, it is worthy of note that the violin family includes the violin itself, the viola, tuned a fifth below the violin, and finally the cello, tuned an octave below the viola. It will be clearly seen that the distance between the viola and the cello (an octave) is greater than that between the violin and the viola (a fifth). Therefore, there is an instrument missing between the viola and the cello — an instrument which would serve the same purpose as the tenor in a vocal quartet. This is what Ritter had in mind when he made the tenor-geige, which brings to mind the short-lived *violoncello piccolo*, having five strings, the four lowest of which were tuned as on the cello, and the highest a fifth higher, thus on *E*, in other words an octave beneath the highest string of the violin.

Another instrument, deriving from the same principle and called the *baritone violin*, was built in 1847 by Charles Henry of Paris, following the directives of the French cellist Bartanchon.

Double flagcolet

Wind Instruments

In the early years of the nineteenth century a long controversy was waged between the Swiss flautist William Gordon, who died in about 1850, and the German Theobald Boehm (1794-1881), also a flautist, as to which of them was responsible for improvements made on the flute which brought this instrument to the highest degree of perfection and resulted from an invention of the greatest importance: this was an ingenious mechanism that was applied to the flute, now known as the Boehm system, which is still used today and has remained essentially unaltered since its appearance; its efficiency made such an impression that soon the oboe, the clarinet and the bassoon were provided with it.

Gordon and Boehm started from the same idea, namely, that in order to build a flute perfectly, or indeed any tubular instrument, it is absolutely essential to bear in mind the laws of acoustics; these laws had not previously been widely observed, particularly in the construction of flutes where the boring of holes (at the time when keys did not yet exist) was carried out rather to facilitate the player's task of blocking them with his fingers without his having to stretch them into an unnatural position. This method of boring the holes, which had been wrong from the beginning, was nonetheless retained after the introduction of keys, even though these would have permitted a more logical placing of the holes.

However, Gordon had become aware of these discrepancies after having referred to Nicholson (whom we mentioned in the last chapter), from whom he had taken the idea that larger holes produced brighter and more powerful sounds, such as were required by the modern orchestra.

For his part, Boehm too knew of Nicholson, but whereas Gordon (who had worked with him) left no specimen of his flute but instead a clumsy and rough drawing, Boehm clearly expounded his ideas in several illustrated works and, still better, brought them to realization. These ideas may be summarized under three heads: 1) the holes should be large; 2) they should be bored according to acoustical laws and not for the convenience of the player, who should consequently be assisted by the use of appropriately designed

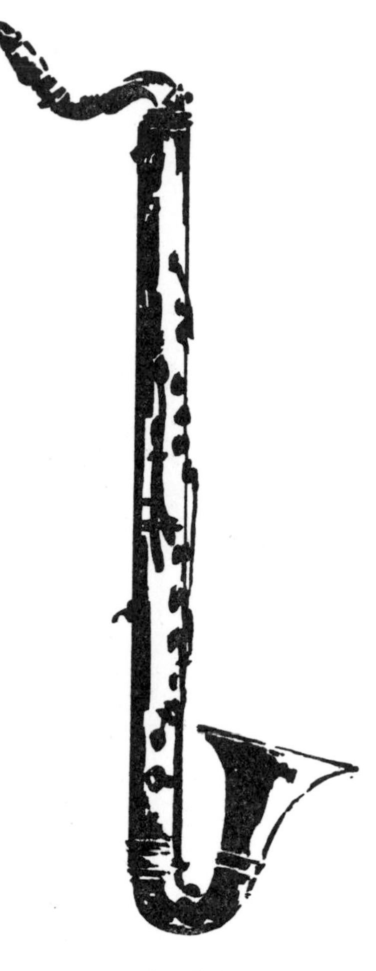
Alto clarinet

keys placed so that they can be operated effortlessly by the fingers; 3) all the keys should be open keys.

Boehm's flute, of which an actual specimen already existed in 1832, was further transformed in 1846, for from that year on Boehm himself built his flutes with a cylindrical bore. A final (and less important) improvement was the suppression of the last remaining bifurcated fingering positions by the addition of the *B♭* key; this improvement was the work of Briccialdi.

From the start, the Boehm flute was received favourably in England and France, but was neglected for a long time in Germany, its inventor's homeland. In England, Rudall Carte made a flute which offered a compromise between the old and the new systems.

For their part, composers were not slow to exploit, bit by bit as they appeared, the technical improvements brought to the flute. Already Beethoven took the instrument as high as a^{III} in his works; Meyerbeer made much use of the now more rounded deeper register, and especially in *Le Prophète* (1849) contrasted this aspect of the flute with the violin. A supreme example of a composer making full use of the versatility the instrument now possessed so as to bring into play its different aspects may be found in the admirable flute solo that opens Debussy's *Prélude à l'Après-midi d'un Faune* (1894).

However, inventors continued to conduct their researches, usually without any noteworthy results. In 1888, in Florence, Giorgi made an ebonite flute having eleven holes, each closed by means of a key, and each corresponding to a semitone; the tenth and eleventh keys were operated by the same finger. In 1911 another Italian, Albi, built a flute which, although it was based on the same principle as the transverse flute, was held vertically in front of the performer thanks to a T-shaped mouthpiece.

To turn to the clarinet. It was, to a point, provided with the Boehm system by Hyacinthe Klosé and Auguste Buffet. This Klosé-Buffet clarinet was very quickly taken up in France; it was less widely used in England and Germany, where an instrument having fifteen keys and two rings was preferred, known as a half-Boehm clarinet.

The *alto clarinet* differed from the normal clarinet not only in its size, but also by the fact that its bell was of metal. From the middle of the nineteenth century on, the basset horn underwent a transformation, for instead of having an angular shape, it now became straight; in fact, it offered the appearance of an ordinary clarinet except that its bore was narrower and its casing thinner.

The *bass clarinet* was invented in 1836 by Adolphe Sax; despite the softness of its sonority, it is capable of producing very powerful notes. Meyerbeer (who, it will be remembered, played no small part in the development of the orchestra by introducing new instruments into it) made use of it, notably in *Le Prophète*.

The *contrabass clarinet*, for which the Paris firm of Fontaine-Besson was responsible, did not make its appearance until 1890. All the same, other makers had tried to make a similar instrument without arriving at a satisfactory result, their attempts dating from as early as the first half of the nineteenth century. In view of its costliness, the contrabass clarinet is scarcely used. Vincent d'Indy used it to good effect in his opera *Fervaal* (1897).

Since the clarinet does not overblow at the octave, but rather jumps straight to the next harmonic, in other words the twelfth, makers sought to construct a single-reed instrument which would overblow at the octave; it was in this way that the saxophone came into existence. This instrument has a conical bore and its inventor, Adolphe Sax, patented it in 1846 at the same time as other instruments he had invented, the *saxhorn* and the *saxotromba*. The saxophone is made entirely in metal; because of its fairly wide bore, and also as a result of its single reed, it gives a fairly full sonority that has an individual flavour, and is instantly recognisable among the brass instruments. It has a family of seven members ranging from the *sopranino saxophone* to the *contrabass saxophone*, though the sopranino and soprano are rarely used.

It seems that the saxophone was used in theatre music for the first time in G. Kastner's opera *Le dernier Roi de Juda*, which was given in Paris in 1844, thus two years before the instrument was patented. However, although it was quickly and decisively taken up by military bands, it was not for several years that it took its place in operatic music. Apart from the exceptional case of the work by Kastner we have just mentioned, it was only after Ambroise Thomas' opera *Hamlet* (1868) that it was used, either alone or in groups of several members of the family, by Massenet, Bizet, Charpentier, d'Indy, and others, in their operas or lyric dramas. Richard Strauss was one of the first, if not actually the first, to make use of it in a symphonic work; thus it is used in a quartet in his *Domestic Symphony* (1904). Since then it has well and truly established itself, and chamber music groups have been formed consisting solely of saxophones, for which composers have been prepared to write interesting works.

Sarrusophone

The family of double-reed instruments also underwent a great development in the course of the nineteenth century. The oboe was improved in 1848 by Frédéric Triébert who reduced its bore in order to adapt the Boehm system to it. In 1870, Victor-Charles Mahillon reconstructed the oboe d'amore so that Bach's works and those of his time in general could be performed with a more appropriate tone-colour. After 1850, the cor anglais became straight, and could thus be easily played by any oboist. The *baritone oboe*, whose lowest note is an octave below that of the oboe, was built in 1889 by the Parisian maker Lorée. Like the oboe d'amore it had a pear-shaped bell, and its length necessitated the use of an S-shaped crook.

Another instrument, fairly similar in shape and called the heckelphone, made its appearance in Germany in 1904; it is said that it was at the suggestion of Richard Wagner that Wilhelm Heckel had the idea of building this instrument, but since Wagner had died in 1883, thus before the instrument came into being, it was Richard Strauss who, in *Salome* (1905), was the first to use the *heckelphone*, an instrument whose tone differed from that of Lorée's baritone oboe.

The bass member of the double-reed family, the bassoon, was also transformed. In fact in 1855 Triébert tried to apply the Boehm system to it, but since in so doing he caused the bassoon's timbre to be considerably altered, this modification was only moderately successful. In Germany, Karl Almenräder (1786-1843) had made an attempt, prior to Triébert's in France, to adapt the Boehm system to the bassoon.

The double bassoon, sounding an octave lower than the bassoon, and whose ancestor was the contrabass pommer, continued to be used, and underwent certain alterations at the hands of various makers among whom were Schöllnast, with his *Universalkontrabass* (1839), Müller, with his *Müllerphone* (1870), and above all the Bohemian Václar Červený (1819-1896), the inventor of a number of models of cylinder mechanisms, who, among his various inventions, went as far as making a *subcontrabassoon* (1873).

The French maker Gautrot the elder built, at the request of his friend Sarrus, a military band leader, a conical-bore brass instrument with a double reed to which he gave the name *sarrusophone* and which he patented in 1856. He manufactured it in nine sizes. Sarrus's idea was to replace the oboes and bassoons of wind bands by an instrument whose mechanism would be simpler and whose sonority more powerful. A point of interest is that Sax brought an action against Sarrus, though without success, claiming that he had used, in making the sarrusophone, certain procedures taken from the manufacture of the saxophone. At all events, as soon as it appeared the sarrusophone proved itself an interesting instrument and yet hardly achieved any success, except in the contrabass model, which many composers and conductors tended to use instead of the double bassoon, whose tone was less homogeneous across the different registers and whose articulation was less supple.

The ophicleide and the serpent were still used, but were gradually to disappear. Wagner still used the serpent in *Rienzi* (1842) as Mendelssohn had in 1836 in his oratorio *Saint Paul*.

The military serpent we spoke of in the last chapter was provided with supplementary keys and thus became the chromatic bass horn of Pace (of London). As for the ophicleide, it made periodic appearances, notably in Meyerbeer's *Robert le Diable* (1831) and *Les Huguenots* (1836) as well as in Mendelssohn's *A Midsummer Night's Dream* (1826-1841).

Of the instruments with brass mouthpieces, the keyed trumpet disappeared in about 1850 to be replaced by the valve trumpet which offered the advantage of greater precision and, above all, a more brilliant tone.

The slide trombone, whose ancestor was the sackbut, continued to be used more or less according to its size. It was the tenor trombone which, because of its great qualities of powerful and majestic tone, was most frequently used in the orchestra. Later, it was also to be taken up in jazz, where its capabilities and, in particular, its *glissando* effects were fully exploited. The bass trombone was held in much lower esteem because it was fairly heavy and was in some respects difficult to play; since it nonetheless possessed a tone of great power and nobility, it was not abandoned, but rather attempts were made to make it more manageable, and this was achieved by the new system bass trombone.

The contrabass trombone which, in view of its excessive length and the unpleasant sounds it yielded, had disappeared since the time of Praetorius's *Grosse Posaune*, reappeared thanks to the improvements made on it by the Parisian maker Asté, in 1855. However, these improvements in themselves were insufficient for, in particular, they did not avoid the snag of the excessive length of the instrument, and it was only by the intervention of two later makers, Fournier (1900) and after him Maquarre, who succeeded in eliminating its chief remaining defects, that the instrument was able to survive. Alto, soprano and piccolo trombones also exist, brought to perfection by modern makers, but of these only the alto trombone is used.

Besides the slide trombones, whose origins go back to the distant past, the nineteenth century saw the creation of valve trombones. Here, we will only mention the bass trombone, which, as soon as it had been invented by the German D. Jahn in 1834, was, in France, given the name of tuba, a name which elsewhere was later to apply to the bass of the saxhorn family.

The origin of the word bugle is not known for certain. It is said to have been applied to a conical-bore instrument with valves which permitted the playing of a chromatic scale. This instrument, of Austrian origin, is said to have probably appeared in about 1827. Later, this name was customarily used for the higher group of instruments in the saxhorn family, whilst the word tuba was used for the lower instruments.

The tuba, an instrument with conical bore, derived from the low-pitched keyed horn or the ophicleide. It was the maker Moritz, of Berlin, who, in 1835, under the directions of Wieprecht who was the general musical director, built the first tuba, using the pistons of broad diameter that have since come to be known as *Berliner Pumpen*. An even larger instrument, the contrabass tuba, was built a few years later by Červený.

Ignaz Stowasser of Vienna made, in 1849, a contrabass tuba whose tube was turned round on itself in a broad arc so that the player could carry it around his body; this was later given the name of *helicon*. The famous American bandleader John Philip Sousa in 1908 commissioned the maker G. C. Conn (of Indiana) to build a helicon with a winding bell so that the direction of the sound could be controlled, and called it the *sousaphone*. It should however be noted that well before this, Sax too had built instruments with winding bells.

The history of the bugle and tuba families cannot be told without mentioning the name of Adolphe Sax, who for the first time tried to unify the making of the whole group; he finally created the family of saxhorns which had seven members ranging from the small saxhorn to the two contrabass models: the *bombardon* and the *contrabass tuba*, whose tone was soft and articulation precise. In reality, the saxhorn was not a new instrument, but rather the bringing to perfection of instruments that already existed, as we have just seen; this explains the different accusations of infringement of copyright that were levelled at Sax by makers who had themselves sought to make innovations in this field when he came to patent his saxhorn in 1845. The precision of its intonation as well as its other qualities led to the immediate adoption of this instrument by the French army. On the other hand, it was Meyerbeer who introduced the saxhorn into opera when he used it for the first time in *Le Prophète*. The Distin family, who were gifted

VI. — 10.

Ophicleide in *B♭* by the Belgian maker C. Devaster, who worked at Malines and at Brussels. The instrument shown dates from his time at Malines (the dates of this maker's birth and death are not known; he lived in the middle of the 19th century). The body is in pinchbeck with nine silver keys worked in a guilloche pattern. Underneath the mark "*C. Devaster, Malines*" on the instrument's body are the letters "AWX". Height: *c.* 44 ins.

M.I., Brussels.
No. 2745.

VI. — 11.

Tenor trombone in *B♭* by Adolphe Sax (1814-1894). The instrument has 7 tubes which are used separately and each of which has a terminal bell. Each tube, except for the seventh and last, has an independent valve. The seventh, by the fact that it is the longest and consequently emits the deepest note, does not require the use of a valve. Here Sax adopted John Shaw's system of ascending valves (1824) which successively shorten the column of air. This system, which works perfectly as far as sound production is concerned, is obviously only applicable to instruments of a comparatively small size.
Height: *c.* 35¾ ins.

M.I., Brussels
No. 2468

VI. — 12.

Sopranine saxhorn in *B♭* by Ado phe Sax. This instrument is provide with 3 descending valves and h in addition 3 keys opening into th bell (this system was patented o February 19, 1859). The invent hoped to combine the advantages both systems — the valve and th key — to make it easier to produ the higher notes. However th combination was abandoned after short time, as it distorted the r sonance of the harmonics.
Height: *c.* 17½ ins.

M.I., Brusse
No. 126

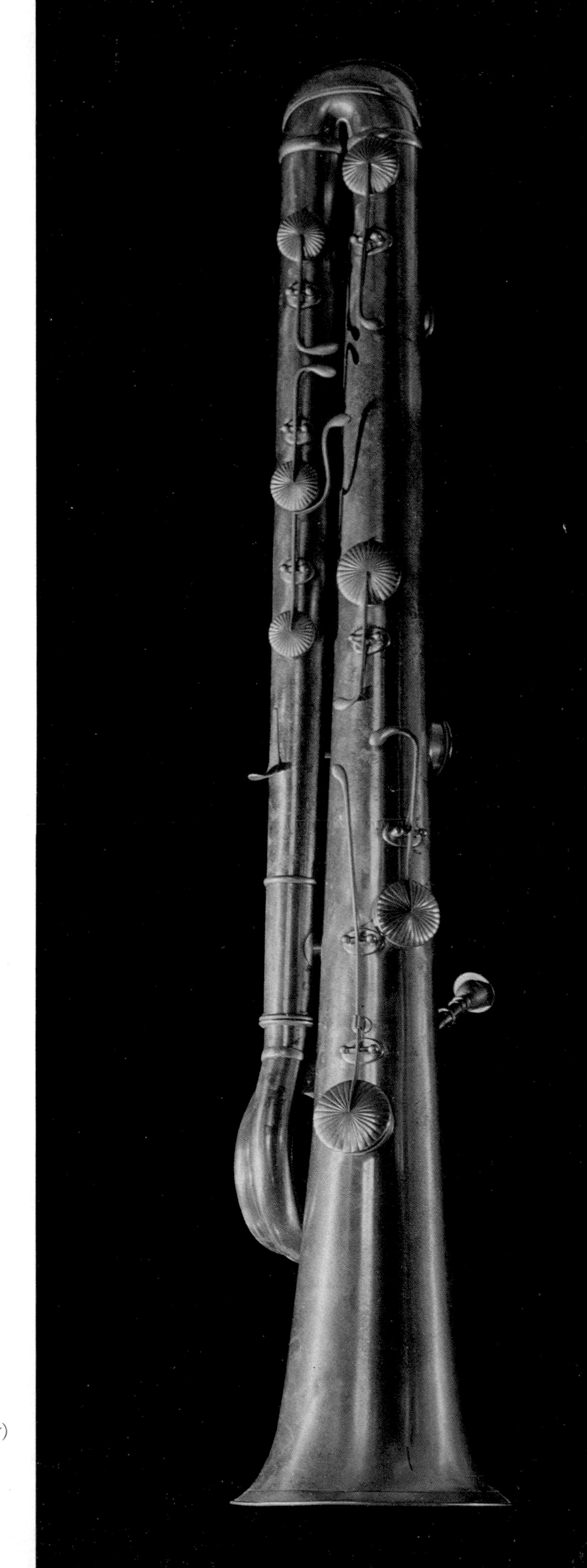

VI. — 10. **Belgian ophicleide** (19th century)

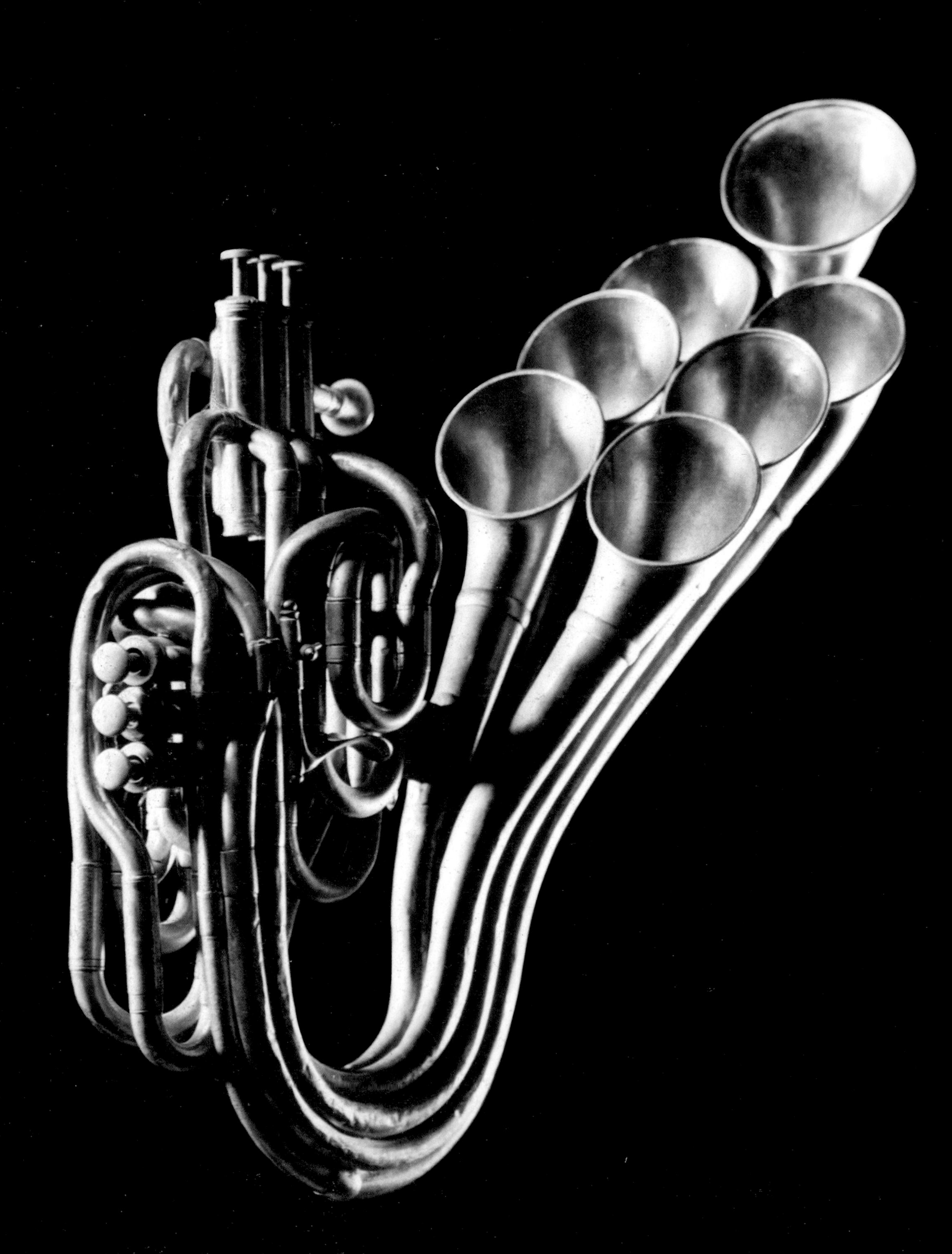

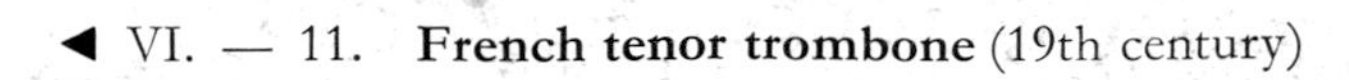

◀ VI. — 11. **French tenor trombone** (19th century)

VI. — 12. **Sopranino saxhorn** (*c.* 1859)

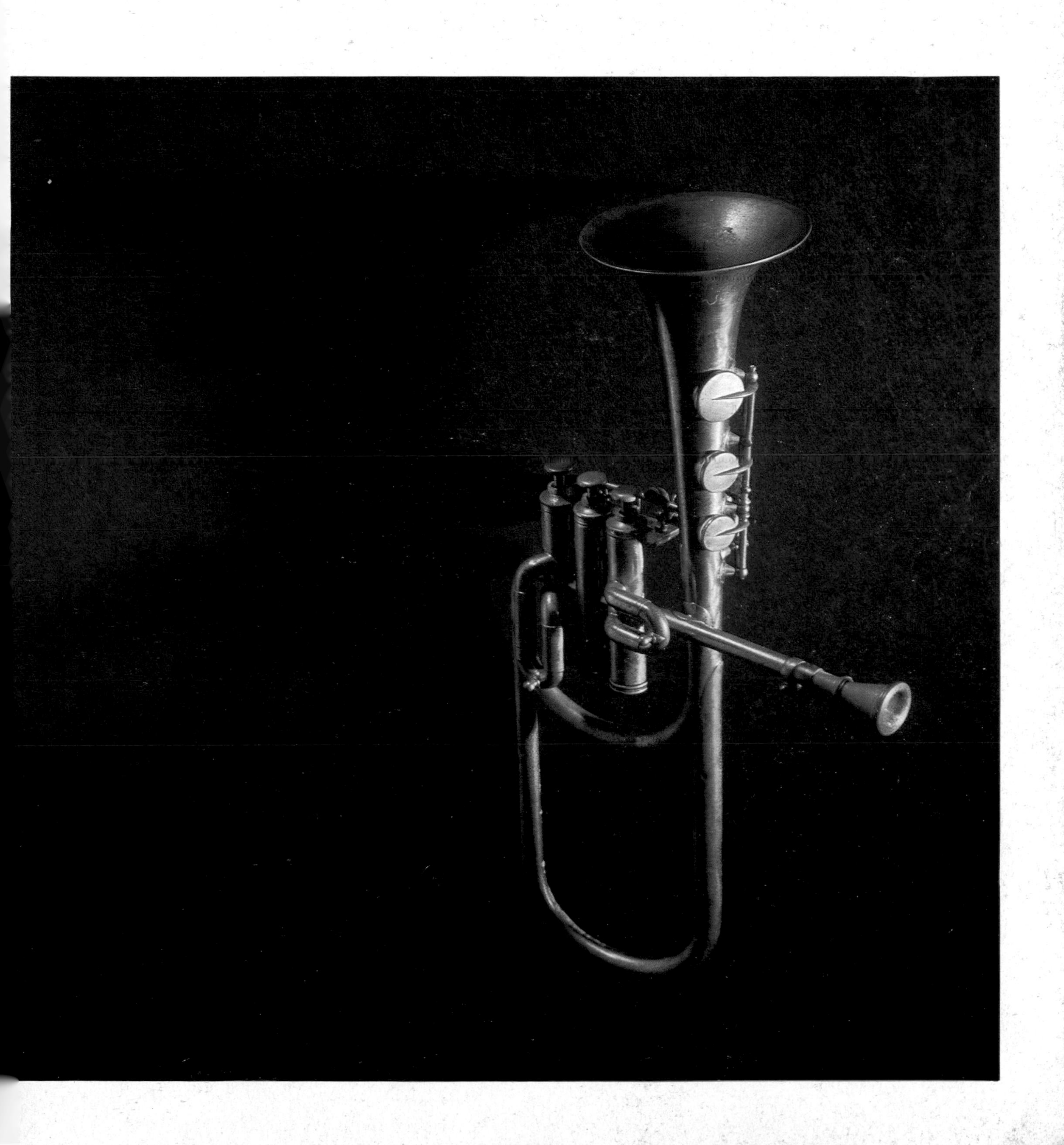

◀ VI. — 13. **German bass tuba** (*c.* 1835)

VI. — 14. **Two kettledrums of unknown origin** (19th century)

VI. — 15. **French harmonium** (*c.* 1870)

VI. — 16. **German Jankó piano** (19th century) ▶

C. Goetze

VI. — 17. **Dutch musical box** (19th century)

VI. — 13.

German bass tuba in ***F,*** dating from about 1835, by the maker C. W. Moritz of Berlin. The 5 valves are of the type invented by C. Moritz and known as *Berliner Pumpen.* With this system of large valves, developed from the rotating cylinder valve, the movement of the piston still remains rectilinear. The accuracy obtained is considerable though certain valve combinations produce too sharp a sound.
Height: *c.* 35 ins.

M.I. Brussels.
No. 1281.

VI. — 14.

Two 19th century kettledrums by an unknown maker. Their skins are of a varying diameter and can be stretched to a certain extent, in order to obtain different notes, by means of a wooden hoop around which the skin is wrapped; this hoop is gripped to the copper bowl in the one drum by 7 large screws, in the other by 8. The hemispherical bowl forming the sound-box rests on wooden feet.
Diameter: *c.* 25⅝ ins. and 24⅛ ins.

Gemeentemuseum, The Hague.

VI. — 15.

Harmonium by Alexandre François Debain (1809-1877). This instrument was built after 1867. Besides its main stop the instrument has another stop, called "expression". The free reeds are provided with a percussive mechanism (invented by Martin of Provins) so as to facilitate their vibration. The instrument's range is five octaves.
Height: 30½ ins.

M.I., Brussels.
No. 3586.

players, helped to propagate it by giving numerous chamber concerts in different parts.

Tubas of narrower bore and with horn mouthpieces were made in 1870 in accordance with the instructions of Richard Wagner, to be used in *The Ring of the Nibelungs.* These Wagner tubas consisted of a tenor and a bass model and combined the agility of the valve cornet with the soft tone of the tuba itself. They were used by Bruckner, and also by Richard Strauss in his operas *Elektra* (1908) and *Die Frau ohne Schatten* (1917). The *cornophone,* produced in 1890 by the Fontaine-Besson workshop of Paris, hardly differed from the Wagner tuba.

A number of specially and originally made instruments saw the light of day in the course of this period, but scarcely met with any success. It is worth remembering the trumpets and trombones with independent valves and seven bells of Adolphe Sax, and the double instruments such as the *doublephone* of the London firm of Besson, derived from the double instrument of the American maker Conn who, in 1880, had combined a valve bass with a trombone.

The horns remained virtually unchanged; the French model generally had a narrower bore than the German model, and was thus harder to play, though the latter, with its wider bore, produced a more vulgar sonority.

Percussion Instruments

Here also there were few changes, except for the kettledrums. These were now tuned by means of keys, used as screws. These would number between 12 and 14. Such a large number made it difficult for the drums to be tuned equally. For this reason, G. Kramer in 1812 at Munich as well as J. Stumpf in 1821 at Amsterdam made attempts to build a drum having a central key which would serve to stretch a cord passing zigzag fashion through rings fixed on the circumference and, by its greater or lesser tension, would to the same extent control the tension and relaxation of the drumhead from which the sound was obtained.

The principle was sound, but its realization left something to be desired, for in spite of everything the tension remained unequal and the sound obtained was correspondingly poor. Because of this, other means of stretching the skin were sought and it was in this way that chromatic pedal-operated mechanical kettledrums were created. On these, the greater or lesser tension of the skin was controlled by a foot-operated cog-wheel which brought into action a ring to stretch the drumhead; furthermore, the needle of a dial placed on the edge of the kettledrum indicated to the player the degree of the tension thus obtained, and consequently told him the pitch of the sound produced by the corresponding amount of tension.

A further very similar system exists in which the cog-wheel is replaced by a pedal which, as in the harp, is connected to a ratchet. This chromatic pedal kettledrum allows the production of certain effects, notably the *glissando,* which it is impossible to play with other types of kettledrums. Richard Strauss and Vincent d'Indy made interesting use of the capabilities of this chromatic pedal kettledrum — curiously, in the same year (1905) — in two important works: the former in the famous dance in *Salome*, and the latter in his symphonic poem *Jour d'été à la montagne*.

The *celesta*, which Widor, Charpentier and many others after them used in their orchestra, resembles a small piano whose strings are replaced by metal blades with brass heads. Invented by Mustel in 1886, it is in some ways similar to the *adiaphone* which was invented in 1882 by Fischer and Fritsch of Leipzig.

Other, rarely used, percussion instruments appeared, such as that used to imitate the sound of hailstones, consisting of a small drum with small hard bullets inside, which strike the skin when the drum is rotated; Richard Strauss used this in his *Alpine Symphony* (1915).

Keyboard Instruments

As we explained in the previous chapter, the development of the piano continued during the first decades of the nineteenth century, and the improvements made to the instrument in those years did not look like being superseded for a long time. And in fact this was to be so, for although many makers subsequently invented numerous models (more than 120 of them) which showed lesser or greater flights of fancy, none of these managed to gain a foothold. Thus we shall mention only those which retain our interest.

First of all it should be noted that in 1839, Pierre Erard built a piano having a bronze stringer which gave it considerable stability; he also made a grand piano with a pedal-board; and in 1843 he applied the double escapement system to the upright piano. This double escapement system, which had been invented by Sébastien Erard, was improved in 1844 by Kriegelstein, who worked in Paris.

In 1849, Mathuseck, a pupil of Pape in Paris, invented an apparatus which facilitated the rapid mass production of mechanisms. Thus, an increasing number of piano makers, finding themselves in need of mechanisms, were able to turn to specialized firms to supply their needs.

Piano making now was something of a craft, though only a few achieved mastery in it, whilst some made accessory discoveries which were taken up by the larger firms. The fact that in the 1951 London Exhibition there was an international piano section demonstrates the important place now held by makers of this instrument.

Although in the Germanic countries the firms of Stein (which had been so highly esteemed by Mozart) and Graf (the firm favoured by Beethoven) remained faithful to the Austrian methods, it was the Anglo-French method of manufacture which soon became dominant. Before long it was to be joined by the American method.

In 1862, the Frenchman Montal invented a third pedal, whose function was to prolong a given note without the notes played subsequently being held too. Mustel, another Frenchman, built a piano in which tuning forks replaced strings. The Hungarian pianist, Emmanuel Moór (1863-1931), built a piano having two manuals tuned an octave apart.

VI. — 16.
Upright piano by th
Goetze (late 19th century), having 6 superposed manuals. This type of piano was invented by Jankó in 1882. It enables the same string to be struck by three different keys each belonging to a different manual. The four upper rows of keys give two repetitions of the lower two. Each key is rounded and fairly narrow so as to enable the hand to stretch over greater intervals. The first piano maker to adopt the Jankó keyboard was the Viennese R. Kurka.
Height of the piano: *c.* $50\frac{7}{8}$ ins.
Gemeentemuseum, The Hague.

VI. — 17.
Musical box by Smulders, a maker living in Maestricht (Netherlands). This has two combs consisting of chromatically tuned metal blades. A spring mechanism turns a disc which has on its back judiciously placed studs. When the disc (which may be replaced by another disc) turns, its studs pluck the corresponding blades, setting them in vibration.
Dimensions: *c.* $21\frac{5}{8}$ ins. $\times$ $17\frac{3}{4}$ ins $\times$ $10\frac{7}{8}$ ins.
M.I., Brussels.
No. 3944.

Double escapement

Previously, the Hungarian Paul von Jankó, taking up Vincent's idea of building a chromatic keyboard had, in 1886, invented a new system comprising six superimposed manuals which he described in his work *Eine neue Klaviatur*, which appeared in 1886. This system, besides reducing the stretch needed to play widely spaced chords on a normal piano, gave scope for many new effects, and particularly chromatic *glissandos* in one or more parts.

During the second half of the nineteenth century Wolfel invented a piano whose keyboard was in the shape of an arc, so as to render the extreme notes more accessible. We should point out that he was the first to use screw tuning pins. It may be noted that it was recently rumoured that the eminent French pianist, Monique de la Bruchollerie had invented a similar piano, but she herself maintains that such a circular, or rather semicircular keyboard is only one of the elements, and not the chief one, of a new piano for which she has already taken out two patents.

The famous virtuoso and professor at the Brussels Conservatoire, Wienawski, apparently wanted for his own use a piano built in such a way as to abolish the distance between the hands in playing the extreme notes and also the necessity for crossing hands. Thus, at his request, the makers Mangeot Frères of Nancy made for him a piano with two manuals, one of which was the reverse of the other. The instrument really consisted of two pianos, one of which was inverted (so that the longer strings were at the right hand side) and placed above the other, having also its own keyboard arranged in inverse order. At present, this instrument may be found in the collection of the Brussels Instrumental Museum. The same Museum also has one of the rare double-manual pianos made by the Pleyel firm, requested and designed by the Belgian engineer Pierre Hans, also a pianist and composer.

For his part, Lyon, who was responsible for the chromatic harp without pedal, sought to avoid the drawback of having to place two pianos together for the performance of duets, and combined them into one instrument having the same sound-board. This piano took the form of a large rectangle composed of two triangles joined together; the two shorter sides of this rectangle were taken up by the keyboards, and in this way the two players would face each other.

It is worth mentioning that the square piano, which had gradually disappeared from Europe during the nineteenth century although still being used in America, was no longer made there after about 1880.

In the course of the period we are dealing with here, the organ saw many improvements that it would be impossible for us to enumerate, and even more so to describe in such a concise work as the present one. We shall therefore merely indicate the most important of them.

By inventing, in 1832, the pneumatic lever, which was applied for the first time in 1841 to the organ of Saint-Denis in Paris by the French organ builder Cavaillé-Coll, the English maker, Barker, effected a veritable revolution. By means of this mechanism, not only was the physical pressure required of the player's fingers on the keys reduced, but it was possible to have a greater number of pallets and valves, so that the instrument could be given a more abundant supply of stops and the air pressure became more regular The principle was as follows: the key opened an auxiliary valve which itself opened a special pipe. Because of this pneumatic mechanism, the manuals could be coupled together without the least effect on the required finger pressure. It was the Frenchman Peschard who, in 1862, first thought of applying electricity to the organ, but it was Baker who, in 1868, patented his electro-pneumatic action, which was, broadly speaking, nothing more than the application of electrical principles to the mechanical part of the former system. Further, it became possible to increase the air pressure, so that new registers could be added, one such being the harmonic flute stop introduced by Cavaillé-Coll.

At Paulinzelle, Schulze made use of a cylinder which opened all the stops consecutively as it rotated.

In America, a pedal-board was used in which the keys radiated in an arc formation, thus facilitating the footwork, since all this pedal-board's keys were readily accessible to the player's feet.

In the nineteenth century, the organ case lost its individuality; this was the age of pastiche. The flamboyant Gothic style was as widely imitated as the Renaissance style, but with less taste; often the cases were enormous and overloaded. But after the end of the century and at the beginning of the twentieth century, whether out of a taste for simplicity or from a desire for economy, they were hardly made any longer; the arrangement of the pipes was the only decorative element.

The physharmonica, of which we spoke in the last chapter, derived from Grenié's *orgue expressif* as well as from the Asian sheng. The orgue expressif was so called because, being the first European instrument consisting entirely of free reeds, it was capable of producing loud and soft sounds, and even *crescendi* and *diminuendi*, according to the amount of air- or breath-pressure setting the reeds in vibration. It was with this instrument as starting-point that the physharmonica was developed, together with still further instruments to which their inventors gave various names, such as *aérophone*, *mélophone*, *harmoniflûte*, etc. But all these paled beside the invention of the Parisian maker Alexandre-François Debain, the *harmonium*, patented in 1840, which for the first time combined several stops.

It goes without saying that, after Debain, the harmonium underwent a number of improvements. Chief amongst these was the conception and putting into practice, by Victor Mustel in 1853, of double expression, in which, by means of a knee-operated mechanism, the production of expressive variety could be made independently in the two halves of the keyboard, in other words, the treble notes could be independent of the bass notes. In this way, it was possible to bring out a melody either in the upper or lower register by controlling the dynamics of one or the other of the half-keyboards, whilst at the same time the degree to which the knee-pieces were moved determined the loudness of the sound.

Mechanical Instruments

Debain's first mechanical piano appeared in 1850. It had the appearance of an upright piano in which there was no keyboard, but instead a metallic table across which passed a series of steel teeth each of which was attached to a hammer by means of a rod. A system of panels containing nails was set in motion on the sound-board by means of a crank. The nails, coming into contact with the teeth and acting through them, caused the hammers to strike against the strings. By and large, it is still the same procedure which operates the mechanical pianos used by itinerant musicians. Debain, who had also applied this system to the organ and to the harmonium, this time using the mechanism to open the valves and allow the air to reach the pipes, christened his invention the *antiphonal*. Another means of activating the hammers was by pneumatic pressure. In this case, the instrument had to be provided with a mechanism comprising, as in the harmonium, two pedals to pump in air from the outside, a component called the flute of Pan which had a series of extremely small holes along all its length, and a perforated strip either of cardboard or of paper. Each hole of the flute of Pan corresponded to a given note of the keyboard. The perforated strip was set in motion, and when one of its holes coincided with a hole in the flute of Pan the force of the compressed air that was thus liberated activated a kind of key, which struck the corresponding key on the keyboard just as a player's finger would. Thus all that was necessary was for the strip to be perforated in the requisite places for the chosen piece of music to figure on it.

In the first place, the perforated strip was formed of squares or of rectangles of cardboard superposed on and joined to each other on one side so as to form a continuous strip; some of this kind may still be found nowadays. However, in 1868 MacTammany began to use a flexible strip rolled round a cylinder which, after passing by the "flute of Pan", rolled itself round another cylinder; it is this system that is normally adopted today.

It would be impossible to study all the technical details which over the years added their contribution to the capabilities of the mechanical piano. However, we may point out that at first this instrument was quite impersonal, for it could only reproduce a composition in a uniform manner; there were no variations of loudness or tempo since, on the one hand, the hammers always struck the strings with the same degree of force, and on the other hand it was awkward for the player turning the crank to slow down or speed up the movement, a defect which partially disappeared when pedals began to be used. It was thus to solving these problems that makers devoted their attention: the shading of speeds and of loudness. When these were solved, human participation partly came into its own again. In fact, although at that time there was still no question of a performer, as we understand the term, since the hammers were operated mechanically, it was up to the player operating the pedals or handles to effect the nuances of tempo as of dynamics so as to obtain the effect he desired.

It was in 1900 that the American Votey invented the *pianola*, which had a very great success. Later came the *player*, the *duo-*

art and the *welte mignon*, built by the American firm of Aeolian, but the most perfected mechanism was incontestably the *Pleyela* of the Paris firm Pleyel, which was not in the body of the piano but rather was placed in front of it, depressing the keys with more or less pressure, as would fingers, with its mobile arms overhanging the keyboard. We may also mention the *odéola* of Herrburger, which was erected inside upright or grand pianos of different makes, mainly German. These procedures were also applied to mechanical organs.

VII - Twentieth Century

VII. — 1. **Duke Ellington at the Belgian Radio, Brussels**

Historical Background

Although the very large orchestras of the end of the nineteenth century were still to be heard during the first decades of the twentieth, there was nevertheless a real development in the use of instrumental forces after the First World War. For economic reasons, composers were led to make considerable reductions in the number of performers they used in an orchestra. Besides, this return to a smaller orchestral ensemble (though a different one from that of earlier years) was part of the normal cycle of events, whereby the simple leads to the complex which in turn reverts to the simple only to change direction and tend yet again towards the complex. Such a state of affairs brought about a reduction of the orchestra's sonority and thus allowed the more refined exploitation of timbres that had never till then been used. Even new techniques of playing were introduced, such as passing the bow underneath the strings of the double bass, or playing on the strings of the violin between the bridge and the tailpiece. Finally, percussion instruments were used in their own right, and were sometimes elevated to the rank of soloists. Besides this, jazz introduced new instruments to the orchestra, such as the rattle, the *vibraphone*, and the *Hawaiian guitar*; strange and exotic sonorities were heard, as were certain rhythms of popular dances and of jazz.

Stringed Instruments

Banjo

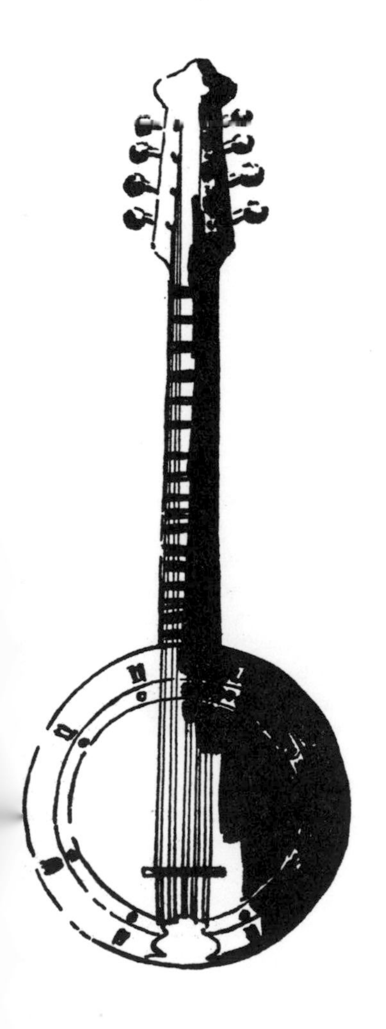

The making of stringed instruments underwent no changes except for an experiment — which was in any case completely unsuccessful — made by the Englishman Stroh of London, who, towards the end of the nineteenth century, introduced a violin without a sound-box; this instrument, in dispensing with the sound-box, substituted a diaphragm which was connected to an amplifying horn, such as those used on the gramophones of the time. Another more recent violin that is rarely encountered was that which had microphones connected to a pedal which could give all the intermediary intensities between triple piano and triple forte. This principle of electrically amplifying an instrument's volume by the use of microphones may be found on numerous other musical instruments, including the harpsichord, the piano and the guitar. The latter is the most familiar, thanks to its use in jazz and in light music. This *electric guitar* is not the same instrument as the Hawaiian guitar, on which the player slides a piece of metal on the metallic strings to give an effect that is similar to that of the Indian *gottuvadyam*.

In the same group of instruments we must mention the *ukulele*, which is a sort of small guitar, originating in Portugal, which was brought over centuries ago to the Sandwich Islanders. It was from there that the ukulele passed over to America to be accepted as a typically indigenous instrument at the beginning of the twentieth century. Another plucked string instrument is the *banjo*, an instrument of Negro origins which was mentioned for the first time during the seventeenth century but did not become widespread until the arrival of jazz. The banjo appears in various forms, in the most authentic of which a wooden neck is fixed on a metal frame over which a membrane is stretched as a sound-board. Its strings are of metal. This instrument, the tuning of which varies, is not played with a plectrum but with the fingers; it lends itself particularly well to the playing of violent and abrupt rhythms and is often used to accompany the singing voice.

Wind Instruments

A few of the older wind instruments have been revived; the recorder, for example, is again used, notably by Orff in his *Schulwerk*. The other wind instruments show no modifications to speak of, although a more highly developed technique of playing allows new effects to be produced; this may be seen particularly clearly in the field of jazz.

Keyboard Instruments

Making use of the principle of microphones picking up the sound of the strings, Nernst built, in 1936, a piano called the *Neo-Bechstein*. Whereas in the normal grand piano there are two or three strings for each note, Nernst only had one or at the most two. The sounds produced by the strings were picked up by 18 microphones. The left pedal operated an amplifier which enabled the volume and the intensity of the sound to be varied without the finger leaving the key. The right pedal lifted the dampers, as on other pianos. The instrument's touch was extremely light.

Before the Second World War, the engineer Pierre Hans had a double manual piano made by Pleyel's of Paris; the same keys of the upper and the lower manual produced notes a semitone apart. When one played on the lower manual those keys on the upper manual which corresponded to the notes sounded functioned automatically. The upper manual still operated independently.

Certain modern harpsichord makers also provide their instruments with microphones so that they can respond more effectively to the demands of large halls. The harpsichord is enjoying a return to favour, not simply in the same way as other instruments of the Renaissance, but also because modern composers, such as Falla and Ibert, have written for this instrument.

There is a return to the organ of Bach's time. This tendency is in evidence particularly in northern Germany, one of the greatest of organ-building regions. Attention should also be drawn to the importance of the organ the Abbé Pujet had built for the church of Notre Dame de Liban in Paris in 1934, which has fifty stops, four manuals and a pedal-board. This instrument was called a *radio-synthetic organ* because, the manufacture of the numerous pipes it was to possess proving too expensive, Pujet resolved the problem by positioning microphones which allowed the production of the necessary harmonics for the mutation stops, and thereby considerably reducing the number of pipes needed. Such an operation was only possible as a result of the use of electrical and electronic resources that had recently been used to good effect. Long before Abbé Pujet, Abt Vogler in Darmstadt had also attempted to reduce the number of pipes. His *Simplifika-*

VII. — 2.

Hawaiian guitar by the firm Melodia. This flat-bodied instrument has 6 metal strings that are plucked by a plectrum of either tortoiseshell or metal. At the same time, with his left hand, the player slides a piece of metal along the strings, producing the characteristic effect of the Hawaiian *glissando*. This guitar may be connected to an amplifier and loudspeakers. Inside the sound-box is a variable resistance which enables the intensity to be varied.
Length: *c.* 26½ ins.

M.I., Brussels
No. 4206

VII. — 3.

Electric harpsichord by the firm Neupert, Händel model. This instrument differs from other modern harpsichords by the fact that the vibrations of its strings are picked up by microphones, thus adapting the harpsichord to the demands of present-day concert halls. In the photograph a box may be seen placed above the strings; in this box are the microphones. Loudspeakers are placed near the lid which in this way serves the purpose it has always had: that of resonating the sound. The usual stops of the Neupert harpsichord are retained.
Length: *c.* 93¾ ins.

Coll. Neupert, Nuremberg

VII. — 4.

Detail of a Hans system Pleyel piano. On this piano the playing of sometimes difficult chromatic compositions is made easier. This instrument offers new and interesting technical possibilities, but up to now has only been played by a few pianists (for example Mme. Scapus and Pierre Hans's friend, Carl Smulders). In fact besides being expensive, large and twice the weight of a normal grand piano, it demands a pianistic technique to which most pianists are hardly prepared to devote the necessary time and effort.

M.I., Brussels
No. 38[illegible]

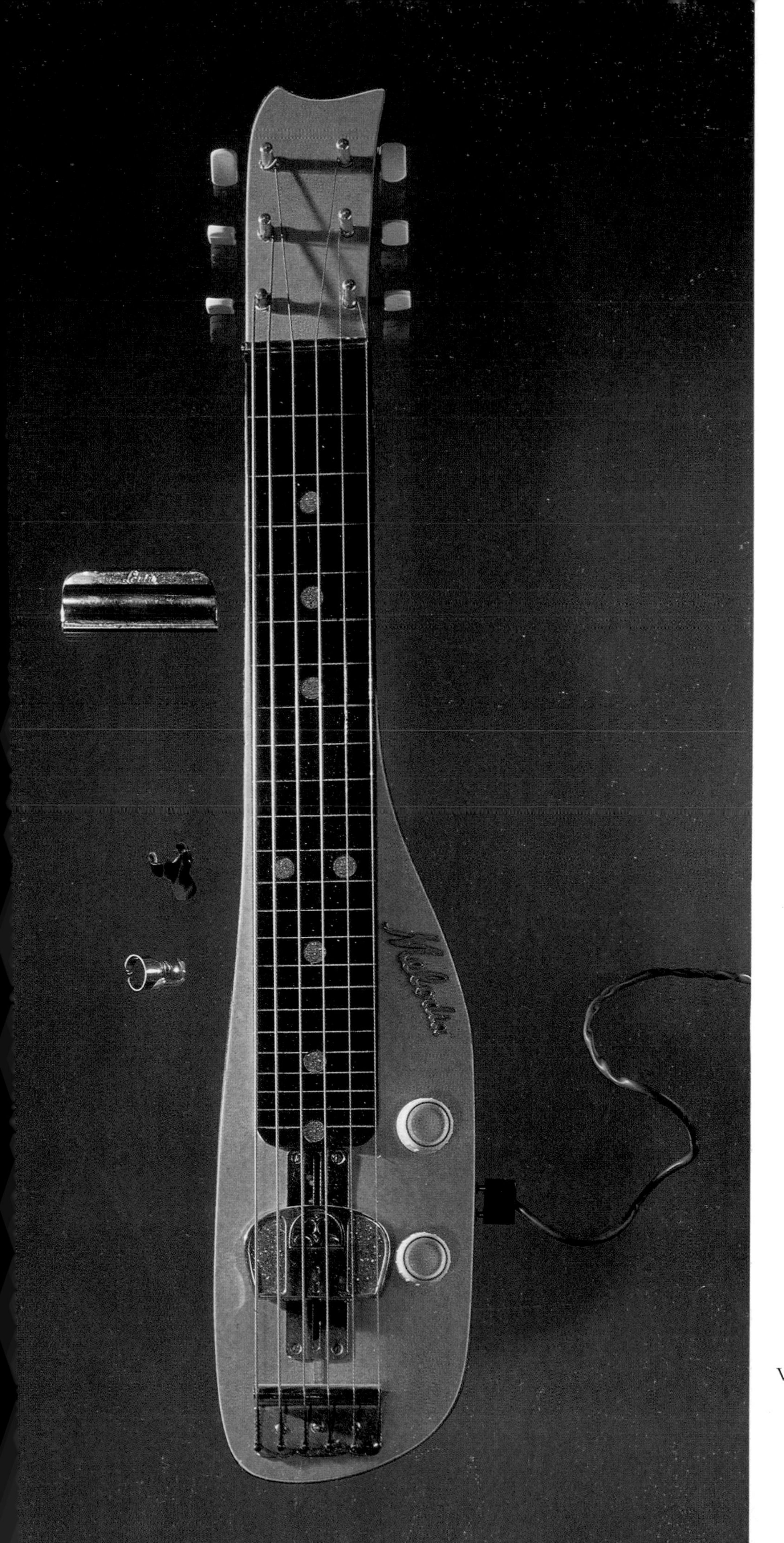

VII. — 2. **Hawaiian guitar**
(20th century)

VII. — 3. **German electric harpsichord** (20th century)

VII. — 4. **Hans system Pleyel piano** (20th century) ▶

CLAVIER HANS

VII. — 5. **French crystal trombone** (20th century)

VII. — 6. **French percussion instrument** (20th century) ▶

VII. — 7. **American Hammond organ** (20th century)

VII. — 8. **Jazz rhythm section** (20th century) ▶

MEXICO
MEXICO

VII. — 9. **Electronic music equipment** (20th century)

VII. — 5.
Crystal trombone by the brothers Baschet. This instrument has twelve crystal rods attached to a piece of metal to which is fitted a polygonal sheet of metal which acts as an amplifier. The player's moistened fingers rub the rods which are thus set in vibration. The sound can be regulated by means of weighted metal rods placed perpendicularly to the crystal rods.
Property of the Brothers Baschet, Paris.

tionssystem was based on the acoustical law, according to which two harmonics cause a deeper harmonic to be sounded. In this way Vogler was able for instance to avoid the use of 32-foot pipes while still using a 32-foot stop.

The "biggest organ in the world" was built at Atlantic City in New Jersey (U.S.) in about 1935 and has 32,882 pipes. It has 1,233 stops and 7 manuals.

Electric And Electronic Instruments

However, the most important invention of this century as far as instrument making is concerned was the application of electrical and electronic techniques to classical musical instruments. We have already seen one example of this with the radio-synthetic organ. As a rule, these techniques are of two types: firstly, the application of electro-acoustical means and, secondly, the electronic production of sounds.

We have already mentioned some of the electro-acoustical instruments, notably the neo-Bechstein piano and the pedal violin. In these cases, the sounds which are initiated in the normal manner struck strings on the piano or bowed strings on the violin are either amplified or transformed into new timbres. We may recall that a sound can be characterised by its pitch (determined by its frequency cycles), by its intensity or loudness (determined by the amplitude of its vibrations) and by its timbre (determined by the form of its vibrations). These three facets can be influenced by electronic intervention; in this way, for example, a violin can be made to give out sounds similar to those of a cello. It should be noted that for the sound to be picked up electrically, metallic strings have to be used.

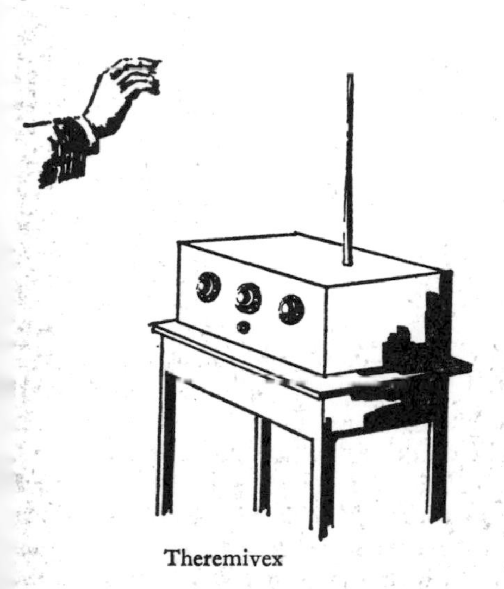

Theremivex

Electronic equipment is capable of producing sounds either by high frequency or by low frequency. High frequency can only be used for generating sounds by means of pulsations.

The Russian, Leo Theremine, introduced in 1924 an instrument he called the *Thereminvox*. Its outward appearance is very simple; it consists of a box having an upright rod projecting upwards. The nearer the performer's hand approaches this rod, the higher is the sound produced. To avoid *glissandos*, the player uses an interrupting button; he can also vary the loudness of the sound by means of a pedal. The principle of the thereminvox is fairly simple; two sound-waves of differing frequencies produce a given note (*Differenzton*). Thus, all that is required for the pitch of this note to be varied is that one of these initial frequencies should be altered. This is made possible by the fact that the transmitter is simply an inductor coil and variable condenser. The interest of the thereminvox is above all historical. It consists of two high frequency oscillators from whose interferences a pulsation is given. This pulsation is amplified and directed through two loudspeakers. The sound produced is similar to that of a pure sine-wave, thus is very poor in harmonics. One of the oscillators transmits a constant frequency.

Sphaerephon

In 1928, Jorg Mager, a German inventor, introduced the *Sphaerophon* at Darmstadt. The modification of frequencies was produced by the interference of frequencies transmitted by a valve oscillator with a basic frequency. By adding filters, Mager could vary the timbre. Mager died in 1939 practically forgotten. The Nazi régime had previously deprived him of his laboratory.

The thereminvox was hardly an ideal instrument, for the use of the hand entailed certain drawbacks and limited the instrument's capabilities. For this reason, ribbons began to be used, these being on the one hand more precise and on the other hand able to offer a certain amount of polyphonic scope. The instruments based on this principle were either monodic, like Martenot's *ondes musicales* (also called *ondes Martenot*, 1928), Langer-Halagyi's *Emicon* (about 1930) and Trautwein's *trautonium* (1930), or had polyphonic capabilities like the *hellertion* of Helberger and Lertes (1928) and the *Hammond organ*. All these instruments operate on low frequencies. They use sine-waves or distortions of them: square waves, saw-tooth waves, etc. The hellertion basically used the latter.

Martenot's starting-point was the principle that, if correctly circuited, valves can produce very pure wave forms; the electronic instrument yields its notes by the interference of two frequencies which are themselves produced by two oscillators. The ondes Martenot has a range of 7 octaves. The player has two possible ways of playing the instrument: there is a keyboard to control the degrees of vibrato and a volume-control button which allows *pianissimos* as well as *fortissimos*, *glissandos* as well as *pizzicatos* to be played. In 1950, Martenot added special loudspeakers. The instrument has been taught at the Paris Conservatoire since 1947. Composers who have used it in their works include Olivier Messiaen, André Jolivet and Arthur Honegger in his work *Jeanne au Bûcher*.

The German H. Genzmer has written a concerto for the trautonium.

The first models of the Hammond organ were based on vibrations produced by light waves. A light ray was projected into 91 revolving discs which intercepted it and in this way produced vibrations which were transformed into audible sound-waves. Each note had its corresponding disc. On each of these discs, by means of perforations, the first six and the eighth harmonics could be obtained. The seventh harmonic was not included because it clashed in dissonance with the first. By means of resistances, these harmonics could be combined with each other, thus forming new timbres. This being the case, here was an organ in which pipes would have been superfluous. All its sounds were produced entirely by electricity. Vibratos and tremolos were also possible.

The great economy offered by these instruments will readily be appreciated. Those mentioned above were not alone in benefitting from the application of electronics. For example, instead of having costly bells cast, they can be cheaply replaced by tubes which are struck and whose sound is amplified and improved by means of microphones, amplifiers and filters.

Today's electronic music calls on still further instruments; the modern composer works in a veritable laboratory surrounded by tape recorders (preferably in quantity), microphones, a number of generators, mixers, audiofilters, amplifiers, channel separators and finally loudspeakers placed in the corners so as to give a three-dimensional effect.

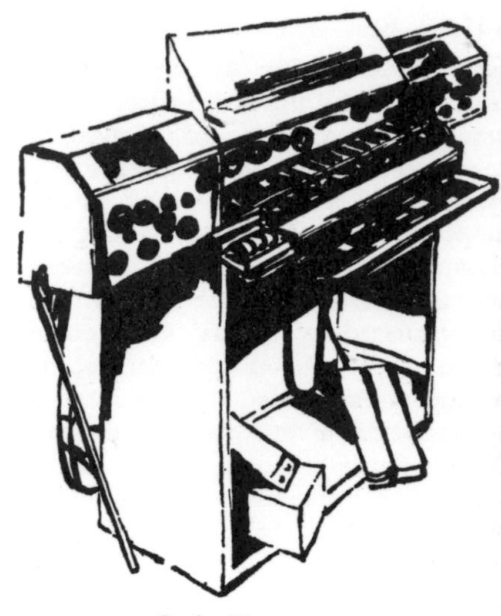

Onde Martenot

VII. — 6.

Percussion instrument by Baschet. It consists of a number of metal rods whose ends are weighted so as to determine the pitch of the sound. They are struck with rubber-headed sticks. The rods are connected on the one side to two cardboard cones which act as amplifiers, and on the other side to two cylindrical barrels acting as resonaters.

Property of the Brothers Baschet, Paris.

VII. — 7.

Hammond organ; the instrument shown here has the same characteristics as had the first Hammond organ. However some of its elements have been improved. This type, E-100 has two manuals of 61 keys and a pedal-board of 25 keys activating 8- and 16-foot stops. Each manual has 9 stops, 3 combinations and 9 registers which enable the harmonics to be regulated. In addition, the instrument has a swell-box. Three loudspeakers are used to distribute the sound.

Dimensions: *c.* $47\frac{1}{4}$ ins. × $47\frac{1}{4}$ ins. × $25\frac{5}{8}$ ins.

Hammond Organ Ltd., U.S.A.

VII. — 8.

Jazz rhythm section comprising a bass drum with pedal, tenor drum, side drum and snare drum, cymbals, a suspended cymbal, maracas, a recco-recco, two claves, a gourd, a wood-block and bongos. On the skin of the snare drum are ordinary sticks and brushes. The drumheads are stretched by screws. The snare drum can, if the player wishes, be turned so that special strokes such as the "rim-shot" can be played. Its special feature is the "snare", a series of metal wires strung under the drum which, when brought into play by a lever, give a characteristic sound often used in drum-rolls. The recco-recco, a hollow rattle, and the claves, small sticks of hard wood, figure in the rumba, as do the maracas and gourd.

M.I., Brussels.
Nos. 3967 - 3983.

VII. — 9.

Equipment used in making electronic music. This set consists of a professional two-track stereo tape-recorder. Above the recorder are placed (*left*) a sine- and square-wave generator and (*right*) an oscilloscope.

Studio for Electronic Music,
Brussels.

Vibraphone

The instruments used in experimental music and in *musique concrète* can be divided into three categories: generators, wave shapers and linear mixing devices.

I. The generators provide the raw material of arbitrarily pitched sounds; they include:

a) natural generators (traditional instruments, voices, noises);
b) oscillators which produce pure sine-waves;
c) timbre generators in which photo-electric cells act on light rays;
d) the electronic instruments mentioned above;
e) digital computers which can create wave forms (used by Matthews and Guttman in the Bell laboratories).

II. The wave shapers serve

a) to define the pitch: the sound or noise should be able to be fixed at the desired pitch. Here, Pierre Schaeffer's phonogen, filters and Heck's ring modulator are used particularly.
b) to define the duration (either psychological or physical) by means of repeating devices (e.g. tape loops), artificial echo effects (obtained by a spaced-out series of play-back heads on the tape recorder) or, finally, by reverberation.

III. The linear mixing devices produce a synthesis of I and II, moulded into a logical structure. Here the composer makes particular use of:

a) multiple-track tape recorders;
b) play-back tape recorders;
c) computers such as Illiac which select, examine, accept or reject about 1000 possibilities a second. Those that are accepted are stored in the computer until the composition is complete. In this way Hiller and Isaacson wrote the *Illiac* suite in 1957.

In France, Barbaud and Blanchard have used computers to explore the possibilities of composing artificial music on machines, using serial music as their basis.

Musique concrète is based on the principle of applying and extending the principles discovered by Abraham Moles at the *Centre National de Recherches Scientifiques* in the field of presenting a three-dimensional music using the following parameters: amplitude, frequency and duration. Thus the sounds or noises to be used can be subjected to a preparative treatment.

Generators produce electric currents. These can be regulated with respect to frequency (pitch), wave form (timbre) and amplitude (intensity). Theoretically there is no limit to the possibilities of obtaining new sounds and effects. In order to be able to work with pure sounds (without harmonics), sine-waves are used. Filters help the composer to add or to eliminate certain effects. Once everything has been recorded, the composer has at his disposal an enormous range of possible ways of working with the raw material he has prepared. In fact it is possible to superimpose tapes, as well as to play them back in canon. The tape can be cut into pieces and stuck together again. The dynamics can be varied; as for the speed, which can also be varied, it not only changes the tempo of a piece but also its pitch range. The tape can be played backwards, and *ostinati* can be produced by using a tape loop. Echos are produced in a special echo chamber or by having two identical tapes playing back slightly out of phase with each other.

Modern experimental music does not stop at using all these procedures. The American, John Cage uses traditional instruments, such as the piano, which he "prepares" by introducing mechanical or acoustical modifications. He has adopted the principle of Henry Cowell, who in 1919 used "note clusters" by striking a number of adjacent piano keys. John Cage has made a systematic exploration of the timbres that are possible if the strings of a piano have been prepared with plumb-lines, knobs, iron balls, etc.

To sum up, we may say that in experimental music there is a discernible pattern of three national schools: in France, *musique concrète* is composed; on the other hand, in Germany the post-war school continues with electronic music; and two tendencies are to be found in the USA with Cage's prepared piano and music for tape (cut up and reassembled).

Other Instruments

Further exotic instruments besides those used in the previous period, such as the vibraphone, have made their appearance in the modern European symphony orchestra. The origin of the vibraphone is in the non-European xylophone. It is a metallic instrument having a pedal to control its intensity. Also, it is worth mentioning the inclusion in the orchestra of the rattle, several drums including the *bongos*, and the *Chinese blocks*.

We may be certain that increasing and deepening intercourse between the peoples of the earth will result in a new type of instrumental ensemble, such as may be found already on a small scale today.

postscript

In closing a work which has given the reader a bird's-eye view of the evolution of musical instruments from prehistoric times till the present day, we may ask what is to be expected of instrument making in the future.

Such a question might well be answered if we base our conjectures on the lessons of the past and the experiments of today. It can be seen that since the earliest antiquity man has never ceased to seek out new sonorities by creating new instruments or by improving the quality of those already in existence. A good number of experiments have led to failure and been quickly forgotten. However, they were not always fruitless, for sometimes they opened up horizons to which would be directed later and more successful experiments by more fortunate and skilled inventors.

There can be no doubt that the traditional instruments such as are today used as solo or orchestral instruments will not quickly die out. They are backed up by a history which has well and truly established them and it will be a long time before they yield to newcomers. Although some of them, such as the violin family, have attained an unsurpassable perfection, others, belonging to the woodwind and the brass, could still be improved from the point of view of their precision and versatility of sound as well as in their ease of handling.

But side by side with these we find new instruments appearing in our music. These should be seen as being of three types: 1) those which, like Baschet's glass organ, are built with the same materials and on the same principles as earlier instruments like the glass harmonica and the mattauphone; 2) those which are taken over from Oriental or African music; and 3) those of electronic origin.

When Baschet called his instrument an organ, he did not intend it to be understood as a normal organ any more than had Hammond, for the elements of the glass organ and of the Hammond organ are quite different and although some of their sounds and timbres are reminiscent of the traditional organ, many others are not at all like it and constitute a hitherto unheard world of sound. This new world of sound grows daily; for example, Baschet, using mainly glass and perhaps a vibrating metal plate or other materials, is extending the scope of his researches as far as percussion instruments. Besides this, experiments are being carried out on the sonorific potential of such materials as bamboo and plastic. With such research in view, laboratories have been set up in various centres, such as those at the Universities of Amsterdam, Utrecht and Ghent.

From the time of Haydn and Mozart up to the Impressionist era, Asian instruments (mainly of percussion) were introduced into European instrumental ensembles, above all to add "local colour". Today this is no longer so: these, and other instruments of African and Latin-American origin, are subjected to the study of their musical characteristics and used for these by composers of the present generation (we need only give, as an example, Stockhausen's use of the slit drums of the Duala). Doubtless Western music of the future will continue to investigate the instrumental resources of other continents and, if need be, adapt them to its own ends.

It is equally certain that electronic instruments will increase in number and diversity, opening up a world of sound of which we can now only have a vague idea. This will only be made possible by the work of engineers and acousticians who will create these instruments. In short, these will be supported by their knowledge of traditional methods of instrument making. However, it is the composers who will remain the true musical creators rather than, as some composers fear, the engineers. But they will have to get to know and make the best possible use of these new instruments, whether they use them on their own or combined with classical instruments as is already the case in some compositions of recent years.

Glossary

Each word followed by a * is described elsewhere in the glossary.

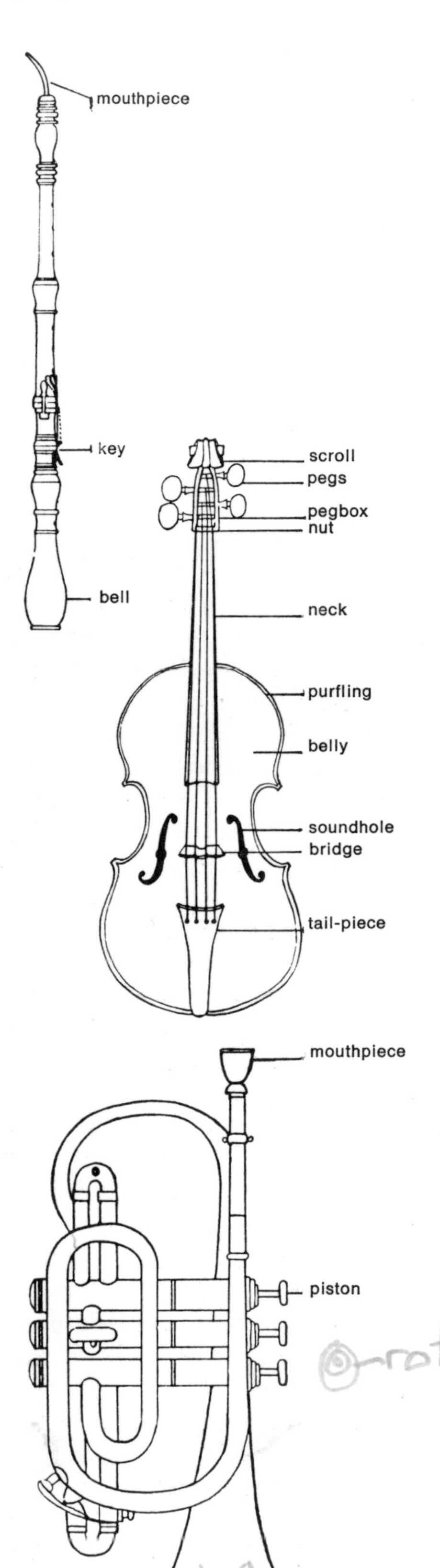

Back. Flat or slightly humped surface forming the underside of the sound-box* of a stringed instrument.

Bass bar. A piece of wood, generally deal, glued to the interior surface of the belly* of a stringed instrument, and stretching almost all its length; in an instrument like the violin, it is placed under the left-hand foot of the bridge*, in other words, on the side of the lower strings, and serves not only to strengthen the part of the belly which is subject to the pressure of the bridge, but also to spread over the belly the vibrations transmitted through the bridge.

Bell. Far end of the tube of certain wind instruments, being flared out or in bulb shape.

Belly. The flat or slightly humped surface above which the strings of a stringed instrument are stretched.

Bore. The proportion existing between the diameter and the length of the interior of a wind instrument; can be cylindrical, as in the clarinet, or conical, as in the oboe. Its form has an influence on the resonance of harmonics* and hence on an instrument's timbre*.

Bridge. A small piece of thin, hard wood placed on the belly of a stringed instrument to support the strings. It is instrumental in transmitting their vibrations to the belly. A bridge is used also in stringed keyboard instruments.

Crook. A small curved tube of copper or some other metal on certain double-reed instruments, such as the cor anglais and the bassoon, on the end of which the reed* is fixed.
Also, in brass instruments, a detachable length of tubing used to alter the instrument's pitch.

Cup. On brass instruments, the part of the mouthpiece immediately in contact with the player's mouth. It can be hemispherical, as in the trumpet, trombone, etc., or conical, as in the horn.

Damper. A piece of felt fixed at the top of a jack* which damps the sound by falling onto a string after it has been struck; on the piano, it takes the form of a length of wood, covered in felt, fulfilling the same function.

Fingerboard. Part of the neck* of a stringed instrument, onto which the player's left-hand fingers press the strings to shorten their length and thus raise the pitch of the note played; can be a part of the neck itself (as on old lutes) or a separate piece, generally of ebony, fixed to the neck (as on the violin).

Flue. Organ pipes, either stopped or open, into which air is introduced without the intermediary of a reed; flue pipes are the organ's basic pipes.

Foot. A term used in defining the register of each rank of organ pipes: a rank is designated according to the length of its longest pipe; hence, one may talk of 1-, 2-, 4-, 8-, and 16-foot stops*. There are also 1-, 3-, 5- and 2-, 2-, 3-foot stops. This terminology is also applied to the harpsichord, by analogy, and not because its longest string is of any particular length.

Frequency. The number of vibrations per second produced by a fundamental*. The higher the frequency, the higher the sound.

Fret. A fairly thin piece of catgut, wood or ivory, a number of which are placed on the neck* of certain stringed instruments marking off the positions the player's left-hand fingers will adopt.
A fretted clavichord is one having more notes than strings.

Frog. A small piece of wood at the lower end of the bow, to which the hair is attached. Also called the nut.

Fundamental. The lowest sound produced by a free vibrating body; all musical sounds consist of fundamenta and their attendant harmonics*.

Harmonics. The higher sounds produced togethe with a fundamental*; their frequencies* are multiple of the fundamental's frequency.

Jack. A small, flat piece of wood placed vertically ove each of the keys* of a plucked string keyboard instrumen such as the harpsichord or the spinet. The jack is nc attached to the key, but when the key is depressed, levers the jack upwards to the string, which is plucke by a plectrum* and subsequently damped by a damper both attached to the jack.

Key. In keyboard instruments, a small lever, mounte on a pivot, upon which the player presses with his fing so as to activate the sound-producing mechanism.
Also, on wind instruments, a mechanism which enabl the player to stop or open a hole without applying h finger directly to it.

Mixture stops. In the organ, the mixture stops ar those which strengthen one or more of the harmonics sounded by the fundamentals* of the flue* stops.

Mouthpiece. A detachable part of a wind instrumer to which the player's lips are applied.

Neck. That part of a hand-held stringed instrume which the player holds, and over which is placed t fingerboard.

Nut. On a stringed instrument, a small piece of wo or ivory placed on the neck* below the head in order lift the strings slightly before they traverse the neck. Also a frog*

Peg. A small piece of wood or metal, conical in sha inserted into the head of a stringed instrument, arou which the string is wrapped (each string having one pe and by means of which it is tuned.

Pegbox. That part of the head of a stringed instrum in many instruments surmounted by a scroll* or ot decoration into which the pegs* are inserted.

Piston. On brass instruments, a feature of valve* mech ism.

Plectrum. A small blade or quill used to pluck strings of certain stringed instruments. In pluck string keyboard instruments, the plectrum is affixed the jack.

Purfling. Inlaid strips of wood set near the edge of belly and back of an instrument, such as a violin, serving protect it from the effects of chips and cracks.

Range. An instrument's range is the distance betw the lowest and highest notes normally playable on

Reed. A small blade of wood, reed or metal, one whose extremities is generally attached to a pipe, and other of which vibrates with the passage of air ei from a player's mouth or, as in the organ, from a wi chest*. Single-reed instruments have a reed which vibr against the entry to the pipe (as in the clarinet): dou reeds vibrate against each other (as in the oboe): free reeds vibrate along their own length, being pla over an aperture through which air is forced (as in accordion).

Register. A term used loosely to define a given sec of an instrument's range*. If the normally used quency* range is split up into registers each comprising an octave, the following table based on the French system of *régions* results:

Région	Lowest Note	Feet	Frequency (Hertz)
02	C''	32	16
01	C'	16	32
1	C	8	64
2	C	4	128
3	C'	2	256
4	C''	1	512
5	C'''	1/2	1024
6	C''''	1/4	2048
7	C'''''	1/8	4096

Also virtually a synonym of stop*.

Rose-hole. A circular sound-hole* in the belly* or sound-board* of a plucked-string instrument, often covered in fretwork in earlier instruments.

Screw. A tuning device fitted to certain instruments, such as hand-tuned kettledrums.

Scroll. The top end of an instrument of the violin familly. This part which is in the shape of a spiral wrapped round a central boss, is generally artistically carved and may help to identify an instrument's maker.

Sound-board. On a stringed instrument, the board over which the strings are stretched; see also Belly.

Sound-holes. Small openings in the sound-boards of hand-held stringed instruments, in the shape of a C, an S or an F, according to the period. The sound-holes allow free passage of the vibrating air from the soundbox; their shape and position on the belly* have an effect on the quality of sound production.

Sound-post. A small cylindrical piece of wood placed a little behind the right foot of the bridge*, between the belly* and back* of a stringed instrument, such as the violin. It reinforces the right side of the belly and at the same time relays its vibrations to the back.

Stop. In the organ, this refers to a rank of pipes of the same type and the same timbre*. The principal stops of the organ are of three kinds: flue* stops, reed* stops and mixture* stops. The term can also refer to a series of strings of the same register or the same timbre on the harpsichord.
The verb, to stop, is used to describe an action - of "stopping" strings (i.e., placing one's finger on a string in order to alter its length and the pitch of its sound), or of "stopping" holes (i.e., placing one's finger or a mechanical substitute over the hole of a pipe, again in order to change the pitch produced) - used in playing certain stringed and wind instruments.

Tail-piece. A piece of wood placed on the lower part of a stringed instrument's belly* to which are secured the strings after crossing over the bridge*.

Tailpin. A small piece of wood or ivory in the shape of a conical peg with rounded head, which serves to attach the tail-piece* to the instrument.

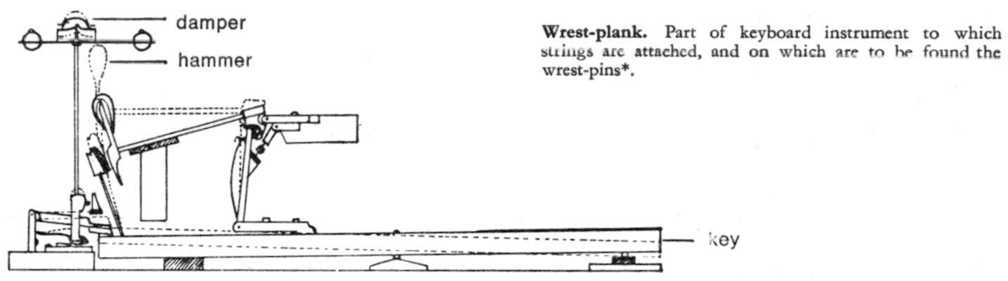

Brinsmead patent piano action

Throat. The narrowest part of a brass mouthpiece leading away from the cup*.

Timbre. The particular quality of the sound produced by a voice or an instrument which distinguishes it from another voice, or from an instrument of a different family; a sound's timbre or colour, depends on the number and intensity of the harmonics* attendant on a fundamental*.

Tuning-slide. In wind instruments, a part of the tubing which is mobile, whose purpose is to maintain the correct pitch of the instrument.

Valve. On certain brass instruments, a mechanism that allows the length of a secondary tubeto be added at will to that of the principal tube thus affecting its pitch; different instruments have a different number of secondary tubes, and consequently a different number of valves.

Wind-chest. A vital part of the organ, situated under the pipes, in which air pressure is built up from the bellows in readiness to enter the pipes.

Wrest-pin. On keyboard stringed instruments, a peg used for tuning the strings.

Wrest-plank. Part of keyboard instrument to which strings are attached, and on which are to be found the wrest-pins*.

Comparative Chronology

Date	Musical instrument	Musical history	Philosophy and the arts
700 B.C.	Seven-stringed lyre Bronze jingles	Assyro-Babylonian bas-reliefs showing martial and festive music	Terpander (Lesbos)
c. 4 0 B.C.	Twelve stringed cithara	The musicians Phryne of Mitylenus and Timotheus of Miletus	Plato (*c.* 427-347 B.C.)
c. 350 B.C.	5 types of aulos		Aristoxenus of Tarentum (*c.* 330 B.C.)
c. 200 B.C.	Hydraulic organ		Terence (185-159 B.C.)
3rd century A.D.	Pneumatic organ	The Celtic Bard Ossian	Origen (*c.* 200 A.D.)
500 A.D.	Harps used by the Irish bards	Boethius: *De Institutione Musica.* Distinction between *musica mundana, humana* and *instrumentale*	St. Benedict founds the Benedictine order.
600	Lyra Triangular psaltery	Gregory the Great	Invention of printing in China (early 7th century)
7th century	Irish harp	Founding of the *Schola Cantorum* in Rome	Caedmon, Anglo-Saxon poet (*c.* 650)
9th century	Lyre-lute	Alcuin: *Treatise on the Modes*	Palatinate schools at Aachen and Tours.
980	Winchester organ	Treatises on the dimensions of pipes and on neumes	St. Mark's, Venice (976)
11th century	Clairsighe	Guido d'Arezzo: *Micrologus de disciplina Artis Musicae*	Death of Avicenna (1037). *Chanson de Roland* (late 11th century).
1250	Manichord	Franco of Cologne, *Ars Cantus Mensurabilis*	Ste. Chapelle (Paris) finished. *Cantigas de Santa Maria* of Alfonso the Wise (1252-1284)
1306	Pedal-board added to organ	Birth of Guillaume de Machaut	Birth of Petrarch (1304). Death of Duns Scotus (1308). *Roman de Fauvel* (1316).
1404	Clavichord first mentioned	Dufay born (1400)	Leipzig University founded (1409)
1413	Earliest drawing of a harpsichord. Flute has an open key.	Joanes Ciconia at Padua (1412)	Excommunication of Huss. François Villon born (1431).
1451	Building of the Blois organ	Conrad Paumann: *Fundamentum Organisandi* (1452)	Botticelli born (1449). Da Vinci born (1452).

1457	Appearance of the kettledrum in the West	*Lochamer Liederbuch* begun (1452). John Dunstable died (1453).	Fra Angelico died (1455)
1493	First known spinet	Heinrich Isaac, *Missa Carminum*	Da Vinci's " Last Supper " painted (1495-1497)
1511	Clavicytherium first mentioned	Sebastian Virdung, *Musica getutscht.* Thomas Tallis born (*c.* 1505) Petrucci of Venice prints music from movable type.	Matthias Grünewald's altar-piece at Isenheim (1510). Erasmus, *In Praise of Folly* (1509).
1519	Earliest picture of a regal organ	Hofhaimer, organist at Salzburg.	Tintoretto born (1518).
1520	Viol introduced to England	*Canzoni* by Willaert published by Antico in Rome. Palestrina born (*c.* 1526).	Raphael died. — Grünewald and Durer died (1521). Pierre de Ronsard was born (1524).
1541	Carillon provided with a keyboard	Ganassi del Fontegne, *Regola Rubertina* (1542).	Michelangelo completes " The Last Judgement ".
1543	First known clavichord	Cavazzoni, *Intavolatura d'Organo* Byrd born (1543).	Tasso born (1544)
1550	Bible regal organ	*Vespers* by Willaert	Vasari, *Vite de 'pittori.*
1572	Cello made by Andrea Amati	De Lassus, *Patrocinium Musices*	Shakespeare born (1564). De Vega born (1562).
1581	Invention of the French flageolet by Juvigny	First *ballet de cour, Ballet comique de la Reine*, by Beaujoyeux.	Montaigne, *Essais.* Tasso, *Jerusalem Delivered.* Franz Hals born (1580).
1600	Carillon provided with a pedal-board	Peri's opera *Euridice*	Malherbe, *Odes.* Calderón born.
1619	Harpsichord by Boni	Landi's opera *La Morte d'Orfeo.* *Fitzwilliam Virginal Book* completed.	Kepler, *Harmony of the World.* Rubens, " The Descent from the Cross ".
1626	*Les 24 violons du Roy*	Mazzocchi's opera *La Catena d'Adone.* First German opera, *Daphne*, by Schütz.	Molière born (1622). Bunyan born (1628).
1643	Cross-strung harp	Monteverdi 's opera *L'Incoronazione di Poppea* (1642)	Corneille, *Polyeucte* (1642). Descartes, *Method* (1636). Rembrandt, " Night Watch " (1642).
1650	French horn	Carissimi's oratorio *Jephtha*	Velasquez, " Toilet of Venus ".
1657	Introduction of the oboe	Alessandro Scarlatti born (1660)	*L'Académie des Sciences* founded in Paris (1658). Molière: *Les Précieuses Ridicules* (1659).

date	musical instrument	musical history	philosophy and the arts
1675	*Hamburger Zitrinchen*	Lebegue, *Premier livre d'orgue*	Bunyan, *The Pilgrim's Progress* (1678). Leibnitz and Newton discover infinitesimal calculus.
1690	Flat trumpet	Muffat, *Apparatus musico-organisticus*	Papin, *Memoire sur l'emploi de la vapeur d'eau.* Locke, *Human Understanding.*
c. 1700	Invention of the clarinet	Kuhnau, *Biblical Sonatas*	Yale University founded
1709	Cristofori's piano	Tomaso Albinoni, *Concerti per Violone*	Goldoni born (1707).
1712	Swell-box on the organ	Handel's opera *Rinaldo*	Watteau's "L'Embarquement pour Cythere". Pope, *Rape of the Lock.*
1716	Marius's piano	Fux, *Missa Canonica*	Vauvenargues born (1715)
1717	Schröter's piano	François Couperin, *L'Art de toucher le clavecin.*	Garrick born
1720	Oboe d'amore. Hochbrucker's pedal harp.	J.S. Bach, *Well-tempered Clavier.* Rameau, *Traité de l'harmonie.*	Defoe, *Robinson Crusoe* (1719). Gibbs begins building St-Martin-in-the-Fields.
1726	Cristofori's piano with double action and escapement	Pepusch and Gay, *The Beggar's Opera*	Vico, *Principles of Philosophy and History* (1725). Swift, *Gulliver's Travels.*
c. 1730	Crenelated bow	J.S. Bach, *Kyrie* and *Gloria* from the B Minor Mass	Prevost, *Manon Lescaut.* (1731)
1743	Puckeridge's angelic harp	Handel's oratorio *Samson*	Voltaire, *Mérope.* d'Alembert, *Traité de dynamique.*
1745	Friderici's pyramidal piano	J.S. Bach, *Well-Tempered Clavier* (Book Two, 1744)	Volta born
1747	J.S. Bach approves Silbermann's pianos	J.S. Bach, *The Musical Offering.*	Diderot, *Pensées philosophiques*
1750	*Harpe* à *béquilles*	J.S. Bach, *Art of Fugue*	Rousseau, *Discours sur les Sciences*
1753	Range of harpsichord five octaves	C.P.E. Bach, *Versuch uber die wahre Art das Klavier zu Spielen*	De Maistre born
1760	English horn. Hampel-system chromatic horn	Leopold Mozart, *Violin Method* (1756)	Voltaire, *Candide* (1759). Rousseau, *La Nouvelle Heloise.*
1761	Franklin's glass harmonica	Gluck's opera *Orfeo* produced in Rome	Petit Trianon built
1764	Four-keyed clarinet	J.C. Bach's opera *Orione*	Voltaire, *Dictionnaire Philosophique*

1769	Glass harmonica given rubbing pads	Rousseau, *Dictionnaire de musique* (1767)	Chateaubriand born (1768)
1770	Basset horn. Prellmechanik given escapement.	Handel's *Messiah* performed in New York. Tartini died.	Goethe begins *Faust*. Wordsworth born.
1774	Six-keyed transverse flute	Gluck's opera *Iphigénie en Aulide*	Goethe, *Sorrows of Werther*
1779	Glass harmonica played with a bow	Gluck, *Iphigénie en Tauride*	Lessing, *Nathan der Weise*
1780	Modern bow by Tourte and by Dodd	Paisiello *The Barber of Seville*	Kant, *Critique of Pure Reason* (1781).
1782	Bassoon with wooden crook. Harp with 14 pedals.	Mozart's opera *Il Seraglio*	Samuel Johnson, *Lives of the Poets* (finished 1781)
1783	Cittern with keyboard. Piano with pedal.	Mozart, Great C Minor Mass	Reynolds paints " Mrs Siddons as the Tragic Muse " (1784).
1786	*F* key added to the transverse flute.	Mozart's opera *The Marriage of Figaro* (1785).	Burns, *Poems*.
1788	Six-stringed guitar.	Mozart, *Jupiter Symphony*.	Blake, *Songs of Innocence*.
1792	Alto clarinet. Bass clarinet.	Cimarosa's opera *The Secret Marriage*.	Paine, *The Rights of Man* (1791).
1807	Piano buffet.	Beethoven's opera *Fidelio* (1805).	Schiller, *William Tell* (1804).
1810	Harp with fork mechanism. Keyed bugle. Metal transverse flute.	Beethoven's music for *Egmont*.	Schlegel, *On Modern History*. Goya's " Execution of the Defenders of Madrid ".
1812	Double-action harp. Thirteen-keyed clarinet. Basse orgue.	Weber s opera *Abu Hassan* (1811).	Byron, *Childe Harold* (1812-1818). Grimm, *Fairy Tales*.
1815	Invention of valve mechanism.	Field, *Nocturnes*. Schubert, *Heideröslein*.	Robert Owen, *A New View of Society* (1813).
1817	Chanot violin.	Clementi, *Gradus ad Parnassum*.	Constable's " Flatford Mill ". Lammenais, *Essai sur l'indifférence en matière de religion*.
1818	Savart violin. Cylindrical valve.	Beethoven, *Hammerclavier Sonata*.	Keats, *Endymion*. Schopenhauer, *Die Welt als Wille und Vorstellung*
1819	Ophicleide.	Schubert, *Trout Quintet*	De Maistre, *Du Pape*.
1820	Chin-rest added to the violin.	Spontini Kapellmeister at Berlin.	Shelley, *Prometheus Unbound*.
1821	Componium.	Weber, *Der Freischütz*.	St Simon, *Le Système Industriel*.

date	musical instrument	musical history	philosophy and the arts
1822	Forvielle bassoon	Beethoven, *Missa Solemnis.*	De Vigny, *Poèmes.*
1823	Clarinet with sliding discs. Double-escapement piano.	Schubert's music to *Rosamund.* Weber's opera *Euryanthe.*	Ingre's " La Source ". Thiers, *Histoire de la Révolution Française* (begun).
1824	Ascending valves	Beethoven, *Choral Symphony.*	Leopardi, *Canzoni e Versi.*
1825	Piano with steel frame.	Beethoven, *Grosse Fuge.*	First railway in Britain opened.
1826	Piano with felt hammers	Weber's opera *Oberon.*	Heine, *Buch der Lieder.*
1827	Austrian bugle	Schubert, *Die Winterreise.*	Poe, *Tamerlane.*
1829	Symphonium	Rossini's opera *William Tell.*	Hugo, *Les Orientales*
1830	Cross-hatched strings on a piano.	Auber's opera *Fra Diavolo.* Berlioz, *Symphonie Fantastique.*	Hugo, *Hernani.* Stendhal, *Le Rouge et le Noir.*
1832	Rotating valve. Pneumatic action on the organ.	Mendelssohn, *Hebrides.* Rossini, *Stabat Mater.*	Pushkin, *Eugene Onegin.* Washington Irving, *A Town of the Prairie.*
1834	Melophone Bass Trombone.	Berlioz, *Harold in Italy.*	Balzac, *Le Père Goriot.*
1835	Bass tuba Berliner Pumpen.	Schumann, *Symphonic Etudes Op. 13* (1834).	Musset, *Les Nuits.*
1836	Sax's bass clarinet	Meyerbeer's opera *Les Huguenots.*	Dickens, *Pickwick Papers.*
1839	Universalkontrabass	Berlioz, *Roméo et Juliette.* Chopin, 24 *Préludes.*	Hildebrand, *Camera Obscura.*
1840	Harmonium	Liszt, *Années de Pelerinage* (1841).	Ste Beuve, *Port-Royal.*
1844	Boehm-system clarinet.	Mendelssohn, *Violin Concerto in E Minor.*	Engels, *Umriss der Kritik einer Nationalökonomie.*
1845	Pape's chromatic harp. Saxhorn.	Wagner's opera *Tannhauser.* Schumann, *Piano Concerto.*	Mérimée, *Carmen.*
1846	Boehm flute. Saxophone.	Mendelssohn's oratorio *Elijah.*	Michelet, *Le Peuple.*
1847	Henry's baryton	Verdi's opera *Macbeth.*	Emily Brontë, *Wuthering Heights.*

1848	Triebert system applied to the oboe.	Wagner's opera *Lohengrin*. Schumann, *Manfred*.	Communist Manifesto.
1849	Octobass.	Liszt, *Tasso*.	Dickens, *David Copperfield*.
1854	Guitar made by Torres.	Berlioz, *Te Deum*.	Viollet-le-Duc, *Dictionnaire Raisonné de Architecture Française*.
1856	Sarrusophone.	Wagner's opera *Tristan und Isolde* (1859).	Baudelaire, *Les Fleurs du Mal*.
1862	Piano with sustaining pedal.	Liszt, *La Légende de Ste. Elisabeth*.	Manet's " Lola de Valence ".
1868	Electro-pneumatic-action organ.	Smetana, *My Fatherland*.	Darwin, *Variations of Animals and Plants*.
1870	Wagner tuba. Heckel's contrabassoon.	Delibes, *Coppelia*.	Schliemann excavates Troy.
1878	Mangeot piano.	Borodin, Symphony in B Minor.	Swinburn, *Poems and Ballads*.
1890	Cellone. Contrabass clarinet (Besson).	Tchaikowsky's opera *The Queen of Spades*.	Tolstoy, *The Kreutzer Sonata*.
1894	Chromatic harp built on Lyon's system.	Dvoràk, *New World Symphony*.	Conrad, *Almayer's Folly*.
1904	Heckelphone	Puccini, *Madama Butterfly*.	Lagerlof, *Legends of Christ*.
1908	Sousaphone	Richard Strauss's opera *Electra*.	Behrens builds in steel and glass.
1924	Theremin.	Webern, *Three Religious Songs*.	Kafka, *Ein Hungerkünstler*.
1928	Ondes Martenot. Hellertion.	Weill/Brecht, *Threepenny Opera*.	Matisse's " Seated Odalisque ".
1930	Trautonium.	Stravinsky: *Symphony of Psalms*.	Ortega y Gasset, *The Revolt of the Masses*.
1934	Radio-synthetic organ.	Hindemith, *Mathis der Maler*. Berg, Violin Concerto.	Cocteau, *La Machine Infernale*.
1936	Neo-Bechstein.	Prokofiev, *Peter and the Wolf*.	Wright builds house at Falling Water.

BIBLIOGRAPHY

- The Prehistoric Ages : The Orient Greece and Rome

BUCHNER, A. — *Musical Instruments Through the Ages.* London, 1956.
FARMER, H. — *The Organ of the Ancients.* Reeves, London, 1931.
GALPIN, F. — *The Music of the Sumerians and Their Immediate Successors, the Babylonians and Assyrians.* Cambridge University Press, 1937.
GRADENWITZ, P. — *The Music of Israel.* Norton, New York, 1949.
IDELSOHN, A. — *Jewish Music.* Tudor, New York, 1949.
SACHS, C. — *The History of Musical Instruments.* London, 1940.
— *The Rise of Music in the Ancient World.* New York, 1943.

I - The Middle Ages

ANDERSON, O. — *The Bowed Harp.* Reeves, London, 1930.
BEDBROOK, G.S. — *Keyboard Music from the Middle Ages.* Macmillan & Co, London, 1949.
BESSARABOFF, N. — *Ancient European Musical Instruments.* Harvard University Press, 1941.
FARMER, H.G. — *The Minstrelsy of the Arabian Nights.* Glasgow, 1945.
GALPIN, F. — *A Textbook of European Instruments.* E. Benn, London, 1956.
GALPIN, F. — *Old English Instruments of Music.* Methuen, London, 1965.
HILL, A.G. — *The Organ and Organ Cases of the Middle Ages and Renaissance.* London, 1883.
PANUM, H. — *Stringed Instruments of the Middle Ages.* London, 1940.
REESE, G. — *Music in the Middle Ages.* Norton, New York, 1940.

II - The Renaissance

ARTZ, F. — *From the Renaissance to Romanticism.* University of Chicago Press, Chicago, 1962.
BAINES, A. — *Woodwind Instruments and Their History.* Oxford University Press, London, 1957.
BESSARABOFF, N. — *Ancient European Musical Instruments.* Harvard University Press, 1941.
BOALCH, D.H. — *Makers of the Harpsichord and Clavichord 1440-1840.* London, 1956.
BROWN, H. — *Music in the French Secular Theatre, 1400-1550.* Harvard University Press, 1963.
CART DE LAFONTAINE, H. — *The King's Musick.* Novello, London, 1909.
GALPIN, F. — "The Sackbut" in *Proc. Mus. Ass.* 1907.
GALPIN, F. — *Old English Instruments of Music.* Methuen, London, 1965.
LEIGH, H. — *Dr. John Bull.* Herbert Joseph, Tonbridge, 1937.
MACE, T. — *Musick's Monument.* T. Ratcliffe & N. Thompson, London, 1676.
NAYLOR, E. — *Shakespeare and Music.* Dent, London, 1931.
NEF, K. — "The Polychord", in *Galpin Society Journal* IV, 23, 1951.
REESE, G. — *Music in the Renaissance.* Norton, New York, 1954.

V - From Monteverdi to J.S. Bach

BABITZ, S. — "Differences between 18th-century and modern violin bowing" in *The Score,* March 1957.
BUKOFZER, M. — *Music in the Baroque Era.* Norton, New York, 1947.
CARSE, A. — *The Orchestra in the XVIIIth Century.* Heffer, Cambridge, 1950.
DOLMETSCH, A. — *The Interpretation of the Music of the XVIIth and XVIIIth Centuries.* Novello, London, 1946.
HELM, E. — *Music at the Court of Frederick the Great.* Norman, University of Oklahoma Press, Oklahoma, 1960.
HUNT, E. — *The Recorder and its Music.* Herbert Jenkins, London, 1965.
JAMES, P. — *Early Keyboard Instruments.* Davies, London, 1930.
KIRKPATRICK, R. — *Domenico Scarlatti.* Princeton University Press, Princeton, 1953.
KLENZ, W. — *Giovanni Maria Bonocini of Modena.* Duke University Press, Durham, 1962.
MENKE, W. — *History of the Trumpet of Bach and Handel.* Reeves, London, 1934.
RUSSELL, R. — *The Harpsichord and Clavichord.* Faber & Faber, London, 1959.
TERRY, C. — *Bach's Orchestra.* Oxford University Press, London, 1946.
TREND, J.B. — *The Music of Spanish History to 1600.* Oxford, 1926.
YORKE-LONG, A. — *Music of Court.* Weidenfeld & Nicolson, London, 1954.
WELCH, C. — *Six Lectures on the Recorder.* Oxford, 1961.

V - The Classical Period

ALTON, R. — *Violin and Cello.* Reeves, London, 1964.

BATE, P. — *The Oboe.* Benn, London, 1956.

BOYDON, D.D. — "The Violin and its Technique in the Eighteenth Century", in *Musi[c] Quarterly,* Jan. 1950.

BURNEY, C. — *The Present State of Music in Germany.* Becket, London, 1775.

CARSE, A. — *The Orchestra in the XVIIIth Century.* Heffer, Cambridge, 1950.

DORING, E. — *The Guadagnini Family of Violinmakers.* Lewis, Chicago, 1949.

FARGA, F. — *Violins and Violinists.* Barrie & Rockliff, London, 1968.

FARMER, H. — *The Rise of Military Music.* Reeves, London, n.d.

HELM, E. — *Music at the Court of Frederick the Great.* Norman, University of Oklaho[ma] Press, 1960.

HILL, W. — *Antonio Stradivari.* Hill, London, 1902.
— *The Violin Makers of the Guarneri Family.* London, 1931.

HOTTETERRE, J. — *Principles of the Flute, Recorder and Oboe.* Barrie & Rockliff, Londo[n], 1968.

MOLLER, M. — *The Violin-makers of the Low Countries.* Moller, Amsterdam, 1955.

MORLEY-PEGGE, R. — *The French Horn.* Benn, London, 1960.

RENDALL, F. — *The Clarinet.* Benn, London, 1957.

RUSSELL, R. — *The Harpsichord and Clavichord.* London, 1959.

VI - Romanticism and Impressionism

ANDSLEY, G. — *The Art of Organ Building.* Dodd and Mead, New York, 1905.

BOEHM T. — *The Flute and Flute Playing.* Cleveland, 1922.

CARSE, A. — *The Orchestra from Beethoven to Berlioz.* Heffer, Cambridge, 1948.

CLARK, J. — *Musical Boxes.* Allen, London, 1961.

DAVIS, B. — *The Saxophone.* Selmer, London, n.d.

EINSTEIN, A. — *Music in the Romantic Era.* Norton, New York, 1947.

GELATT, R. — *The Fabulous Phonograph.* Cassell, London, 1956.

GREGORY, R. — "The Horn in Beethoven's Symphonies ", in *Music & Letters,* 1952.

HARDING, R. — *The Piano-Forte.* Cambridge University Press, 1933.

HIPKINS, E.J. — *How Chopin Played.* London, 1937.

VAN DER STRAETEN, E. — *The History of the Violin.* Cassell, London, 1933.

WELCH, C. — *History of the Boehm Flute.* Rudall, London, 1896.

VII - The Twentieth Century

CAGE, J. — "Experimental Music ", in *The Score,* 12: 65, 1955.

COWELL, H. — *New Musical Resources.* A. Knopf, New York, 1930.

DORF, R. — *Electronic Musical Instruments.* Radio Mag. Inc., New York, 1954.

DOUGLAS, A. — *The Electronic Music Instrument Manual.* I. Pitman & Sons, London, 195[-]

EBY, R.L. — *Electric Organs.* Wheator, Illinois, 1953.

HILLER, L. & ISAACSON, L. — *Experimental Music.* McGraw-Hill Book Co., New Yo[rk], 1959.

WHITWORTH, R. — *The Electric Organ.* London, 1948.

INDEX OF INSTRUMENTS

Index of Makers